P9-DUA-474

Seeking Identity

302.54
B417

SEEKING IDENTITY

Individualism versus Community in an Ethnic Context

Raymond A. Belliotti

WITHDRAWN

University Press of Kansas

LIBRARY ST. MARY'S COLLEGE

©1995 by the University Press of Kansas
All rights reserved

Published by the University Press of Kansas (Lawrence, Kansas 66049), which was
organized by the Kansas Board of Regents and is operated and funded by Emporia
State University, Fort Hays State University, Kansas State University, Pittsburg State
University, the University of Kansas, and Wichita State University

Library of Congress Cataloging-in-Publication Data

Belliotti, Raymond A., 1948 –
    Seeking identity : individualism versus community in an ethnic
context / Raymond A. Belliotti.
        p.   cm.
    Includes bibliographical references (p.   ) and index.
    ISBN 0-7006-0729-3 (cloth: alk. paper). – ISBN 0-7006-0730-7 (pbk.: alk.
paper)
        1. Individualism.   2. Anarchism.   3. Community.   4. Italian
American families.   5. Italian Americans – Intellectual life.
I. Title.
    JC571.B455   1995
    302.5 – dc20   95-31444

British Library Cataloging in Publication Data is available.

Printed in the United States of America

10 9 8 7 6 5 4 3 2 1

The paper used in this publication meets the minimum requirements of the American
National Standard for Permanence of Paper for Printed Library Materials
Z39.48-1984.

For Marcia, Angelo, and Vittoria

Cent'anni dopo che un Siciliano muore, ancora si ricorda

CONTENTS

PREFACE

Throughout history, writers have argued that existential tension is at the heart of human experience: our yearning for intimate connection with others and the recognition that others are necessary for our identity and freedom coalesce uneasily with the fear and anxiety we experience as others approach. We simultaneously long for emotional attachment yet are horrified that our individuality may evaporate once we achieve it. This disharmony may never be fully reconciled; we find ourselves instead making uneasy compromises and adjustments as we oscillate between 'radical individuality' and 'thorough immersion in community.' This existential tension replicates itself at numerous levels: the individual confronts family, the family confronts village, villages confront wider society, and society confronts the state. The antinomies generated by the individual's confrontations with communities of various sizes and influences provide the unifying themes of this book.

The individual confronts other people at many different levels. When we meet others at institutional levels, the stakes rise in some respects. Our need to retain individual freedom and resist coercion intensifies when our relations are impersonal, when we experience less direct control over our destiny, and when entrenched bureaucracies seem ready and able to usurp our autonomy. Circumscribed by socioeconomic reality, the relentless socializing of the established order, and the inherent inertia of the masses, our sense of possibility nevertheless resists extinction and thereby honors the human craving for transcendence.

Moreover, the individual confronts several different, often conflicting communities. She faces the intimate aspirations of family; the often conflicting ultimatums of ethnicity, gender, and race; the stirring, history-laden, patriotic implorations of country; and the more distant claims of the international order. Clearly, the individual-community continuum expands in several dimensions. In fact, only in the simplest cases is it ever one-dimensional. As such, contexts such as family, ethnicity, gender, politics, and war multiply the tensions, exhilarations, fears, and hopes invariably embodied by the continuum.

This book is not a typical philosophical monograph. First, I do not assume that the proper use of abstract reason will result in unadulterated truths embodying necessary moral and political implications. Instead, I try to illustrate the powers and limitations of abstract reason, its glories and tragedies alike. Too often, invocations of abstract reason obscure the concrete circumstances and history that imbue our lives with meaning. Moreover, reason cannot by itself advance one world view to which all humans must subscribe. There comes a point where reason runs out, where we must appeal to a self-evident principle, accept an unprovable assumption, or take a leap of faith. Although reason sets the boundaries of plausibility, there may well be several conflicting world visions that do not violate general moral principles. Philosophy then becomes less of a deductive enterprise and more a project of wisely adjudicating normative puzzles. The significance of analytic philosophy may therefore reside in its potential for stimulating participants to alternate ways of thinking and experiencing—intellectual creativity as a redemption of spirit and flesh. From this perspective, philosophy aids individuals to arrive at temporary solutions to life struggles, instead of exemplifying the demands of Reason itself and coercing participants to specific conclusions.

Second, I do not purport to have written the book from an ahistorical, aridly impersonal, effetely impartial perspective. I include several personal narratives that reflect the prejudices, biases, and descriptive and prescriptive world views that necessarily color my work. Too often, I admit, I revert to the noble "we," implying that I speak authoritatively for all right-thinking scholars or all members of the moral community in good standing or from the view from above. I was trained well in the rigors and conceits of analytic philosophy; old habits are difficult to break. The book thus mirrors my own ambivalences, dimly understood conflicts, and deepest personal commitments.

Third, I have not confined the book to philosophical inquiry alone. Historical, sociological, and political descriptions and speculations intrude freely, for I believe that scholars should underscore the counterproductiveness of rigid disciplinary boundaries, which too often emerge from particular historical, personal, and contingent circumstances soon forgotten.

Fourth, I have not written the book from a contextless vantage point. Italian-American experiences are the ballast that supports my philosophical speculation. I chose this context because I was tired of pretending that my philosophical reflections were autonomous from my moral experiences, because Italian-American experiences have contributed so greatly to my identity, because the immigrant experience teaches so much about the human condition, and because it was time for me to pay tribute to the giants on whose shoulders I have stood. Even more important, my overall strategy is animated by the firm conviction that comparative examinations of specific Italian-American contexts and their correlated philosophical debates can produce a rewarding conversation between concreteness and abstraction.

Fifth, the book addresses a variety of concerns: family relations and obligations, feminist epistemology and interpretation, government authority, war and pacifism, and personal and ethnic identity. These issues, at once disparate and overlapping, touch on both classical and contemporary problems of human identity. To formulate at least a semi-coherent life and sense of identity we must scrutinize such issues as a group rather than in isolation.

In Chapter 1, the individual confronts family, and the family confronts wider society. I outline the unwritten but deeply ingrained system of moral rules the southern Italian immigrants brought to the Americas. This system, *l'ordine della famiglia*, prescribed relations and responsibilities within the family and appropriate conduct toward those outside the family. I use *l'ordine della famiglia* as a point of departure to examine a current debate in moral theory between partialists, who champion the conventional moral wisdom that we owe more to those close to us than we owe to humanity in general, and impartialists, who argue that we must attach no special weight to our own interests or to the interests of those close to us when determining proper moral action. I also argue for a version of partialism that includes numerous noncontractual moral obligations. Finally, I evaluate the morality of *l'ordine della famiglia* in light of the partialist-impartialist debate.

In Chapter 2, the gendered self confronts the family. I explain and discuss three common images of Italian immigrant women found in the literature: the woman as stabilizer, as cultural transformer, and as matriarch. Trying to unravel these somewhat overlapping, somewhat conflicting images raises fundamental issues in epistemology and value theory that underlie much of the interpretive enterprise. I assess these issues in the context of contemporary debates between feminist thinkers and analytic philosophers: Is there a "woman's perspective"? Must knowledge be objective? What if anything in feminist epistemology is new and valuable? What are the prospects for reconciliation between mainstream analytic philosophers and feminist epistemologists? The answers to such questions facilitate a deeper understanding of the interpretive project and of the celebrations and disappointments of Italian immigrant women.

In Chapter 3, the individual confronts the state. I discuss Italian and Italian-American anarchical experiences in the late nineteenth and early twentieth centuries. I then explore several historical strains of political anarchism: individualistic anarchism, mutualism, collectivism, anarchist-communism, anarchosyndicalism. Finally, I analyze the anarchical instincts of contemporary social philosopher Roberto Unger. Although as a developed political theory and prescription, anarchism has at best a limited practical application, its animating spirit and distinctive moral posture retain robust vitality today. Analyses of the general theories of anarchism, Italian and Italian-American anarchical experiences, and Unger's contemporary political vision combine to cast light on the features of anarchism that embody enduring appeal and reveal much about the human need for individualism.

In Chapter 4, the individual confronts the nation and the nation confronts the international community. I describe the symbolic importance of Giuseppe Garibaldi, the military hero of Italian unification in 1860, to the southern Italian immigrants. I then examine a host of issues in the philosophy of war that emerge from the work of contemporary philosopher Robert Holmes: Is the killing of innocent persons in war ever justified? Is modern war presumptively unjust because it necessarily involves such killing? Can and should we adopt pacifism as a form of nonviolent resistance to aggressors and as an inherently salutary way of life? Finally, I touch upon the perceived values and evils of war in the context of looming postmodernism. The specter of war forces individuals into clearly demarcated political units engaged in zero-sum struggles for the highest stakes. Here the individual is often forced into communal projects to survive.

In Chapter 5, individuals confront their ethnic group and the ethnic subculture confronts society. I begin with an explanation of Christopher Columbus as an Italian-American ethnic symbol, then I discuss ethnicity generally and provide the latest and most reliable statistical analyses of Italian-American attitudes, behavior, and ideology. Finally, I advance a normative vision of ethnicity in which group pride and solidarity do not degenerate into prejudice, in which the group's past is honored but not sanctified as necessarily definitive of its future, in which a group celebrates its historical legacy without forsaking allegiance to its adopted homeland. Ethnicity, which straddles a fine line between group pride and prejudice, conjures unique hopes and fears for individuals and their communities.

In some respects the version of self I explore here is deeply situated: socially embedded in contingent family, ethnic, and national understandings. But in other respects the self is adrift and never fully resolved: it struggles to define and redefine itself along the numerous dimensions of the individualism-community continuum. In one sense, we all live alone, but in another sense the self finds itself deeply situated in contexts not of its making. These contexts can be reimagined and remade over time, but the self cannot ascend to pure context-lessness. This book chronicles the morally ambiguous results of the coping strategies the self employs to mediate the anxieties of the human condition.

ACKNOWLEDGMENTS

Giuseppe Leonardo and Grazia Giordano Leonardo immigrated to this country from Valguarnera, Sicily, in 1912. Angelo Belliotti, Gaetana Zaso Belliotti, and Rosario Belliotti arrived from Cerda, Sicily, in 1896. Rosario met and married Agnes ("Daisy") Rizzo in the United States and together they raised five children, one of whom was my father, Angelo Belliotti. Giuseppe and Grazia raised nine children, one of whom was my mother, Louise Leonardo Belliotti. This book is my tribute to them.

I have numerous people to thank. Without the support and encouragement of my wife, Marcia Dalby Belliotti, this book would not exist. Her unwavering love and faith bind our family together. Our children, Angelo and Vittoria, merit special mention, for they are the prime reason why I write: one day they will have to read my books, and I will experience the ultimate parental revenge. Deep appreciation also goes to Mary Ann Belliotti Conroy, the sister who taught me many years ago how to read. Back then we did not have sophisticated reading programs, and my sister taught me by the Sicilian method. She would teach me a word, and if I erred when that word appeared in a text, she would grab her instrument of terror, the wooden spoon, and crack me over the head. I had to either learn quickly how to read or suffer a fractured skull.

Cynthia Miller, my editor, provided wise counsel, a cheerful disposition, and firm resolve. She and the other members of the production team made the process an enjoyable adventure, rather than the tedious chore it could easily have become. Thanks also to Barbara Dinneen for copyediting the book. The two anonymous readers who evaluated this book for the University Press of Kansas were extraordinarily insightful: open to innovative presentations of philosophical material, generously thorough in their analyses, yet sharply critical where appropriate. I was fortunate to have drawn them.

Many of the ideas in this book and the impulse to write it emerged from a course I team-taught in the fall of 1993 called *The Italian Americans.* I want to warmly acknowledge Dr. Richard A. Leva, Associate Professor of Psychology, for his massive contributions to that course and to the celebration of Italian-American culture in Fredonia. Also, special gratitude goes to Giulio and Silvia Mannino, who helped me put a necessary finishing touch on the book.

Finally, I would like to thank the editors of the following journals for permission to adapt material from my articles: "Contributing to Famine Relief and Sending Poisoned Food," *The Philosophical Forum* 12 (1980):20–32; "Honor Thy Father and Thy Mother and to Thine Own Self Be True," *The Southern Journal of Philosophy* 24 (1986):149–162; "Parents and Children: A Reply to Narveson," *The Southern Journal of Philosophy* 26 (1988):285–292; "Blood is Thicker Than Water: Don't Forsake the Family Jewels," *Philosophical Papers* 18 (1989):265–280; "Beyond Capitalism and Communism: Roberto Unger's Superliberal Political Theory," *Praxis International* 9 (1989):321–334; "Are All Modern Wars Morally Wrong?," *Journal of Social Philosophy* 26 (1995):17–31. Special thanks also to Temple University Press for permission to adapt a few pages of my *Justifying Law* (1992).

Seeking Identity

CHAPTER 1

FAMILY CONFRONTS SOCIETY

Moral Reasoning and *L'ordine della Famiglia*

When I was twelve I was caught stealing from a local merchant. After making restitution and rendering an effusive, albeit disingenuous, apology, my real punishment commenced. For thirty minutes that seemed like six hours, I endured a parental grilling on the responsibilities of childhood. My mother, who was especially graced in techniques of frightening interrogation, made several familial verities painfully clear: I had besmirched the family name and reputation, I had brought irredeemable dishonor to the extended kinship network, I had inadvertently reinforced the criminal image of Italian Americans in Anglo-American minds, and I had repaid the ongoing sacrifices of my parents and grandparents with disgraceful action. In sum, the message was loud and lucid: in one fell swoop, my self-indulgent greed had taken down an entire family network. I had committed the ultimate *infamia* ("vile deed"): I had placed corrupt individual desire above family honor. Worse, I was so untutored in and oblivious to *ben educati* ("proper behavior") that I was antecedently unaware of what was at stake. I absorbed these charges without rejoinder, for I had no plausible justification. I never stole again. The family survived. I must add that my mother, with her unwavering intuition for familial reconciliation, symbolically welcomed me back into the fold that very night without further words: she baked my favorite Italian cookies and placed them on the table as a snack. I was still her son.

In this chapter, I outline the family code the southern Italian immigrants brought to the Americas, using that code as a point of departure to examine a contemporary philosophical debate between moral partialists and moral impartialists. I then argue for a version of partialism that includes noncontractual moral obligations. Finally, I morally evaluate the family code in light of my conclusions on the partialist-impartialist debate.

By invoking a dialogue between a specific Italian-American context and an abstract philosophical discussion, I explore the subtle antinomies generated by two fundamental dimensions of the individual-community continuum: the self struggles with the family and the family confronts society.

L'ORDINE DELLA FAMIGLIA

The immigrants from the *Mezzogiorno*[1] brought to the Americas an unwritten but deeply ingrained system of rules, *l'ordine della famiglia*, prescribing their relations within and responsibilities to their family and their appropriate conduct toward those outside the family. *L'ordine della famiglia* apportioned the world into four morally significant spheres of social intimacy: The social group of paramount value was the family, which consisted not only of immediate members (the nuclear family) but also of relatives often extended to the third or fourth degrees. The exact degree of kinship determined reciprocal duties and privileges. The welfare of the family, taken in this extended sense, was the primary responsibility of each member. The next degree of intimacy was embodied in the system of *compareggio* that, among other things, served as a limited check and balance to family policies and practices. This sphere can be subdivided into *compari* and *commare*, and *padrini* and *madrine*. The former were literally "coparents," usually one's peers and intimate friends, and often the godparents to one's children. *Padrini* and *madrine*, by contrast, were venerated elders prized for their demonstrated wisdom, prestige, or power. Strikingly, the system of *compareggio* admitted few vicissitudes: intimate friendships were permanent. Marginal adjustments could be negotiated between the parties, but their intentions to rescind their relationship, even if reciprocal, could not sever what were taken to be enduring bonds. The third sphere of concern involved *amici di cappello* (those to whom one tips one's hat): people outside the scope of intimacy, friendly acquaintances. The final and by far the largest group is composed of *stranieri* (strangers): everyone, known or unknown, who falls outside the three other classes.[2]

L'ordine della famiglia was at once simple and complex, protective yet isolating, humanistic but distrustful. Its simplicity is apparent in the clear-cut demarcations among people: one was either part of the family, an intimate friend, a friendly acquaintance, or a stranger. Little nuance or ambiguity was recognized. Moreover, if one were a member of the family or an intimate acquaintance that relationship was, at least in principle, inalienable and immutable. The complexity of the code manifests itself in the intricate rituals and negotiations deemed suitable for members of the first two classes. For example, fathers were ostensibly entrenched as the powerful leaders of the family to whom obedience was owed, yet wives were expected to assert their dominance in numerous everyday matters, and children, at least sons, were subtly encouraged to exercise independent judgment, even disobedience, to learn and practice the skill of *furberia* (shrewdness) necessary for worldly success.

The code was clearly protective in that it created, at least in theory, an intimate shield, a zone of security, against the oppressive economic and social structure of the *Mezzogiorno*. But the isolating and parochial implications of the code were equally stark: *stranieri* were neither to be trusted nor consulted; *amici di cappello* were to be regarded at a distance with cool politeness. Not only was there no concept of an international brotherhood and sisterhood, there was little appreciation of those outside one's village.

Yet the code reflected a deep humanism, often demanding strenuous sharing and contributions to joint interests within one's circle of intimates. Such parochialism, however, simultaneously deepened and legitimated existing cynicism toward outsiders. There are two obvious contemporary postures one might assume when confronting *l'ordine della famiglia*. The first, and probably most common, is dismissal: Here is a clearly primitive code that right-thinking people would now reject straightaway as unsophisticated tribalism emerging from an uneducated people's struggle with overwhelming economic and social forces. Are we not fortunate to claim membership in a more progressive polity under more salutary socioeconomic circumstances? The second contemporary response is sentimentalization: The *l'ordine della famiglia* was a better, more spiritually rewarding, historical moment when a code of affection transcended socioeconomic oppression and pointed the way to a true family ethic, a microcosm of successful human relations in existential crisis. What have westerners gained by purchasing better material conditions with their souls? Has the disintegration of family values proven perhaps too high a price to pay?

The dismissal and sentimentalization both embody more powerful forms in the philosophical debate between impartialists and partialists. Moreover, a deep understanding of the sources and possible justifications of *l'ordine della famiglia* can illuminate that debate. Accordingly, an examination of the specific Italian-American context and the abstract philosophical debate can nurture a reciprocally enriching process of clarification.

THE IDEAL OF IMPARTIALITY:
THE TERMS OF THE DEBATE

Moralists who subscribe to the ideal of impartiality can point to a distinguished history for support. In the West, we are familiar with the biblical injunction to love they neighbor as thyself.[3] This moral ideal was clearly meant to extend self-love to all other humans, or at least to all those with whom one comes into contact.[4] At its most uncompromising, this injunction commands us to manifest the same degree of concern to others that we lavish upon ourselves. Although inartfully crafted – it holds out the possibility that if one is filled with self-hate or ersatz self-love such dispositions are legitimately transferred to others – it offers a powerful moral aspiration. In the eyes of the Supreme Being we are all equal, and none of us merits privilege on the basis of identity. Instead, humans all share claims to equal mutual concern based solely on their humanity. In the language of affection, love for all humanity must be unconditional and unwavering.

But one need not subscribe to this strain of Judeo-Christianity to find historical support for impartiality. Four hundred years before the birth of Christ, the Chinese sage Mo Tzu counseled a universal human love that did not distinguish between families, friends, and strangers.[5] Mo Tzu explicitly advised us to have as much regard for strangers as for our immediate families and suggested that until we renounce partiality to immediate families, we will be saddled with an incoherent and inferior moral code: recognized duties among family members could only be understood coherently as particular cases of our duties to humanity.[6] Thus, to differentiate strongly between the degree of concern we show to intimates and to strangers undercuts the ground of all morality and fragments social life.

The impartiality thesis requires us to assume the perspective of an ideal, detached observer when arriving at moral judgments: I must attach no special weight to my own interests when determining moral action. Moreover, the fact that another person is my spouse, my child, or my intimate friend is morally irrelevant: it provides no moral reason to favor such a person over a complete stranger. Eighteenth-century English philosopher William Godwin exemplifies this position in a discussion of whom he should save in a fire, an archbishop or a chambermaid, when he can save only one: "[If the chambermaid is my wife or mother] that would not alter the truth of the proposition [about whom to save] for of what great consequence is it that they are mine? What magic is there in the pronoun 'my' to overturn the decisions of everlasting truth?"[7] We may from a moral viewpoint discriminate between people—Godwin would save the archbishop not the chambermaid—but only on the basis of *nonrelational* characteristics that would attract the assent of an ideal, detached observer.

Several of our most influential moral theories embody forms of the impartiality thesis. Utilitarianism, the view that an action is morally right in the instant circumstances if and only if no other action available to the moral agent in those circumstances produces a greater balance of good consequences for those affected by the action, demands that we adopt the principle of equal consideration of interests when making our moral calculations. A contemporary Australian philosopher, Peter Singer, interprets this to mean that "we cannot, if we accept the principle of equal consideration of interests, say that doing [a particular] act is better . . . because we are *more concerned* about Y than we are about X. What the principle is really saying is that an interest is an interest, whoever's interest it may be."[8]

Kantianism grants humans moral standing in virtue of their rationality and capacity for autonomy. To respect someone as an equal subject of experience is to recognize that she has value independent of whatever uses I might conjure for her and independent of my goals and purposes. Kantianism thus demands impartial treatment of persons and impartial judgment of cases. Moreover, moral judgments must be based on a categorical imperative that purports to test universalizability and logical consistency. Finally, the only unconditional good is a good will: performing an action because one recognizes it is the right thing to do based on the categorical imperative and for no other primary reason. Thus, performing an act because I love the other person or because the other person is my intimate friend is an unreliable moral guide. Accordingly, Kantianism is often perceived as an ethic founded on an impartiality that makes it difficult for us to justify our preferential behavior within personal relations.[9]

Liberal-contract theory also embodies a form of the impartiality thesis. As John Hardwig contends: "The whole point of contract theory is to try to get us to abstract from our particular characteristics, wants, goals, and values, in order to ascertain what any self-interested, rational being would want and, given those wants, would agree to. Not surprisingly, such depersonalized contractors agree only to principles for impersonal and quasi-impersonal relationships."[10] Sometimes based on a form of atomistic individualism, contract theory conceives my well-being as apart from the well-being of others: the well-being of others is not antecedently part of mine. Although contract theory implicitly rejects the injunction to love thy neighbor as thyself, clearly repudiates utilitarianism's tacit assumption that we are all antecedently connected, and replaces Kantian duty with strong notions of voluntarism, it may share with these other theories a reluctance to accept personal relationships as bearing special moral currency. A contemporary Canadian contractualist, Jan Narveson, states: "That blood is, as they say, thicker than water may be true, but if so it is an emotional truth, rather than one with a firm basis in reason."[11]

In fact, to present the problem as "partialists versus impartialists" is misleading. Most philosophers who ponder the issues described here accept some version of both ideals. The real debate surrounds the relative domains and the specific justifications of each ideal. For example, virtually everyone who writes on these matters accepts impartiality at a general level: moral rules and principles must apply universally; I cannot make myself an exception to the moral law. Moreover, most thinkers also accept at least a limited notion of partiality: at least on some occasions I can prefer my interests or those of my intimates to those of strangers, perhaps on grounds of a geographic proximity that facilitates better knowledge of the interests of those I know, thus creating a greater likelihood that my efforts will succeed.

When assessing claims about impartiality, we must recognize distinctions among different levels of generality in moral theory. Although most of the major Western philosophical traditions emphasize notions of impartiality, under certain interpretations they can all be reconciled with a consideration of personal relationships. For example, the Christian tradition, although advancing the commandment to love one's neighbor and the parable of the good samaritan, has moderated the requirement of strict impartiality and has been a bastion of "family values" that support partiality in personal relations.

Likewise, a utilitarian might accept a rule permitting partiality in personal relations, if general compliance with that rule would produce a greater balance of good consequences for all those affected than the balance generated by strict impartiality.[12] Kantianism, too, may accommodate actions taken from the motive of intimacy, as long as the agent's will also exhibits the paramount motive of duty.[13] Contractualists can also accept actions of partiality exhibited in personal relations, as long as the actions are based on permissible voluntary transactions or chosen by rational moral agents operating from an ideal and impartial vantage point.[14]

Nevertheless, disagreements between impartialists and partialists persist on the level of concrete moral action, for all of the main secular philosophical traditions hold partiality in personal relations hostage to other conditions. Thus, utilitarians such as Singer demand the fulfillment of two external conditions – that people are more aware of and more willing to fulfill the interests of those close to them, and that the distribution of resources between families is not significantly unequal – prior to embracing the partiality that is part of common thinking and practice. Unsurprisingly, Singer concludes that "in the world as it is presently constituted the first condition seems to hold, but not the second. For that reason I do not think that the subordinate principles [of partiality] mentioned correctly set out our present moral responsibilities, though they could do so if resources were more evenly distributed."[15]

Likewise, Kantianism seems merely to tolerate motives of affection and intimacy that often characterize actions done by those in personal relations. The real key for Kantians still is the good will, which presumably ensures that even if I did not esteem a person I would have still done the action. Inherent moral worth of motives of personal connection is either unrecognized or marginalized. On the level of concrete action, then, partiality is morally permitted only where it is generally allowed on grounds other than those emerging from personal relations. The motives of personal connection are not real factors in the moral calculus.

Finally, contractualists recognize no antecedent personal bonds, no moral responsibilities based on who we are rather than what we do. Worshipping at the altar of voluntarism and often tacitly underwriting atomistic individualism, contractualists must be convinced that ideal observers would choose principles of partiality from an ideal vantage point. Conversely, partialists insist that some personal relations, particularly those attending blood ties, are not chosen but are antecedent attachments that partially but importantly constitute who we are. To partialists, who we are affects what we must do: moral obligations cannot be dismissed merely because we did not choose them.

Accordingly, there is much at stake in the debate between partialists and impartialists: Do our moral obligations arise from only one source? What moral currency, if any, do personal relations bear? How can the constitutive attributes of the self translate into moral obligations? Can the seemingly abstract claims of humanity taken as a whole properly regulate the conduct of common people? Is what we can provide our families from a moral point of view determined not merely by the resources we acquire but also by the general distribution of social goods in the world? How does the debate between partialists and impartialists bear on *l'ordine della famiglia?*

THE CASE FOR IMPARTIALITY

Impartialists can point to much in our moral traditions that supports their position, although, at first glance, their position seems completely ridiculous at the level of concrete moral action. Few aspects of human experience are celebrated as intensely as family love and intimate friendships. What could be more preposterous than morally requiring that one treat one's child no differently from an utter stranger? Can even a plausible case be made for such a posture?

James Rachels argues that the partialist position, even if deeply embedded in conventional moral wisdom, is fatally flawed because it wrongly privileges irrelevant considerations, such as luck, with moral significance: "Suppose a parent believes that, when faced with a choice between feeding his own children and feeding starving orphans, he should give preference to his own. This is natural enough. But the orphans need the food just as much, and they are no less deserving. It is only their bad luck that they were not born to affluent parents; and why should luck count, from a moral point of view?"[16] Rachels endorses the view that "universal love is a higher ideal than family loyalty, and that obligations within families can be properly understood only as particular instances of obligations to all mankind."[17] Finally, the conception of morality captures "something deeply important that we should be reluctant to give up. It is useful, for example, in explaining why egoism, racism, and sexism are morally odious, and if we abandon this conception we lose our most natural and persuasive means of combating those doctrines."[18]

Rachels advances a number of insights here. First, he disparages good fortune as morally irrelevant. In a world with radically unequal distribution of resources, a world that lavishes encomiums on the partiality shown by parents to their children and by intimate friends to one another, a child's well-being is wrongly connected to facts beyond the child's control: initial starting position, material circumstances of birth, and the genetic lottery. Here Rachels is tacitly accepting one of Singer's criteria: partiality could be justified only if the distribution of necessary social resources were relatively evenly distributed. That distribution is radically uneven, however, and moral partiality is therefore unjustified under current conditions. There is also an implicit consequentialist claim here: if more (most? virtually all?) people were to adopt an impartialist outlook an overall social gain would be made by the world's people as a whole.

Second, when he describes family duties as derived from more general duties to all humans and impartiality as essential to blocking racism and sexism, Rachels is emphasizing that the entire history of progressive moral thinking is a story of widening our circle of concern. Tribalism is dangerously parochial from a social and moral standpoint. Carving out carefully and narrowly circumscribed loops designating "them" and "us" fosters misunderstanding and inhibits deeper moral sentiments. We might expect this mentality from gangs of socially deprived adolescent boys, but not from moral philosophers.

Partialists, however, often rejoin by claiming that impartialists have an impoverished concept of the value of personal relations. In this vein, Thomas Donaldson asks us to imagine a hypothetical world, "Equim," in which impartiality is the dominant norm. In Equim, our natural desires do not translate into behavioral partiality: "People *do* have desires; indeed they are fond of people and enjoy their company. It is rather that they are equally fond of everyone, for a stranger as much as their own child. Self-interest is the only exception to this rule. That is, impartiality in Equim does not extend to the *self*."[19]

The inhabitants of Equim, then, achieve a sort of universal benevolence and sympathy, and intimacy, in the sense of exclusionary and partial relations, vanishes. Donaldson further stipulates that the aggregate happiness in Equim is somewhat greater than in the world we know because the undesirable effects of racial, ethnic, familial, religious, and marital partiality disappear. He then asks whether we would choose Equim over our present world. Noting that in Equim aspects of life that are deeply embedded with moral significance are relinquished, Donaldson answers that "the overwhelming majority of people would choose the present world over that of Equim. A world of no friendship and of no neighborly or family affection is one few would choose to inhabit even on the condition that it yielded slight gains in overall happiness."[20] Impartiality, then, is conflicts with the sort of personal relations that "the overwhelming majority" of us prefer.

Impartialists point out, however, that this objection is fatuous. For example, Marcia Baron argues that "it is no violation of impartiality to see certain people as special if this means that we enjoy their company more than that of others, mourn their losses more (or in a different way) than those of others, and rejoice in their happiness and successes in a way in which we do not rejoice in those of others. Nor is it any violation of impartiality to spend more time with those whom we see as special and to look after them in circumstances or in ways in which we would not look after others."[21] Baron is emphatically denying that impartialists are committed to a radical undifferentiation of allocation of their emotional and spiritual resources.

At least two questions emerge from the Donaldson-Baron debate. First, is it so obvious that the "overwhelming majority" of us would choose our present world over Equim? It may well depend on whom we ask. Certainly those of us who have a reasonably satisfying network of personal relations would agree with Donaldson; but those of us who suffer from intense, unsatisfied basic needs and who have experienced mainly stormy, frustrating personal relations may dissent. In world survey, which group predominates?

Second, although Baron argues persuasively that impartialists can accommodate the type of personal relations many of us cherish, what is the relationship of intimacy, in the sense of one's emotional and spiritual allocations, to the distribution of one's material and service goods? It may well be true that impartialists can "see certain people as special," "mourn their losses more than those of others," and "rejoice in their happiness," but can they also distribute more material goods to their intimates than to others? Can they remain impartialists yet, unlike Godwin, rescue the chambermaid who is their mother and not the archbishop? The task here is to unravel the connection between acting on emotional and spiritual levels as if someone is your intimate friend and thus special, and remaining impartial when allocating material and service goods. Is it plausible to act as if someone is your friend, to tell that person that you are friends, yet at the moment of need toggle to a default moral position of impartiality? ("Mary, we have been close for years, we have shared a common history and exchanged numerous intimacies, but, hey, you are only a chambermaid and the other guy is an archbishop! I must either be a Godwinian and save the chief or remain fully neutral and flip a coin to see whom I should rescue. Either way, our friendship of many years cuts no moral ice!")

In sum, Donaldson has not shown conclusively that our world is preferable to Equim, and Baron, although she makes a strong case that impartialists can absorb personal relations on the emotional level, has not shown clearly that impartialists can reflect their alleged concern on the more practical level of allocation of material and service goods. If impartialists must embody a moral schizophrenia toward their family and friends then they have still not answered the more general criticism—that impartialists cannot truly integrate a coherent understanding of personal relations—that philosophers such as Donaldson have lodged.

Three Kinds of Impartialism

The first interpretation can be called *strict theoretical impartialism*. It holds that the existence of a personal relationship between X and Y does not of itself furnish either party a morally relevant reason to prefer advancing the interests of the other to advancing the interests of a stranger. Obviously, a more rigorous formulation of this stance would have to take into account situations that by their very nature differentiate (e.g., Mother's Day, family reunions, allocations of one's personal emotions, and so on). But the point is that this interpretation would not consider the presence of a personal relationship morally relevant in assessing, for example, which competing interest of two parties we should advance when we can only advance the interests of one party. It is unclear, the biblical injunction notwithstanding, whether anyone has truly held this view. Perhaps William Godwin came the closest when he suggested that if the chambermaid were his mother he would still save the archbishop. (Would he have saved his mother if she also were an archbishop?)

The second interpretation can be called *strict contingent impartialism*, which concedes that partialism can be justified but only if the world enjoyed a relatively equal distribution of material and social resources. Until then, we should at least strive for an impartialism that aspires to satisfy interests according to the methodology of the utilitarian calculus and on the basis of need. The presence of a personal relationship provides no *independent* reason of moral significance. There may be times when our moral calculus decrees that in a conflict we advance the interests of a relative or close friend instead of the interests of a stranger, but only because of our geographical proximity to the former and thus our greater prospects for effectiveness, not because the personal relationship itself registers moral weight. Peter Singer comes closest to embracing this interpretation.

The third interpretation can be called *moderate contingent impartialism.* Like strict contingent impartialism, this view accepts that partiality could be justified in a world of relatively equal resource distribution. However, unlike strict contingent impartialism, it recognizes that personal relationships embody a degree of independent moral relevance. The work of James Rachels represents this view.[22]

It may seem that the third interpretation coincides with the basic tenets of partialism and thus lacks distinctive status. But this appearance is deceiving, for this interpretation still embraces a moral ideal that conflicts with partialism. In this vein, Rachels describes a utopian vision that undermines several distinctions of our world, distinctions that partialists hold dear: "In [this utopia] children with living parents able to provide for them would be raised by their parents, who would give them all the love and care they need. Parents who through no fault of their own were unable to provide for their children would be given whatever assistance they need. Orphans would be taken in by families who would raise and love them as their own. The burdens involved in such adoptions would be shared by all."[23] This ideal conflicts with partialism in that it makes equal provision for the needs of all children and eliminates, or at least softens, the role luck plays in the satisfaction of those needs.

Furthermore, moderate contingent impartialism tempers the utopian vision by transporting it to our real world and offering a concrete proposal in conflict with partialism. The proposal distinguishes between different levels of need and between different degrees of importance for goods provided: "When considering *similar* needs, you may permissibly prefer to provide for the needs of your own children. For example, if you were faced with a choice between feeding your own children or contributing money to provide food for other children, you could rightly choose to feed your own. But if the choice were between some relatively *trivial* thing for your own and *necessities* for other children, preference should be given to helping the others."[24]

Obviously, the line between the trivial and the important is highly contestable, but the main thrust of this proposal is that partiality, at least in the allocation of material benefits, must be limited to situations where the needs of conflicting potential recipients are similar. When one potential recipient has greater need than another, the fact that the latter is my child or intimate friend is morally irrelevant. Accordingly, a proponent of this proposal would rescue his mother the chambermaid, not the archbishop, in the knowledge that the presence of personal relationships triggers moral currency only when the needs of the potential recipients are similar.[25]

Moderate contingent impartialism, then, challenges the partialist to advance a persuasive case that providing our children or our intimates luxuries, however one defines them, is morally justified in a world where the raging, unsatisfied needs of others are well known.

THE CASE FOR PARTIALISM

Partialists generally underscore the following arguments in making their case.

Morality Presupposes Personal Relations

Impartialists claim that moral obligations within families and intimate relations can only be understood coherently as a special case of general obligations to humanity. Partialists, conversely, argue that the moral enterprise, understood properly, presupposes partiality in personal relations. That is, the sorts of dispositions and virtues that comprise the moral enterprise can only be learned from personal relations characterized by partiality. Personal relations are nonfungible: if X has a personal relationship to Y, then Y is one of X's ends and that end is precisely Y and not any other person.[26]

In this vein, Hugh LaFollette clarifies the paradox in which impartial moral principles may presuppose partiality in personal relations: "Intimacy promotes honesty, caring, loyalty, self-knowledge, patience, empathy, etc. These are significant moral values by anyone's lights—values which arguably are best promoted by intimate relationships. So by this line of reasoning impartial moral principles dictate that we pursue intimacy. Since intimacy requires partiality, it is legitimate to treat intimates preferentially."[27]

This line of thought bears currency, but it is not the conclusive argument one might first suppose. If it were true that the world is better off with our dominant understandings of morality and if it were true that these understandings are initially grounded in the partiality of personal relations, then impartialists would have a powerful reason to accept at least a limited version of partiality in personal relations. Impartialists argue, however, that an even better world is one in which impartialism is strictly complied with; or that the amount of partiality justified by the need to develop proper moral dispositions is much less than commonly thought; or that a limited partiality is acceptable only because of the special assigned roles society designates for parents. Accordingly, impartialists would claim that the partialist's argument demonstrates less than is commonly supposed and that the partialist's empirical assumptions are greatly exaggerated.

A partialist might respond that she has at least driven a wedge into Godwin's uncompromising version of impartialism: we cannot acquire the knowledge, nurture the proper dispositions, or develop the proper motivations for moral action under obdurate versions of impartialism. Thus, the implacability of strict theoretical impartialism is ultimately self-defeating.

We must recognize that the unique and valuable ends of family and personal relations cannot be achieved without the socially recognized institutions of family and friendship. Although the precise nature and strictures of these institutions are reimaginable, *some* form of family and friendship are necessary lest important values evaporate. By viewing morality merely as a set of abstract principles, impartialists open themselves to the charge that they ignore paramount functions of morality such as developing personal relationships and trusting local communities. Accordingly, a powerful burden rests on impartialists to show how their ethic is compatible with forms of friendships and family that preserve important values.

Impartial Principles Undermine True Intimacy

Partialists also point to the alleged poverty of viewing the value of personal relations in purely instrumentalist terms. If some impartialists are willing to admit a certain level of partiality only because doing so has an instrumental value for the general moral enterprise, they miss the mark. There is also much inherent value embodied by personal relations. Imagine being in a personal relationship and discovering that the other party has done certain actions for you only out of a sense of Kantian duty or from an ideal of universal beneficence or for reasons of general moral development. You would likely conclude that the other has misunderstood the nature of personal relations.[28] The question here is whether a purely instrumental acceptance of partiality in personal relations is self-defeating. Under the partialist's argument, a proper understanding reveals both the inherent value and inherent partiality of personal relations.[29]

The partialist contends that personal relations have an inherent value and a phenomenology that transcends the requirements of instrumental impartiality. Personal relations are not merely different in degree from impersonal relations, they are metaphysically different in kind: the metaphors of mutual bonds, connectedness, attachments, although faintly capturing the truth, are too effete. Here two slogans of *l'ordine della famiglia* can be most helpful in expressing the metaphysical differences between familial and impersonal relationships: *sangu du me sangu* ("blood of my blood") and *nun aviri famigghia e comu essiri un nuddo miscatu cu nenti* ("to be without family is to be a nobody mixed with nothing").

In reality, we may find families much less of a haven of mutuality than what some partialists suggest. Moreover, it is unclear whether this argument, even if accepted in its most celebrated form, destroys impartialism. Remember, both Rachels and Baron accept a limited partiality in personal relations, and Rachels does so on explicitly noninstrumentalist grounds. Nagging questions remain for impartialists, however: Can we have deeply felt love-bonds but still remain impartial when meting out our resources and service goods? Is the partial bias permitted by moderate contingent impartialism—I may prefer my family and intimates to strangers only when the conflicting interests at stake are equally important, or when family interests are nontrivial and stronger than the competing interests—sufficient to rescue the impartiality thesis from the charge that it wrongly devalues and misunderstands intimacy?

Partiality is Presupposed by Personhood

There is a related objection that partialists levy against impartialists: to require people to determine all of their important decisions by impartial consideration of global needs is to destroy personhood itself. The assumption here is that personhood presupposes partiality in the sense that one's identity and personal integrity must consist in part of projects, aspirations, and life's plans that have unique status in one's priority of values simply because they are hers.[30]

An interesting question arises here. Could an impartialist reply that with proper moral education and socialization the general welfare, at least insofar as it involves satisfying the basic needs of everyone, could in fact become our project and highest aspiration? Is there necessarily an incompatibility between thinking and acting impartially and one's integrity? Could it not be that partialists now suspect that there is such an incompatibility because as an empirical and contingent matter most people are radical partialists? Is this an inevitable feature of human nature? Or is it a sad commentary on the primitive, parochial level of our moral education and socialization?

John Cottingham, a contemporary English philosopher, would be unconvinced by the questions I have raised on behalf of impartialism: "A world in which I accorded everyone at large the same sort of consideration which I accord to myself, my children, and my friends would not be 'one big happy family'; it would be a world in which affection no longer existed because the sense of 'specialness' had been eliminated. It would be a world where much of what gives human life preciousness and significance had disappeared."[31]

One of Cottingham's points, an echo of Donaldson's concerns, is that an impartialist ethic makes each of us a dispassionate, bloodless, conscientious bureaucrat who never displays favoritism when allocating public resources. Partialists consider this even-handedness a feckless moral ideal because two of the paramount points of the moral enterprise are personal transformation and social nonfungibility.[32]

We return to the questions that haunt impartialists: Despite their protestations to the contrary, can they truly accommodate a moral universe where individuality and intimacy remain? Is a universe of impartiality truly a better world on balance than the partialist world that presently dominates our moral thinking?

Impartialists can retort that many of the charges of partialists are question-begging. They may assert that partialists presuppose the values of the dominant social order and then simply show how the impartialist moral ideal fails to instantiate those values. The partialist thus has done no more than to show that when judged by partialist standards, impartialism will fail. But after all, part of the impartialist program is to unsettle and transform precisely those partialist values and standards. The impartialist may argue that instead of exposing embarrassing implications of impartialism, all the partialist has done is restate part of the impartialist program and register shock. But this response was to be expected from the outset: the entrenched social order is unlikely to welcome a threatening challenger.

Practical Problems with Impartiality

Partialists also insist that impartialism is utopian in a pejorative sense. John Cottingham reminds us that impartialism "urges us to transcend our selfish nature and adopt the life of universal agape; yet few or none of the proponents of that life have even come remotely near to putting it into practice . . . we devote indefinitely more time and resources to our own plans and projects, to our own self-development and fulfillment, than we can even begin to conceive of devoting to the needs of humanity at large."[33]

In an empirical sense, Cottingham is, of course, correct. But surely no impartialist denies his description of current and past practice. The real debate is whether our dominant social practices can and should be transformed. Cottingham takes the prevalence of such practices as strong (dispositive?) evidence that the impartialist ethic is beyond our grasp. Because he also is firmly convinced that any concentrated effort to strive for the impartialist ethic is accompanied by devastating costs – loss of genuine personal relationships, compromise of the individual's integrity and self-identity – he argues that the quest for this impossible dream is ignoble: we cannot achieve impartialism and we should not struggle for it.[34]

The impartialists ask us to look around this world and see what the dominant practices have wrought. They perceive partialists as overly pessimistic and point out that general acceptance of impartialism would not hurt any one individual, group, or nation, and would facilitate great overall benefits in the world. Instead of viewing prevalent past and current practices as data for circumscribing what is possible, impartialists view them as embodying moral errors that should be repudiated.

Impartialists, however, face a deeper problem. The radically counterintuitive features of their program call into question at least two of their methodological assumptions: their belief in the strict epistemological priority of the general and abstract over the concrete and particular;[35] and their unwavering conviction in the moral authority of grand theory.[36] Both assumptions are highly contestable. Rather than showing, as impartialists often claim, the inadequacy of particular judgments about concrete cases based on prejudice, bias, and unreflective moral conventionalism, the conflict between impartialism and partialism may demonstrate the utter poverty of trying to apply directly abstract moral theory to particular cases. Accordingly, impartialists may exaggerate the moral force of grand theories and the epistemological power of logical abstractions.

THE BURDEN OF PERSUASION

Most readers probably find themselves favoring a version of the partialist position, for most of you, by virtue of being in a position to read literature of this type, are not engaged in a brutal struggle for survival. Your probable distance from necessity permits innovative reflection on the terms of social life. But you also have or possess a reasonable chance for a network of relatively satisfying personal relations and have deeply assimilated dominant social and moral norms. You are the readers to whom Donaldson could so confidently appeal when favorably comparing "our" world with the impartialists' Equim. You appear to have much to lose and relatively little to gain, both materially and emotionally, from a conversion to Equim. Furthermore, even if you sympathize with the impartialists' aspirations, and I speculate that most of you do, you will probably suspect that the burden of persuasion rests with the impartialists. That is, no conclusive argument is available on questions such as, is human nature inherently and inevitably partialist? Can personhood exist in Equim? Can intimacy persist where we favor some people in terms of emotional and spiritual goods, but not in terms of material or service goods? and therefore impartialism must convince us to change our minds because our default mindset registers partialism. Moreover, you are undoubtedly very skeptical that the institutions of family and intimate associations can be restructured in a way that preserves their unique values to personal integrity and growth, yet embody an impartial ethic regarding allocation of resources and personal goods.

You will recall even the most plausible version of impartialism, Rachels's moderate contingent vision, demands that the basic needs of strangers morally trump all desires of family and intimates that cannot be legitimately charac-terized as basic needs. The rhetorical trick here is to label the latter luxuries, a phrase that carries morally pejorative baggage and obscures the real choices most parents face. Moreover, basic needs are construed only in material terms, though in fact children and other intimates have numerous emotional and spiritual basic needs that often require our time, money, and attention. Any reasonable interpretation of where to draw the line between basic needs and luxuries may leave most parents, even those antecedently drawn to impartialism, with precious few material and emotional resources to even consider allocating to the basic needs of strangers. The irony here is that the plausibility of impartialism increases the more liberally it defines basic needs, but its conceptual distinctiveness and practical significance simultaneously decrease. It may seem to degenerate into either one of two disreputable images: wild-eyed fanaticism at its most uncompromising or Simon-says timidity at its most plausible.

By virtue of enjoying an occupation that permits me to write essays such as this, I am one of you. Impartialists focus on the principle of equality as definitive of morality. In fact, that principle is only one of many principles required for full moral assessment. Thus, impartialists generate disturbing implications only because they wrongly reduce morality to one of its components. Although I am not convinced that impartialism can be proved logically unsound or empirically impossible, neither can impartialism persuasively alter, on the basis of a disputable abstract reason, our default moral theory and practice. Paradoxically, impartialism might be most successful in an atmosphere of relatively abundant resources where universal benevolence would be less taxing for us all: precisely the atmosphere where impartialism would be least necessary. Where impartialism is most needed, in circumstances of deprivation and scarcity, it may be least persuasive because great numbers of people are preoccupied with a brutal struggle to obtain life's necessities.

This paradox suggests another facet of the problem: a serious coordination problem attends impartialism. Even those who deny Donaldson's conclusion that our world is preferable to Equim must grapple with the fact that an individual's choice is not simply between our world and Equim; instead, the choice is between our world and acting *as if* we are in Equim. Acting as if Equim existed does not, in the absence of millions acting likewise, establish the impartialist paradise. The real question is whether I prefer acting in accord with the partialist norms of this world or acting in accord with impartialist norms while the overwhelming number of others are acting in accord with the partialist norms of this world. Accordingly, even someone who is moved by the impartialist ideal and who is seduced by its transformative possibilities has a further question to address: Does it make moral and practical sense for me to act on that ideal while millions of others remain partialists?

NONCONTRACTUAL PARTIALISM

As I mentioned previously, the major arguments within moral theory are not merely those between partialists and impartialists. Most thinkers accept elements of each ideal, although they differ as to the scope and to the justification of each ideal. There is also an interesting debate within partialism between contractualists and noncontractualists.

Contractualists argue that our moral obligations arise from the voluntary agreements and commitments we make. In its strictest form, contractualism denies that we are antecedently bound to others: in the absence of voluntary acts and mutual commitments – activity that the moral agent has chosen and for which she is therefore responsible – no moral obligations exist. Contractualists of this sort revere the ideals of human autonomy and rationality as distinctively human and the foundation of all morality.

Strict contractualism poses difficulties for an ethic of personal relations. Children, for example, do not choose their parents, their ethnicity or race, their cultural heritage, their initial communities, and so on. Parents often (but not always) choose to have children but not the particular offspring that result. Intimate friendships may largely be chosen, but contractualism seems to reduce the ground for the ensuing obligations to what underwrites impersonal agreements such as business contracts. It may seem that strict contractualism must conceive personal relations on the model of commerce "writ small." If so, part of the richness of the experience of personal relations is lost.

Consider the case of the phenomenology of personal relations, the ways they are experienced and internally develop. Can volition and cognition account entirely for the nature and mutual obligations of personal relationships? Thomas Donaldson astutely points out that "we cannot *choose* to possess a genuine and primitive concern for the welfare of our children over that of others, any more than we can choose to possess it for our friend or for our family members. In order for familial affection to be true, it must be primitive rather than derivative, and spontaneous rather than chosen. Similarly, the personal concern characteristic of friendship cannot be chosen as a matter of duty; it emerges spontaneously in the activity of friendship."[37] Donaldson questions whether a strict contractualist ethic can account for the concern and affection that seem integral to successful personal relations.[38]

Blood is Thicker than Water

Elsewhere[39] I have argued against strict contractualism. As a prelude to assessing *l'ordine della famiglia*, I will resketch that argument here. My thesis is that certain demands of morality do not arise from explicit and discrete volitional acts. Humans have a general moral requirement to preserve and maintain value; constituents of personal identity such as our inherited legacy (genetic make-up, family, nation, culture, and traditions) and noninherited attachments, commitments, and properties possess value independently of whether particular individuals explicitly acknowledge that value; moral requirements are generated in part by the fact that as the repository of such value I am better placed than others to understand and to preserve it simply by being who I am; and as the repository of that value I therefore bear a special responsibility to a particular segment of the shared human heritage. Thus, my metaphysical constitution—who I am—has moral implications for what I must do.

People who subscribe to a contractualist version of the self assume unanimously that the volitional acts of self create moral requirements—my expressions of free will and choice are morally binding. But if the acts of self create moral requirements, why cannot the self embody moral requirements by its very nature—being one kind of repository of value rather than another; being comprised of certain valuable constituents rather than others? I claim that the acts of self both manifest who we are and help forge who we are to become, and if the acts of self create moral requirements (as is universally accepted) then the other constituents of self can as well.

The self is given in and through a social context and is not a fixed, complete entity at a certain specified time. Others make us who we are; we share and participate in a common identity and tradition that comprises one segment of the human heritage. We enter the world already laden with history, traditions, prejudices, and community structures. Their moral force results from the recognition that they are indispensable in forging the particular people that we are and in constituting the particular value we embody.

These elements, which engage our identities and inspire our allegiance, are never finally and permanently fixed, but are always open to growth and transformation. We cannot, however, renounce entirely our metaphysical constitution, or reimagine and remake our personal identities sharply and suddenly. Thus, we cannot cast off moral requirements generated by our constitutive attributes merely by impulsively renouncing our inherited legacy, ongoing attachments, and core commitments. Gradually, as the self is reimagined and remade, such moral requirements may well fade away or change.

The self, constituted and nurtured by social interaction and participation, remains unique. The specter of the destruction of "individuality" because of appeals to such sociality must be exposed as a false terror. This notion of self seeks only to refine the nature and quality of social participation as a way of recognizing the reality of the development of concrete persons, rather than focusing on the illusions of the abstract, unencumbered, atomistic self so familiar in contractarian literature. The individualistic emphasis on choice and freedom must be muted by recognizing that personal autonomy is only possible in communal settings. Our social context establishes the structures and arrangements that make individual rights possible, provides alternatives, and socializes us to favor certain alternatives over others. Therefore, the individualistic myth — that social life is developed from characteristics that adhere to humans in isolation — is false and dangerous.

Our personal identities are thus linked intimately and necessarily to our relations with other people, traditions, and institutions. My argument is that one source of our moral requirements concerns our identities and involves the way other people and traditions satisfy the conditions of the Contribution to Self Principle (CSP):

> If entity Y (a person, tradition, culture, family, and so on) either has made or is making a morally valuable contribution, in an otherwise morally permissible way, to person X's identity either by (a) being part of X's genetic make-up or inherited legacy, or (b) being an attachment or commitment, or providing a property constitutive of X's personal identity, then X owes a prima facie moral requirement of care to Y. The relative strength of the requirement owed is proportionate to the extent and value of Y's contribution to X's personal identity at the time of calculation and the extent of Y's effort/ sacrifice/burden in making the contribution to X.

The moral requirements at issue embrace partialism: providing resources for the care of biological and rearing parents, as well as for others with whom we have significant relationships or who have contributed significantly to our personal identity; preserving and maintaining cultural traditions and embodied values; and allegiance to one's nation. Like virtually all moral requirements, these obligations are prima facie and can be overridden by our own limited resources, sphere of inviolable personal concern, and conflicting moral requirements. Moreover, CSP is a bottom-up moral principle: although general and abstract, it is derived inductively from interpretations of concrete social relations, rather than concluded deductively from ethical theory on a grand scale. Finally, we need not view CSP as the sole source of familial obligations.

Although an adequate explanation of CSP demands intensive technical analyses, I will not address such technical questions here, nor will I further illustrate CSP, for I have done so in detail elsewhere.[40] The purpose of this section of the essay is merely to introduce a version of noncontractual partialism that can lead to a fuller understanding of *l'ordine della famiglia.*

The Grounding of CSP

The reasons why CSP generates moral requirements differ according to whether the contribution to self concerns an inherited legacy or noninherited personal attachments, commitments, or properties.

Our inherited legacy consists of the family, culture, nation, and traditions into which we are born and raised. Some of our moral requirements are grounded in our metaphysical constitution — who we are — which makes us the repository of certain value rather than other value. This basis for moral requirements is independent of the contractualist ground of reciprocity. The Contribution to Self Principle is grounded here on the following Principle of Preservation:

If moral agent X is in a favored position to maintain and preserve Y, which possesses value V and which partly constitutes X's personal identity, then X, as the repository of Y, is the custodian of Y and bears special responsibility R for Y. The magnitude of R that X bears is directly proportionate to the amount of V possessed by Y and the extent to which X's personal identity is constituted by Y.

These moral requirements cannot be based on contractualist grounds, because we do not choose our parents, ethnicity, or cultural heritage. Such constituents of self transcend volitional acts and contractual interactions. Nevertheless, our inherited genetic make-up and formative culture contribute greatly to who we are. We cannot ground the moral requirements at stake here on feelings of affection because such sentiments are unreliable. Lacking an antecedent notion of what is genetically and culturally due to one from one's parents and formative environment, we can in every case fantasize about what we might have been and be resentful of being short-changed and deprived, rather than thankful for who and what we are. If preoccupied by the gap between our real selves and our fantasized selves, we are likely to blame the imagined discrepancy on the parents and cultural traditions that appear responsible. Thus, the traditional approach of contractualist ethics cannot account for the existence of the moral requirements at issue in those cases where we are unappreciative. Paradoxically, if affection were necessary for these moral requirements, we could lessen the number and gravity of our moral requirements by our own lack of moral sensibility.[41]

At best, certain interpersonal relations are characterized by intimate feelings—love, deep mutual affection, recognition that the interests of the other is part of my good, the experience of forming a subjectivity wider than myself, and so on—but even where such feelings are absent, moral requirements may reside. The Principle of Preservation accounts for such requirements on the basis of our assumed general human imperative to preserve and maintain value, a requirement especially relevant to those values we are in a favored position to realize; on the fact that humans are valuable, and their specific identities are constituted partly by the aforementioned inherited legacies; and on the fact that our inherited legacies thereby possess value of which we are custodians because we are the repositories of that value. In fulfilling these moral requirements, we are, literally speaking, being true to our selves.

I assume here that families, cultural traditions, and national heritages are valuable because of their role in constituting personal identity. Humans are valuable, and without social attachments and connections, some of which arise nonvoluntarily, we would all stand alone, naked before a terrifying and seemingly all-powerful universe. Not to belong to a nation, tribe, or parents—to be stripped of our metaphysical constituents—is to be nobody. (Once again: *un nuddo miscatu cu nenti.*) We all draw strength from and are constituted by our inherited legacy, and to be uprooted, to belong to no place, is the great tragedy of displaced persons, refugees, and aliens. Such people suffer grave and frightening identity crises because they have lost some of their most valuable characteristics, those pertaining to membership and belonging. Our inherited legacy thus fulfills necessary psychological functions.

To say that a moral agent is in a favored position to preserve and maintain value might suggest criteria relevant to resources such as wealth, or the possession of special skills and abilities, or situational advantages such as geographical proximity or being privy to certain information not accessible to everyone. But the more fundamental criterion here is one's metaphysical constitution. The values of a certain inherited legacy *are* "me" and as the repository of such values I am better placed than others to understand and preserve them simply by being who I am. One bears a special responsibility to the particular segment of the shared human heritage that one embodies and thus is in a position to cherish, regardless of whether one wants to cherish it or not.

Our noninherited attachments, commitments, and properties are also important constituents of self. If others contribute to our personal identities, we owe them moral requirements in return. One ground for these moral requirements is a contractualist appeal to reciprocity, combined with the acknowledgment of the Principle of Preservation that we all embody value—regardless of whether we are precisely who we would like to be, who we might have been, and regardless of the presence or absence of affection toward those who have contributed to our identities. We owe moral requirements, based on our benefactors' contributions to the person that we are and the value we thereby embody, as a demand of justice. Thus, our metaphysical constitution and our embodiment of certain value have moral implications in concert with generally accepted liberal principles of justice.

Note that liberal-contractualist appeals to justice have more force in a discussion of noninherited attachments and commitments than when in an analysis of inherited legacies. The contractualist rubric of rational choice-agreement-voluntary interaction is much more applicable to noninherited constituents of self where elements of rational autonomy, so prized by contractualists, play a more significant role than they do in constituents of self that transcend choice such as much of our inherited legacies.

I urge readers to imagine the moral requirements generated by CSP as located on a continuum. We owe more to those who fulfill the conditions of CSP than we do to those who do not, and the strength of the moral requirements varies proportionately to the extent of our benefactors' contribution to and nurturing of our identities. The justification for so acting stems in part from an acknowledgment that (1) the boundaries of self are drawn mainly by convention, not by requirements dictated by nature, but some parts of nature are closer to "me" than others;[42] (2) the considered moral judgments of common morality, with the exception of implausible versions of impartialism, admit the egoist insight that, other things being equal, we are often morally permitted to advance the interests of the self rather than the interests of others; and (3) the grounding provided by the preservation principle for our inherited legacies and by contractualist principles of justice for our noninherited attachments transforms the moral permissions generated by the egoist insight into moral requirements.

Comments on Method

Jan Narveson argues that I fail to provide a "foundation"[43] or a "clear logical entailment"[44] demonstrating that, on the basis of CSP, children have moral requirements to their parents based on the latter's contribution to the former's personal identity. My position is that reasons, considerations, and arguments can clothe what begins as the bare intuition that children have duties to their parents. I do not suggest that a "foundation" resting on an unassailable deductive argument can be advanced. Indeed, I reject foundationalism, by which I mean any moral theory that our knowledge claims can ultimately be tested by certain foundational truths that are immune from revision. Such foundational truths may be indubitable or incorrigible, or they may be presuppositions of rationality itself.

Often we philosophers claim to be providing deeper arguments and building foundations for our claims, whereas in fact we make a series of lateral rhetorical moves. Not even the formal system of two-value deductive logic can be proved in any truly foundational sense, for we all know that under incessant questioning of our claims – Why? Why? Why? – we soon begin repeating ourselves or reiterating previous claims in slightly different words.

Moreover, much of morality is embedded in the structure of society, not in the structure of human cognition. Social relations may play a greater role than we minions, of abstract rational principles may often suspect. Thus, Anthony Cortese writes: "Relationships, not reason nor justice, are the essence of life and morality. Conceptions of justice are merely abstract and reified rationality; they remove us from the real world in which we live, and separate us from real people whom we love. Relationships provide the context and the basis for any type of justice, any code of moral principles for which we live. Relationships provide the context for all of our sets of belief, value systems, and behavioral norms."[45]

Narveson also castigates thinkers who would derive moral theory from a theory of human nature and includes me among that ignoble group.[46] I agree with Narveson that such a derivation cannot be made without something more: a first principle or axiom that itself cannot be proved, an appeal to social practice or custom, reliance on the dictates of a supreme being, a leap of faith, or some other maneuver. This admission may seem abhorrent to those of us who pretend to avoid contaminating our conclusions with emotion and passion and claim instead to discover through conceptual analysis the secret demands contained in the strongbox of Reason.

I, however, am much more suspicious of moral theories that purport to make no appeal to a theory of person. Theorists of this ilk all too often smuggle into their analyses covert interpretations of human nature, which they shield from critical scrutiny by protesting that no appeal to a theory of persons is being made. I do agree that we cannot appeal to an antecedent and disembodied theory of persons as an axiomatic starting point in our quest for moral theory. Rather, a theory of persons partly constitutes particular versions of moral theory, and the acceptability of a moral theory helps determine the acceptability of its component theory of persons. The notion of "acceptability" here is much looser and contestable than standards of deductive logic: it appeals to concrete experiences of human personality more than formal categories.

Lacking a belief in a pure, neutral Reason that might adjudicate conflicting value claims once and forever, I perceive normative disputation as an exercise in persuasion, neither completely rational nor purely emotional. We all know that a valid deductive argument can be construed for any conclusion, no matter how preposterous. To assess the soundness of such arguments we go beyond merely applying the demands and logical entailments of pure Reason. Thus I reject the artificial dilemma between "foundationalism" and "bare intuitionism."

Why Contractualism Goes Wrong

Radically impartialist moral theories, which advise us to treat the desires and satisfactions of all humans (or all sentient beings) equally, or which counsel us to genuflect in supplication only before the authority of moral principles themselves, degenerate into formal and thus meaningless abstraction. These theories gain their universality by plundering individuals of their distinctive metaphysical constituents and thus impoverish our concept of personhood.

Partialism based entirely on contractualism, however, grounds morality on uncoerced agreements that underscore the importance of free choice, volition, and rational agency. It begins in a vision of humans as radically distinct individuals, concentrates exclusively on those aspects of experience that separate us, emphasizes our uniqueness and mutual divisions, and ends in the negative freedom of the minimal state. The theory thus provides an important service and corresponds to our felt need to maintain a distinct place in the world and to affirm our irreplaceable specialness. Still, partiality based entirely on contractualism yields only an unfinished picture of our being.

We also experience a competing and equally real yearning to recognize intimate connections and bonds with others, attachments not always created but sometimes discovered. This communitarian impulse affirms our commonality and acknowledges our membership in and alliances within a wider subjectivity. To ignore or understate this experience is to renounce part of our human condition. Noncontractual partialism aspires to complete the contractualist picture without falling prey to the excesses of impartialism: it honors the reality of our biological and social development.

Throughout our lives, we oscillate constantly and uneasily between the attractions of individualism and the seductions of wider communities; we can never resolve this existential riddle. But to ignore in moral theory the presence of these dual longings, to limit the source of moral requirements to the prescriptions of the contractualist's rubric, and to advance such an undifferentiated and one-sided picture of reality as an ahistorical imperative of Reason, is to do violence to our concrete social experience and ultimately to denigrate ourselves.

L'ORDINE DELLA FAMIGLIA REVISITED

In a controversial book,[47] Edward Banfield argued that the southern Italians he studied exemplified "amoral familism," behavior consistent with the following rule: "Maximize the material, short-run advantage of the nuclear family;

assume that all others will do likewise."[48] Banfield insisted that "one who follows the rule is without morality only in relation to persons outside the [nuclear] family—in relations to family members, he applies standards of right and wrong."[49] He argued that the rule of amoral familism generated at least seventeen "logical implications" that explained the behavior he observed in southern Italy.[50] Most strikingly, Banfield claimed that amoral familism, the ethos of the nuclear family, caused the seemingly ineradicable social problems that plagued the region. Moreover, he claimed that southern Italians in the past were as amorally familist as they were in his 1950s research findings. If he is correct, a strong concomitant claim could be lodged against the morality of the entire family structure as partialism run amuck and ironically turned against itself. Moral progress would demand that the southern Italian family structure be not venerated but transcended, be not perpetuated but destroyed.

Banfield's critics, however, far exceed his supporters and they have lodged a number of interconnected complaints. First, even if we entirely concede the soundness of Banfield's argument, it may not follow that his description and analysis of the Montegranesi apply to the entire *Mezzogiorno*.[51] Second, some social scientists have argued that Banfield's description of the Montegranesi as "amoral familists" is inaccurate and unsupported by his own data.[52] Third, other critics have argued that his own theoretical model contradicts his findings.[53] Fourth, some respondents argue that Banfield misunderstands the nature of social values and familial ethos.[54] Fifth, many critics contend that one of Banfield's major suppositions, that the form of the southern Italian family is nuclear, obscures the reality of extended kinship relations.[55] Sixth, even if Banfield's descriptive account of amoral familism is accurate, he has reversed the proper causal priority: it is not the family ethos that causes socioeconomic "backwardness" but objective socioeconomic conditions that facilitate the family ethos.[56] Finally, several responses demonstrate that whatever persuasiveness Banfield's findings embody in the 1950s, they do not accurately describe the behavior patterns of late nineteenth- and early twentieth-century southern Italians.[57]

After a thorough examination of the relevant literature, I am convinced that the most common form of southern Italian family in the late nineteenth and early twentieth centuries was extended, not merely nuclear, and that there exists a mutually constitutive relationship between the family ethos, major social structures, and primary economic forms. This relationship is more dialectical than linearly causal, although economic forms have the highest causal priority.[58] Thus, Banfield's thesis is seriously, perhaps fatally, flawed.

There nonetheless remain serious questions of moral assessment: Even conceding a rich network of extended relations involving blood and voluntarily contracted ties, was *l'ordine della famiglia* a morally flawed form of partialism? Did the family code, even when understood more extensively than Banfield's "amoral familism," too narrowly circumscribe the range of moral concern?

The moral code of *l'ordine della famiglia* embodied a series of moral judgments and practices indigenous to particular existential conditions. The disenfranchised sons and daughters of the *Mezzogiorno* endured especially brutal life prospects.

Booker T. Washington, a man who knew slavery firsthand and fought against it, visited Italy and concluded: "The Negro is not the man farthest down. The condition of the coloured farmer in the most backward parts of the Southern States in America, even where he has the least education and the least encouragement, is incomparably better than the condition and opportunities of the agricultural population in Sicily."[59]

Karl Marx, whose scientific socialism was to energize over 40 percent of the world's population at the height of its influence, once wrote that "in all human history no country or no people have suffered such terrible slavery, conquest and foreign oppression and no country and no people have struggled so strenuously for their emancipation as Sicily and the Sicilians."[60]

Although Sicily provides the most extreme example, much the same conditions could be said to prevail in the other provinces of the *Mezzogiorno:* common people had virtually no chance for upward mobility; only regional loyalties were possible in the absence of a unified Italy; there existed a brutal scarcity of resources; peasants had access only to the most primitive systems of communication and transportation; formal education was woefully inadequate and virtually impossible in an environment where the maximum number of family hands were required for manual labor; criminals often brazenly plied their trades, with a wink and a nod from bribed law enforcement officials; and government was accurately perceived as the paramount part of the problem, certainly not as a treasure chest of enlightened solutions.

Over the centuries, the *Mezzogiorno* had been invaded by Vandals, Greeks, Romans, Byzantines, Arabs, Spaniards, French, and Normans. After the fall of the Roman empire, Italy had divided into several regional political units. By the late fifteenth century, the time of Machiavelli's call in *The Prince* for Italian unification, there were fifteen recognized political regions. In the late eighteenth century, with the invasion of Napoleon, the map of Italy was reimagined and redrawn. At Napoleon's defeat, the Congress of Vienna in 1815 restored much of the earlier demarcations. For the next forty-five years most of the *Mezzogiorno* continued under the rule of the Bourbons. In the 1850s the House of Savoy in the independent state of Piedmont initiated the movement for Italian unification, *Risorgimento*. In the *Mezzogiorno*, where the people's disdain for government had been keenly honed for centuries, the *Risorgimento* was experienced more as an opportunity to retaliate against the current oppressors, the Bourbons, than as a chance for an emotional reunion with central and northern Italians.

The people of the *Mezzogiorno*, tempered by centuries of fragmentation and pernicious hierarchy, could not perceive themselves as part of what they never were; instead, they saw themselves as what they always were and what they seemingly would always be: Sicilians, Neapolitans, Calabrians, Apulians, Campanians, Abruzzese, Lucanians, and so on. More accurately, the people saw themselves as inextricably part of a village or town within these regions; they tended to view even those from other parts of their region with distrust and suspicion, as *stranieri*.

Predictably, the success of the *Risorgimento* in the 1860s not only brought the *Mezzogiorno* no relief from oppression, it exacerbated social tensions in the south. The new federal government was dominated by Piedmontese, northerners with little knowledge of and limited sympathies for southern problems. The distribution of material resources worsened: taxes levied by the central government were heavier in the south than in the north, whereas allocations from the government to the south were more parsimonious. The areas that suffered the most pressing social problems were not accorded commensurate federal support. Fueled by lack of knowledge, knuckling under to political pressures in the north, and harboring long-standing prejudices against southerners, the new federal government sent its message early and often: the problems of the *Mezzogiorno* were not even on the margins of the national agenda, they had been pushed right off the page.

It is dangerously easy to portray this situation one-dimensionally: innocent, noble peasants at the mercy of avaricious, unfeeling local land barons and exploitive northern politicians. In fact, much of the problem involved the deeply entrenched social system in the *Mezzogiorno*, a system in which common people were thoroughly implicated. As with most social situations, the characters in the drama of *Mezzogiorno* cannot accurately be clothed exclusively in either white or black hats.

During the great period of southern Italian emigration to the Americas, from 1880 to 1930, the *Mezzogiorno* was a rural, mainly agricultural, highly stratified society. Moreover, the peasants lived in towns, not on the land they worked. The social hierarchy could be categorized roughly as follows: the *galantuomini* were the gentry, substantial landowners mainly, but also the few professionals, such as doctors, lawyers, pharmacists, and teachers, who were available. The highest gentry were the *latifondisti*, large estate owners who commanded great respect and deference because they controlled southern Italy's most prized and tangible resource, land. Below the landowners and professionals were the *artigiani*, the artisans, such as skilled craftsmen, businessmen, and service workers, who were not engaged in agricultural labor. Far below the higher classes was the largest group, the *contadini*, all the people who worked the land. Some agricultural workers owned modest amounts of land, but most peasants were landless and had to work the land of others. Also included in this class were sheep and goat herders and fishermen. At the bottom of the class structure were *giornalieri*, day laborers whose employment was always hostage to short-term, seasonal demands. This class structure thoroughly permeated the social life of the *Mezzogiorno*.

Agricultural life was particularly severe because centuries of exploitation had resulted in deforestation, erosion of topsoil, and scarcity of water, conditions exacerbated by the semitropical climate. Moreover, the system of share-cropping and short-term leases often found on large estates contributed to inefficient agriculture: the *contadini* felt intense pressure for immediate harvest that often irreparably damaged the best long-term agricultural interests. As late as the 1970s Rudolph Bell described the *la miseria* endured by southern Italian peasants for several centuries: "Houses with cracked and crumbled walls, unborn children you know will be malnourished, abandoned lands, hostile lands, faces and hands burned by the sun. *La miseria* is a disease, a vapor arising from the earth, enveloping and destroying the soul of all that it touches. Its symptoms are wrinkles, distended bellies, anomic individualism, hatred of the soul, and the cursing of God."[61]

Within this context stood the family structure and its elaborate code of rituals and obligations. Luigi Barzini eloquently summed up the importance of the family:

> The Italian family is a stronghold in a hostile land: within its walls and among its members, the individual finds consolation, help, advice, provisions, loans, weapons, allies and accomplices to aid him in his pursuits. No Italian who has a family is ever alone. He finds in it a refuge in which to lick his wounds after a defeat, or an arsenal and a staff for his victorious drives. Scholars have always recognized the Italian family as the only fundamental institution in the country, a spontaneous creation of the national genius, adapted through the centuries to changing conditions, the real foundation of whichever social order prevails. In fact, the law, the State and society function only if they do not directly interfere with the family's supreme interests.[62]

Family structures, Italian or not, are universally susceptible to mythologizing. The Italian family, as Barzini himself otherwise sees clearly, was never simply a "stronghold in a hostile land" or merely a salutary "refuge." It also embodied strictly defined gender and generational roles, congealed hierarchy, and often suffocating tribalism. For purposes of this chapter, however, I assess *l'ordine della famiglia* in respect to its alleged lack of concern for nonfamily members. I do not assess the code in respect to its understanding of proper relations within the family.

The bare sketch of life in the *Mezzogiorno* is sufficient for my larger purpose: an assessment of *l'ordine della famiglia.* My thesis is that this code produces morally ambiguous effects and it is difficult to fully justify or fully delegitimate *l'ordine della famiglia* given the social circumstances from which it arose.

We must distinguish from the outset arguments that the code was justified from arguments that it was merely morally excusable. When we judge an action morally excusable we are saying that the action was morally wrong but under the circumstances its agent bears no moral culpability or disapprobation. When we judge an action morally justified we are saying that the action was morally permissible under the circumstances in which it took place.

Talk of moral justification in particular social circumstances may lead some readers to suspect that I am subscribing to an empty-headed normative relativism in which a culture's or subculture's understandings are morally self-ratifying: what people think is morally right becomes morally right, at least for them, simply because of their social understandings. I wish to distance myself from this self-defeating view, certainly. Some codes of conduct are wrong wherever and whenever they occur, and some principles of morality are required in all social contexts. But much of morality is legitimately subject to varying social interpretations. Part of my argument is that the code of *l'ordine della famiglia* falls within that portion of morality subject to cultural interpretation.

The argument that the code was morally justified is based on several considerations. First, the scarcity of resources in the *Mezzogiorno* facilitated a brutal competition for survival. Any appeal to impartialism or to broad partialism under such circumstances is virtually incoherent. The *contadini* did not have to worry about the allocation of their "luxury" spending because they were fortunate to accumulate enough material resources to fulfill their basic needs, even when we construe basic needs as narrowly as possible. Southern Italians sliced their world into layers of social intimacy: in a world of dehumanizing struggle one needed at least a small network of trustworthy confederates. And what better network than one founded on blood and marriage? Thus, the family was understood in an extended sense to include one's immediate family, first and distant cousins, and the extended family of one's spouse. A distinct sense of obligation to family members was recognized, although the obligations were directly proportional to the degree of kinship.

Second, this sense of family was not experienced merely as an impersonal network serving self-interest. Instead, it was felt as membership in a wider subjectivity: one's identity is related directly to social context. Under *l'ordine della famiglia*, a person experienced his or her well-being as part of a larger organic entity – as part of a family in the wider sense sketched above. I am not harkening back nostalgically and prescribing a return to an allegedly utopian experience of family relations. My point is that the moral self-understandings of those Italians embracing *l'ordine della famiglia* may have a justificatory grounding in some of the principles of morality and noncontractual partialist moral theory I advanced in earlier sections of this essay.

Third, peasants in the *Mezzogiorno* had no opportunity to extend their horizons by interacting significantly with people of different backgrounds and outlooks.[63] Lacking the means to communicate with and observe the world outside their village, residents of the *Mezzogiorno* lacked the correlated opportunity to develop a more cosmopolitan moral outlook.

Fourth, local and federal governments had in fact been archaic, corrupt, and distant from the problems of the *contadini*. Under such circumstances, self-reliance and smaller group affiliation naturally replace allegiance to official authorities. More strikingly, there was great hostility, founded on experience, toward wider institutions: *la legge va contrai cristiani* ("the law works against people").[64]

In sum, in the world of the *contadini*, the burdens and solaces of the extended family were tangible, accessible, comprehensible, reliable, and proximate. To the extent that moral responsibility is linked to such notions and to the extent that noncontractual partialism embodies moral currency, *l'ordine della famiglia* builds a strong prima facie case that it is a morally justified outlook given the social circumstances in which it arose. Under those circumstances, any pleas for impartialism or cosmopolitanism must be seen as abstract, incoherent, inherently uncoordinable, and thus, practically speaking, impossible.

The problem is, however, more nuanced. Although it is easy to idealize *l'ordine della famiglia* as a bastion of personal virtue in an otherwise heartless atmosphere, such sentimentalization misses part of the picture. It is inaccurate to view the family code as a reaction to the separate and larger social atmosphere; in fact, the family code is partly constitutive of the larger social arena.

Thus, the argument against the moral justification of *l'ordine della famiglia* begins with its deleterious wider effects. As Barzini puts it: "The strength of the family is not only . . . the bulwark against disorder, but, at the same time, one of its principle causes. It has actively fomented chaos in many ways especially by rendering useless the development of strong political institutions."[65] We cannot accurately portray the family code as a blameless victim of wider social ravages. The code itself in a complicated way is both a contributor to and mediator of wider social injustice. Contending theories of obligations, like conflicting social classes, do not come neatly packaged in white and black.

The family code retards wider national and world identifications at the same time it nurtures the extended subjectivity of the family unit; while it poses an obstacle to civic virtue, it confers strict understandings and a workable moral system for family members; as it mocks genuine nationalism and the social welfare, it sanctifies family loyalty as true patriotism; while in times of war the code produces soldiers who are only minimally committed to the national cause, it generates people who, at their best, in peacetime will endure draconian sacrifices and unspeakable dangers for the sake of their immediate families. In this fashion, through narrowly circumscribed spheres of concern, carefully understood burdens and privileges, and assiduously cultivated self-identities, *l'ordine della famiglia* both promotes and represses the cardinal moral virtues.

In the language of moral theory, impartialists would criticize the extreme partialism manifested to family members and the clear estrangement from outsiders, whereas most noncontractual partialists would praise the virtues cultivated within the family but still argue for the moderation of attitudes toward outsiders. Most noncontractual partialists would suspect that *l'ordine della famiglia*, although nurturing numerous important values, excludes other prominent values, such as those values connected with strong national institutions.

The moral irony of *l'ordine della famiglia* — its simultaneous promotion in the family and repression on other social levels of the cardinal virtues — is accompanied by a psychological irony: on the one hand, the code provides spiritual sustenance and the foundations of personal identity in an otherwise hostile world; on the other hand, the code facilitates lingering dependencies and helps ensure that the outside world will remain hostile.

Accordingly, no unambiguous moral assessment of *l'ordine della famiglia* is persuasive. I conclude that individual families and individual practitioners of the code are certainly morally excused. Given the scarcity of resources, lack of adequate transportation to and communication with the outside world, and the other social conditions, not even the strictest moralist could stigmatize a typical *contadino* as morally culpable. Moreover, that same social context together with the overwhelming coordination problems accompanying massive social change should imply that the code was morally justified when adhered to by the common people. It would be worse than puritanical to argue that a typical *contadino* could have been morally justified only if he advocated and practiced an ethic of wider social concern in an atmosphere pervaded by *l'ordine della famiglia*. Such action is better characterized as either supererogatory — exceeding moral obligation — or as stone-cold foolish, for a peasant who would act with such social deviance and with such self-sacrifice would place his family's welfare in severe jeopardy. Thus, on the level of individual families and individuals, I conclude that given the social circumstances and context, the practice of *l'ordine della famiglia* was morally justified: the formal principles of noncontractual partialism, like the principles of any philosopher's moral theory, must be interpreted by means of the specific structures of a community.

The more difficult question is how to assess the morality of *l'ordine della famiglia* as a whole. Paradoxical as it may sound, individuals might be morally excused or justified in practicing a code that itself is morally inadequate. People as individuals bear limited responsibility for unilaterally changing society if for no other reason than the sheer impossibility or danger of doing so. Again, we encounter the problem of social coordination and how it may exonerate.

I have already discussed the mixed blessings embodied by *l'ordine della famiglia*. Moreover, I have argued that merely imagining a better social world is insufficient. We need to have at least an inkling of how we get from a currently flawed context to our presumed utopia. Thus, our overall evaluation of *l'ordine della famiglia* hinges on intractable empirical questions: To what extent would renunciation of the code, on a socially coordinated level, disaggregate pernicious community conditions and augur better social contexts for all? Could the requisite social coordination itself occur only if community conditions had already been significantly transformed? To what extent is the code an unwitting collaborator in *la miseria?* To what extent does it moderate *la miseria?* In short, we would need to unravel a mass of intertwined social questions to determine the independent moral currency of the code.

Although we cannot hope to untangle the know here, we can observe that the code was transported to the Americas by Italian immigrants and through the first generation replicated its morally ambiguous effects in the new world. It prevented the first generation from achieving full social integration but it also provided strong spiritual comfort in the strange new world; it prohibited many immigrants from immediate upward mobility but it simultaneously promoted the transition to a strange land; it grounded the second generation's personal identity but ultimately exacerbated tensions between the immigrants and their children. Thus, even in the new world, *l'ordine della famiglia* retained a measure of its genius and mystique—its moral inscrutability.

The family code of the Italian immigrants, moreover, illustrates general human paradoxes and conflicts. Many philosophers argue that existential tension is at the heart of human experience: our yearning for intimate connection with others and the recognition that others are necessary for our identity and freedom coalesce uneasily with the fear and anxiety we experience as others approach.[66] We simultaneously long for emotional attachment and are horrified that our individuality may evaporate once we achieve it. This disharmony is never fully reconciled.

With rapidly developing transportation and communication systems, intermarriage, greater educational opportunities, and the alleviation of brutal economic and social oppression, *l'ordine della famiglia,* in its most uncompromising forms, was doomed to extinction in the United States. As the third and fourth generations and their children take their place in American society, only vestiges remain of the code, relics of the past trotted out only when we seek to amuse at family reunions by remembering the loving idiosyncrasies of our immediate ancestors.

But somewhere deep in the collective consciousness of Italian Americans the sentiments of *nun aviri famigghia e comu essiri un nuddo miscatu cu nenti* still resonate, like the episodic rhythms of a surrealistic montage. I will always embrace these sentiments, and I will teach them to my children, but they must be tempered by an awareness that the family requires numerous myths, taboos, and tribal conventions that sometimes cultivate psychological distortions and impede full intellectual development. Humans must distance themselves from their families, at distinct times and to various degrees, to actualize fully their potential. There is no escape from the individual–community continuum.

CHAPTER 2

THE GENDERED SELF STRUGGLES WITH THE FAMILY

Feminist Epistemology and *Una Buona Femmina*

Throughout her married life, my mother, formally educated through only the eighth grade, was convinced of several inexorable truths: she kept the cleanest home, she was the best cook, and she was the hardest-working woman in town; she was the shrewdest handler of money and cleverest bargainer in the marketplace; she would tolerate little nonsense and apologize not one bit for her expansive temper; she would protect and love her family in unsurpassed fashion; she would enforce the family code and respond to her children's transgressions with her weapon of choice, the wooden spoon; she could guarantee that her children would go off to school impeccably groomed; and she could double-guarantee that her children would someday graduate from college. These were not latent truths. My mother often explicitly stated them, sometimes humorously, and even more frequently exemplified them by deed. She challenged all family members to provide even one shred of evidence against her claims. None of us ever could. Her truths were unassailable.

By the time she was forty-six, my mother suffered from an especially debilitating form of rheumatoid arthritis. By the time she was forty-nine, she was withering and confined mainly to her chair or bed. She died at sixty-two. Was my mother a victim of the legacy of the pernicious southern Italian patriarchy? Was she an illustration of the stolid virtues of a better time? Was she a feminist hero?

In this chapter, I explain and discuss three common interpretations of the relationship between Italian immigrant women and their families. I then raise some theoretical issues in epistemology and value theory that underlie much of the interpretive enterprise and assess their relationship to contemporary debates between feminist thought and analytic philosophy. Finally, I reassess the three interpretations of Italian-American women in light of my conclusions about interpretive projects. In so doing, I focus on a special dimension of the individual-community continuum: the gendered self confronts the family.

IMAGES OF THE GOOD WOMAN

Once we exclude false and pejorative stereotypical images, the literature reveals three main visions of immigrant Italian-American women: the stabilizer, the cultural transformer, and the matriarch. Before explaining and analyzing these visions, I must issue several caveats. First, the three visions manifest areas of overlap. Second, rather than conceiving the three as different in kind it is preferable to understand them as different in degree. Third, it must be clear that just as there was no single, simple mold to which all Italian-American families conformed, so too there was no standard Italian-American immigrant woman. Fourth, all historical recreations, such as the instant case, that suffer from a dearth of sociological data are especially susceptible to retrospective falsification and ideological interpretation: some writers are prone to nostalgia and sentimentality as they longingly conjure an idealized past; others are inclined to harness the past in service of an ideological agenda in the present. Fifth, Italian-American women did not confront a unitary reality in the new world: many labored in urban ethnic sanctuaries in the northeast; some settled on the Pacific coast; others lived in rural America. Thus, differences in climate, class, working conditions, and population density further belie the possibility of a standard Italian-American immigrant woman.

The Stabilizer

The roots of this normative vision of womanhood were sown in the unique culture and history of the *Mezzogiorno*. Lydio Tomasi describes the fundamental role of mother in the southern Italian peasant family:

The mother rules the home merely as an interpreter of her husband's wishes; even when he does not deserve it, she loves and obeys him. She has two other outstanding functions: to select wives for her sons and to hold the family purse. She takes charge of her husband's earnings and those of her unmarried children.[1]

Here Tomasi depicts an aspect of a radically patriarchal family: father has high status; mother is the center of the home only, rarely works for wages outside the home, and is educated for marriage only. Interpersonal relations are characterized by the greater value perceived in boys, a highly parent-centered family, the selection of children's mates by parents, a deeply stable family that defines the way of life, and limited contact with people residing outside one's immediate village.[2]

According to this view, women enjoyed only derivative status: the contributions of males were more highly valued than those of women, whose prestige was proportional to their proper discharge of nurturing and caretaking functions within the family. Wives were regarded as valuable possessions who embodied useful instrumental goods: producer of children, sustainer of family, and provider of domestic services. Accordingly, mothers were perceived as the heart of the family, and qualities such as steadfastness of purpose, purity, and self-sacrifice assumed primary importance. Husbands, however, remained the ultimate source of social power and control on the basis of their role as economic provider and physical protector.[3]

The portrayal of radical patriarchy prefigures its own transformation in the New World. Socially constructed and functioning in the highly stratified, provincial, neomedieval context of the *Mezzogiorno*, the Old World patriarchy was fated for reinvention in the radically different context of the United States.

The first-generation southern Italian family in America experienced a loosening of strict patriarchy, increased mobility, decrease in the status of the father, more frequent occasions of the mother working for wages and receiving formal education, and increased conflict within the family as *la via vecchia* ("the old way") clashed with New World values. Because of these cultural and familial transformations, the role of women became more complicated.[4]

Richard Gambino provides by far the clearest and most powerful image of the Italian-American immigrant woman as cultural stabilizer.[5] Gambino's ideal purports to exemplify aspects of the reinvented family. The first-generation southern Italian family in America immediately adapted, to varying degrees, to its new context. In contrast to the negative stereotype of the Italian mama—invariably overweight, obsessed with food, buffoonishly happy, guileless, and simpleminded—Gambino emphasizes the virtues of *la serieta*. He portrays the woman as the center of the immigrant family: serious, active, embodying acute practical wisdom.

> The role of women was no less than to anchor the family in the power of their own beings and warm *l'ordine della famiglia* by their emotions and love . . . the necessity always to be clever [*scaltra*] was felt more keenly by the women even than by the men . . . artfulness was always required and could never be relaxed . . . they took great pride in their ability to bargain advantages for the clan . . . the world was made up of foxes and their prey, and *una buona femmina* was a vixen par excellence.[6]

Thus, the Italian-American immigrant woman played paramount economic and social roles: mediator of internal familial conflict; transmitter of *l'ordine della famiglia;* nurturer and caregiver responsible for the family's central physical and psychological needs; manager of family finances; possessed of seriousness and inner toughness; courageous, determined, clear-headed, and willing to sacrifice; often employed, but only in contexts (e.g., homework, canning, garment work) that caused minimal disruption to family life;[7] publicly deferential to her husband but privately possessing much say in family affairs;[8] and keenly concerned with household neatness and cleanliness as symbols of the condition of the family itself.

Moreover, this image of the Italian-American immigrant woman acknowledges the great burden placed on the mother as expresser of the entire family's emotional state. For example, at funerals women were responsible for manifesting the sorrow of the entire family. As death has not merely taken an individual but has also torn asunder necessary familial bonds, it must be personified and raged against.[9]

This image underscores above all the degree to which the Italian-American immigrant mother was responsible for stabilizing her family in a new context.[10] She was charged with facilitating *la via vecchia*—values centered on family solidarity, practical wisdom, and self-contained sexual pride—in a foreign setting. Resulting conflicts between the first and second generations were inevitable. Because of the more excessive social restraints placed on adolescent females, the conflicts were perhaps most keenly felt between the women of those generations.

For example, second-generation women were instructed that certain modes of behavior were strictly forbidden: public informality, residing outside the family home, public arguments with family elders, American-style dating, and tardiness in returning home from school. Naturally, the second generation rebelled against such old-world prohibitions, regulations that lacked robust social meaning in the New World. This rebellion implicated the deepest identities of the second generation: Were they Americans? Certainly not to those outside the Italian community. Were they Italians? Certainly not in the eyes of their parents.[11]

Gambino contrasts *una buona femmina* ("a good woman") with the pejorative *mala femmina* ("bad woman"). Although the latter term is literally understood as connoting sexual wickedness, it is more commonly used in the *Mezzogiorno* to mean "a useless woman, a woman who cannot or does not fulfill her complicated role as the center of *la famiglia.*"[12] Thus, the expression evaluates particular women unfavorably against the ideal of womanhood indigenous to the *Mezzogiorno*: "Although the ideal [of womenhood] includes the ability to bear children and household skills, it goes much further. It includes life-supporting qualities which run deep into the being of a person."[13] Accordingly, the ideal of woman as stabilizer served, among other things, as a normative vision that measured women's most profound constitutive attributes.[14]

There are, however, at least two surrealistic qualities to this vision: first, it is not clear that it is an accurate description of the experiences of first-generation Italian-American women; second, it is not clear that it is an acceptable normative ideal to which women should have aspired.

Helen Barolini attacks the ideal of woman as stabilizer in this way:

[Gambino's] espousal of *"La Serieta"* . . . becomes a too idealized vision of woman's place . . . she is seen reducing the importance of sexuality and taking on the mater dolorosa ["mother of sorrows"] role. True, she was the center of life of the whole ethnic group; true, it was she who expressed the emotions of the men; true she must be useful to her family, for her value is based on practical usefulness; but it is less true to women than to men like Gambino that this ideal of *serieta* was the be-all and end-all of a woman's life.[15]

Barolini protests the identification of womanhood with family service: "Everyone leaned on her for support, she was supposed to be permanently accessible and permanently unchanging. She could not exist as an individual with autonomous needs and wishes, for that would have undermined the common good."[16]

At first blush, Barolini's critique seems normative: professional apologists, such as Gambino, for the first-generation southern Italian immigrant family in America obscure the terrible emotional, psychic, and physical harms[17] women experienced in striving to fulfill the ideal of *serieta*. Presumably, while Gambino cheerfully celebrates the selfless, skillful mother, he masks how she was wrongfully immersed in service to others at great harm to her own individuality. In sanctifying the mother to the status of a Madonna, Gambino's vision itself constitutes a false and dangerous stereotype: it shrouds the reality of women's experiences behind the smoke and mirrors of images idealized from a male perspective.

Barolini presses the point that even with its presumed loosening of patriarchy, when contrasted to the family structure in the Old World, the first-generation family unit was stultifying, ego threatening, and emotionally debilitating because it militated against the real possibility of individual assertion. She conjures all of the horrors of the gendered self's excessive immersion in community: loss of self-identity, suffocating psychic pressures, hopeless subjugation to perceived destiny, forfeiture of volition and exercise of free choice, and inevitability of settled expectations. Her critique underscores the violence to freedom and self-development such immersion in community perpetrates on its victims. Moreover, Gambino and others who conceal this reality by their pious idealizations commit an additional affront: by discounting the disproportionately negative effects on women, they confer normative imprimatur on a strikingly deficient way of life.

Barolini's critique also includes a descriptive component. In her view, Gambino's vision is narrow: at best, he describes merely part of the reality of the first generation immigrant woman. Through the lens of his sanguine masculinity, Gambino filters out those portions of *la serieta* that would blemish his sentimental recollections. Thus Barolini retorts: "The professors and other professional apologists of the Italian family had better listen to the women and their literature—to the voices of women writers who are telling it as it is. Home life was never so solid and satisfying as the men said it was; it was what it was for historic and social reasons that are now surpassed."[18]

Not only is Gambino's portrayal descriptively deficient in terms of the negative effects on women it ignores but also in terms of the idealized characteristics it attributes to women: "Contrary to folklore, stereotypes, and compelling portraits of the appealing, traditional Italian woman as pillar of her family, Italian-American literature abounds with portraits of other women who are harsh, frequently cruel, crushing, unfeeling. They are embittered and malevolent; and, given the strictures of their own lives, there is plenty of reason why."[19]

Barolini, then, attacks both descriptively and prescriptively what she perceives as the myth of the Italian-American family: "There never was that perfect state of warmth, security, emotional support [in the family]. There was an uneasy balance of trade-offs in which 'family' cost 'freedom' . . . If one were different, there was *no* supportiveness or family loyalty after all, only emotional blackmail . . . Life, then, was conflict or keeping quiet."[20]

In some respects, Barolini's critique of the ideal of woman as stabilizer is uninspired. For example, her insistence that some first-generation Italian immigrant women fell short of *la serieta* is downright banal. Certainly, Gambino does not assume that his descriptive picture captures all women in its lens. It would be a miracle, and a disappointing one at that, if any description of the Italian-American family or the Italian-American immigrant woman could accomplish such a feat. It would be a double miracle if *all* women in fact achieved a particular prescriptive ideal. Moreover, Barolini often obscures the differences between the inadequacy of the ideal of *la serieta* in contemporary Western settings and its deficiencies in the context from which it emerged. At times, she may be charged fairly with the fallacy of anachronism: applying the sense of possibility and opportunity prevalent today to castigate the social practices of earlier periods. Surely, Gambino would not insist, even at his most sentimental, that the ideal of *la serieta* constitutes an ahistoric, Archimedean standard by which Italian-American (or all) women should be measured. Instead, he is more charitably interpreted as highlighting the paramount values the ideal advanced as Italian immigrants struggled through the difficult transition of becoming Italian Americans or simply Americans.[21]

Having said this, however, I must not minimize the power and vitality of Barolini's perceptions. She is unassailably correct and at her rhetorical best when she mocks the partiality of Gambino's portrayal of Italian immigrant women. Indeed, he does give us an overly cheerful and dangerous rendering of immigrant life. Whether from subconscious retrospective falsification, or out of gratitude for the benefits his own family conferred upon him, or from ethnic pride, Gambino ignores much of the horror of the transition period and the disproportionate suffering women bore. Furthermore, Barolini underscores the unrelenting struggle between individualism and community in the context of immigrant women. She is unquestionably correct when she bewails the lack of freedom and limited opportunities for self-development the women endured.

A recurrent theme of this book is that part of the human condition is the struggle we all necessarily undertake as we move along the continuum between individuality and community, knowing always that each stop along the way is momentary. Although this existential condition may seem a curse, given that our paradox appears unresolvable, it nevertheless provides important transient opportunities for transcendence as we contemplate, negotiate among, and choose from the myriad possibilities along the continuum.

Barolini's position unveils a debilitating aspect of the immigrant family: Italian women were denied these opportunities for transcendence by their social circumstances. Their individuality was submerged in the family unit; their roles were mainly nonnegotiable and hostage to settled expectations; their opportunities were defined by family needs.[22] To put a finer point on it: Italian immigrant women were denied the full experience of the human condition because they had access only to a thin slice of the existential continuum, the attenuated area closest to the end point of "community" defined by "family."

Although this limited access resulted from complex historical, economic, and social reasons, Barolini's critique is most powerfully understood as a reminder of the dangers and falsities of idealizing and sentimentalizing the Italian immigrant family. Those of us who are or border on being "professional apologists" for *l'ordine della famiglia* need a dose of Barolini's chilling realism as an antidote to the (usually male) partiality of our effusive interpretive reconstructions.

The Cultural Transformer

The image of woman as stabilizer acknowledges familial conflicts that resulted from the struggle of an old-world culture to adapt to a new social context. The image, however, portrays these conflicts as marginal to the overall stability of *la famiglia*. Proponents of the image emphasize that Italian immigrants, especially women, preferred work, such as homework and cannery labor, that permitted them to maintain family relationships. They also underscore the immigrants' understanding of the family, not the individual, as the fundamental social unit.

By contrast, other writers portray Italian immigrant women as cultural transformers. These writers take familial conflict as the norm and family stability as vastly overrated. Thus, Elisabetta Vezzosi claims, "[the typical] analysis is valid if 'united family' means one which stays together physically. It is no longer meaningful if instead the quality of the relationship within the family is considered. In this case, work in the canneries was strongly disruptive, not only in regard to the family but to the community as well."[23]

Conflicts within the family, fueled partly by the employment that brought immigrant women in contact with wider notions of social possibility, dialectically generated cultural transformations of Italian immigrants. To put the point in the terms of this book: social forces in America, especially factory work, contact with non-Italian women in the workplace, and exposure to social workers, sowed the seeds of vital individualism within immigrant women. For perhaps the first time in their lives, they conceived their identities outside the strict bounds of the immigrant family, they glimpsed visions of personal happiness and fulfillment, and they imagined themselves agents of salutary change.[24]

This interpretation turns the image of woman as stabilizer on its head: rather than applauding the immigrant family and its values as a refuge from a hostile world, it exalts the personal empowerment women experienced as agents of cultural transformation.[25] Here the family is understood as a source of conflicts, rather than a unity of fused interests. In sum, this interpretation contends that the immigrant women's contact with American women fostered a redistribution of power within *la famiglia.* Maddalena Tirabassi adds:

Americanization meant consumerism and development of individualistic liberal values and so helped women to reject premodern values and traditions, especially when the Americanizers pushed for education, birth control, home economics, modernization of housework, childrearing theories, the right to vote, the right to work and to control money earned and, in a more general sense, development of personal autonomy.[26]

The image of women as cultural transformers is most persuasively seen as one aspect of the immigrant experience, rather than as a complete, typical rendering of Italian women. The main phenomena that allegedly animate this image—extensive outside work experience and contact with American social workers – were not part of the lives of most Italian immigrant women. The power of the image, however, rests in its understanding of the connections between such experiences, the redistribution of familial power, and cultural transformation. The old-world ethos could not remain unaltered in a radically different social setting. The unyielding patriarchy of the *Mezzogiorno* almost immediately reinvented itself and, as the traditional repositories and sustainers of culture, women were an important engine of social change. Although the extent, timing, and nature of this transformation remain in dispute, it is undeniable that Italian immigrants, especially women, confronted social challenges: remain enmeshed in secure but increasingly irrelevant old world values, or remake family power structures to conform to new-world possibilities.[27]

Neither choice was unambiguously preferable, and each triggered the deepest insecurities and fondest expectations of the individual-community continuum. At stake was not merely the continued vitality of a certain set of values, but the immigrants' ability to simultaneously maintain their integrity while occupying a larger portion of the individual – community continuum.

The Matriarch

A third image of Italian immigrant women denies the predominance of patriarchy that is typically taken for granted. This image underlines the difference between public perception and private reality: when outside the home, wives acted deferentially to their husbands who, in the spirit of grand theater, would preen and strut while effusively declaring their authority; in reality, however, women assumed control over all the practical aspects of life. Males were permitted, even encouraged, to exhibit their face-saving *gallismo* (the Italian version of *machismo*), but real family power was held by women.[28] Advocates of this image do not merely claim that women, as center of the family, exerted great influence within the home, but also that they held the balance of family power.[29] One of the most radical proponents of this view is Ann Cornelisen, who contends that the matriarchy was prevalent even in the *Mezzogiorno*.

> [Matriarchy] is a de facto system, one that is felt by everyone, that functions every day, but is not codified . . . It is simply there. There are no large decisions to be made by the men and day-to-day existence is left to the women, who unconsciously take over all the practical aspects of life . . . [The wife] has also slowly replaced her husband's mother, and he, accustomed as he is to the strength of women, does not

notice it . . . In any formal situation the women will go to great lengths not to mar the picture a husband has given of himself and his supremacy within the family.[30]

Susan Berkowitz refuses to accept Cornelisen's widesweeping revision of the conventional view. First, she notes the limited and idiosyncratic nature of Cornelisen's sample: "The women whose portraits she draws had husbands who were either sporadically employed or migrant workers; consequently, they [the women] tended to shoulder a disproportionate share of the work and responsibility involved in maintaining their households."[31] Second, Berkowitz's own research in southern Italy found that "peasant families with independent access to land and resources tend to conform far more to the patriarchal ideal, with the father overseeing key decisions about division of tasks, investments in goods and equipment, marriages of children and the like . . . husbands were generally quite powerful."[32]

Moreover, Berkowitz contends that Cornelisen obscures the reality of how women's influence in the *Mezzogiorno* is dependent on their attachment to males. Thus, women without husbands were pitied because, in an important sense, they were powerless and adrift.[33] In Berkowitz's view, Cornelisen's claims of matriarchy are exaggerated, limited to a particular subset within a particular class, and distorted by undue attention to the unsettling effects of seasonal migrant labor on family dynamics.[34]

Robert Orsi, however, echoes Cornelisen's theme of matriarchy in his analysis of immigrants in Italian Harlem:

Women were the powers to be reckoned with in the domus, the sources of authority and tradition . . . Italian women lived under the pressure of two dangerously conflicting demands: that they exercise their power in the domus and that they appear powerless. Their exercise of power, therefore, was frequently clandestine. They attained their ends by manipulation and indirect influence or they acted through a specially chosen surrogate, such as their oldest son or brother. This kind of power, however, generates bitter suspicion toward those compelled to wield it and provokes the fiercest resentment.[35]

The picture Orsi paints of the father is decidedly unflattering: obsessed with the false public image of strict disciplinarian and authority figure; addicted to intricate, public displays of respect; detached and distant from other family members, yet insistent on ritualistic shows of deference.[36] Orsi offers a chilling image of men trapped by their own illusions. Lacking any real social power outside the home, these men took solace in pathetic theatrics and fatuous posturing: the father as *cafone* ("buffoon").[37]

Yet in bittersweet irony, the notions of power and powerlessness are more than they first appear. As transmitters of domus-centered culture, women had to cater to numerous complex and often contradictory male sexual and psychological needs. This situation required that a woman cultivate the reputation of *una buona femmina*, which demanded that women sustain and conform to a rigorous and iron-clad set of social practices. In contrast to the image of women as cultural transformers, Orsi highlights the stifling and imprisoning features of a deeply solidified subculture.[38]

Orsi also underscores two additional themes: pervasive family conflict and the lack of a sense of individuality. Family conflict took a variety of forms. First, there was alienation between the immigrants and their American-born children as the values of *la via vecchia* clashed with the wider sense of possibility embodied by America.[39] This estrangement often generated fierce rivalries for power among family members.[40] Second, the structure of the domus itself, as the paramount unit of personal affiliation and the primary source of human sustenance, stretched the nerves of all members. The priorities of the domus promoted intense inward preoccupation, closely knit associations, and little personal privacy.[41]

The lack of a sense of individuality within the family[42] sounds again the existential difficulties of immigrants. On the one hand, the family often degenerated into bitter conflicts emerging from its demands for a suffocating conformity. On the other hand, one's family was never merely one's family: to sever one's connection to family implied a deeper alienation of the self and exile from the only tangible source of human community. Thus, one's fundamental identity and most profound self-understanding resided inextricably in *la famiglia*.[43] Few historical occurrences illustrate so well the Janus-faced character of the end points on the individual-community continuum. The family, here representing community, embodied the deepest human values—intimacy, human attachment, source of personal identity—while simultaneously intertwined with the deepest human fears—personal suffocation, denial of autonomy, self-estrangement. Allegiance to *la famiglia* promised fulfillment of the most poignant human aspirations but risked frightening disappointment. Forsaking *la famiglia*, however, although experienced initially as empowering self-assertion, too often matured into isolation and lost identity.

In fact, if Orsi's portrayal is accurate, escape from the mentality of the domus was rare.[44] All family members had so deeply internalized the values and mindset of the domus that such perspectives partly constituted who they were. To flee the domus mentality under such circumstances would have been a radical disruption of self.[45]

Again, in stark contrast to the image of women as cultural transformers, Orsi accentuates the ensnaring and unliberating features of the Italian immigrant subculture. He compares the power of the domus to an oriental finger trap: the harder one struggled, the more deeply ensnared one became. Moreover, the domus was the site of ubiquitous familial conflict and identity crises that produced high levels of guilt, frustration, anger, and insecurity.[46]

We are left, then, with three interpretations of Italian immigrant women: skilled stabilizers of enduring familial values that constituted sanctuary from an often hostile New World; as cultural transformer, who understood viscerally that clinging to *la via vecchia* was anachronistic in the New World; and enigmatic matriarchs, brokers of pervasive family conflict, at once empowered and imprisoned by the old way.

Which image best captures the reality of Italian immigrant women and their family life? The answer to this question requires first answers to larger epistemological and normative questions: What interpretive methods are best able to discern the truth? What standards are humanly accessible to evaluate different social arrangements? How can a critic of the status quo legitimately assert that her views embody higher cognitive and normative status? Contestable but profoundly interesting, the answers to these questions greatly influence conclusions about the proper evaluation of the experiences of Italian-American women.

CONTEMPORARY FEMINIST THEORY

Although a varied movement, feminism is vivified by several general themes: a deep suspicion of socially constructed gender roles, a demand for the full inclusion of women in the public sphere, a call for the obliteration of power differentials between males and females, and a distrust of claims venerating current social practices as necessary or inevitable. At its most general, feminism is committed to ending the oppression of women by explaining the causes and raising our consciousness of women's subordination, by exploring possible solutions, and by acting directly to liberate women from political and social subjugation.

At the heart of these hopes and activities is the firm conviction that political and social life is thoroughly permeated by gender differentiation that invariably undermines the power of women as a class. As a precondition of its practical task, feminism focuses on the importance of women's experiences and the inability of much traditional Western thought to account for those experiences. Indeed, feminists argue that mainstream (male) theorizing is inclined strongly to deny or marginalize women's personal narratives, particularly in two areas of special concern to women: motherhood and sexuality. Women are therefore often alienated because of the dissonance between their subjective experiences and dominant social theory and practice.

Several versions of feminist thought stigmatize the quest for universal legal and moral rules that claim to go beyond and control the results of particular cases. As I explain the most uncompromising and interesting such version, the "feminism unmodified" of Catharine MacKinnon, I will also invoke the views of Ann Scales.

Women's Perspective

Is there a unique and irreducible "women's perspective," a "women's point of view" that can serve as a critical and external standpoint from which to evaluate the status quo? I do not find the thesis of a women's perspective to be a helpful analytic instrument. On the one hand, advocates of the thesis may intend only to highlight the ways women's voices and experiences have been hitherto marginalized in our culture. Moreover, the thesis may underscore the importance of certain reproductive and sexual phenomena experienced exclusively by women. This weak version of the feminist thesis is laudatory, indeed unassailable, but does not require the invocation of a mysterious women's perspective.

On the other hand, advocates may intend a stronger thesis: men and women are trapped in separate and unequal realities, incommensurable points of view that ensure radical conflict between the sexes. This strong thesis is uncommonly interesting but thoroughly problematic. First, by talking about women qua women, the women's perspective implicitly demeans social, economic, ethnic, racial, and religious differences among women, implying that they are irrelevant.[47] Furthermore, feminists who brandish women's perspective often assume that they speak for all ("real") women, or all right-thinking and thus worthy women, or all politically correct women. Ironically, this assumption is redolent of the arrogant false imperialism that feminists otherwise accuse dominant men of embodying: an allegedly pernicious objectivism that mocks and trivializes contrasting viewpoints.

Second, the women's perspective is too facilely taken as self-ratifying: "men's perspective" is thoroughly contaminated with patriarchal aggression and domination, whereas women's perspective germinates from women's experiences and is thus purified and morally superior. Under this corollary, as Jean Grimshaw notes, the two perspectives are commensurable: " 'Man's perspective' is morally self-invalidating, the mirror of patriarchal oppression, and 'women's perspective' captures the moral ideal as it emanates from the experiences of the victimized. This characterization may strike numerous critics as naively reductionist, but, worse, it may need the support of an essentialism that proclaims that 'women are somehow naturally virtuous and men naturally wicked.' "[48] Again, the irony is striking: feminists otherwise view appeals to essentialism as false metaphysics, and they observe that such appeals have traditionally served to disadvantage and oppress women.

Third, advocates of the women's perspective may backtrack to the incommensurability corollary: the different perspectives of the two sexes simply make veridical communication impossible. But the corollary is fragile because members of each sex often report genuine communication with members of the other sex. Moreover, if we take incommensurability too seriously we descend into false necessity: women and men can never speak the same language and therefore can never resolve questions of sexual oppression through communicative means. Only armed insurrection, evolutionary metamorphism of the human species to androgyny, or political revolution offer paths to social equality for women.

Fourth, advocates of the strong thesis may retreat from charges of false imperialism by accepting the validity of multiple female realities. Thus, they would abrogate talk of the one women's perspective and speak instead of various women's perspectives. This strategy, however, would still beg the question of what morally ratifies women's viewpoints and not those of men. Furthermore, this strategy might still have to be supported by either essentialism or an overly sanguine perception of victims' experiences as self-ratifying.[49]

I must emphasize that my critique proves no inherent defect of feminist theory as such; it serves only the limited purpose of stigmatizing a minor and unnecessary rhetorical device employed by some feminists. The absence of this rhetorical device does not necessarily disable feminists from advancing rich and unsettling critiques of the social and political status quo.

But the fundamental question remains whether invocation of women's perspective tends to highlight disproportionately the experiences of white, educated, middle-class women. Several African-American women, for example, have pointed out how their special experiences of race and gender discrimination are often obscured by their separation into the paradigmatic models: their experiences of gender discrimination are assimilated into the paradigm based on the circumstances of white women, and their experiences of race discrimination are assimilated into the paradigm based on the circumstances of African-American men. At best, well-meaning feminists, civil libertarians, and officials add up the two types of discrimination when assessing the burdens of African-American women. The addition is erroneous from the outset because it fails to capture the unique, compounded prejudices African-American women often confront.

The sum of such a calculus is invariably incorrect because neither of its additives is accurate. Kimberle Crenshaw argues that

Black women are regarded either as too much like [white] women or [male] blacks and the compounded nature of their experience is absorbed into the collective experiences of either group or as too different, in which case black women's blackness or femaleness sometimes has placed their needs and perspectives at the margin of the feminist and black liberationist agendas . . . The paradigm of sex discrimination tends to be based on the experiences of white women; the model of race discrimination tends to be based on the experiences of the most privileged blacks. Notions of what constitutes race and sex discrimination are, as a result, narrowly tailored to embrace only a small set of circumstances, none of which include discrimination against black women.[50]

Scholars such as Crenshaw advance a more general point: a robust notion of feminism must be defined narrowly enough to highlight women's special experiences, concerns, and interests, yet broadly enough to comprehend the interconnectedness of sex, gender, race, class, and religion. Unless such themes receive special attention, feminism may unwittingly replicate the elitist excesses it disparages in patriarchal ideologies.[51]

Does MacKinnon's unmodified feminism merit the charge that it marginalizes or ignores the intersection of gender, race, class, religion? Yes. First, MacKinnon devotes little or no space to the problem. Although she is undoubtedly aware of the relevant special concerns, particularly the issue of class, she fails to highlight and grapple sufficiently with them. Second, she too often invokes her brand of feminism as *the* veridical perception of women's situation. Even the name "feminism unmodified" registers a certain imperialistic tone: here is the real thing, unadorned, uncontaminated by the typical modifiers ("liberal," "Marxist," "socialist," and so on), simply feminism as such. There is a peculiar haughtiness to MacKinnon's work that suggests she has special insight into the burdens of *all* women and that this insight will be apparent without special attention to the way discrimination against women differs substantially when gender intersects with race, class, religion, and other constitutive attributes.[52]

Critique of Abstraction and Objectivism

Feminist opposition to the traditional standards of rationality in the Western world takes a variety of forms. First, feminists often resist the exclusionary tendencies of traditional standards that marginalize women's perspectives by devaluing their sources of knowledge. Second, feminists recoil at the conservative (in the sense of "preserving the status quo") bias of traditional standards, which accepts, reflects, and sustains institutional power relations that disproportionately privilege white males.[53] Third, feminists rebel against the ways traditional standards allegedly mask their own reinforcing effects.[54] By sanctifying certain facts, institutions, and power relations as objectively sound, traditional standards insulate them from robust ideological dispute: to the extent that current power relations appear natural and inevitable, people who resist them seem misguided, obstreperous, and immature.[55] Accordingly, members of privileged groups will themselves be blinded to the contestability of their own assumptions as their world view solidifies into objective fact.[56]

Depending on which of these three types of opposition a feminist chooses to emphasize, she will be drawn to a variety of counterstrategies: retention of the traditional standards but full inclusion of women's experiences and perspectives; development of an alternate feminist reason to challenge traditional standards; abrogation of the traditional standards combined with the recognition that all perspectives are partial and subject to political resolution; and revelation of the conservative bias and pernicious reinforcing effects of traditional standards as a first step to demystifying their social conclusions.

A deeper theme underlies these charges and counterstrategies. The conclusions and norms embodied by traditional epistemological standards present rationality in terms appropriate to ideal social roles for men, and in contrast to social roles appropriate for women. Women are thus forced into a double-bind: if they aspire to fulfill traditional standards, they distance themselves from their socially defined "femininity"; if they resist traditional standards, they retain their femininity but remain unempowered. Moreover, traditional standards introduce themselves not as male standards but as human standards. Women are often implicitly viewed as ersatz humans when they best fulfill socially defined ideals of femininity. In subtle ways, then, traditional standards of rationality and prevalent power relations in society form a (largely unconscious?) conspiracy that ensures the continued subordination of women.

Paradoxically, many feminist counterstrategies, if successful, would efface the very distinction that feminism currently presupposes for its own vitality. Sally Haslanger observes that "if feminism is successful, there will no longer be a gender distinction as such — or, allowing that there are a plurality of relations that serve to constitute gender and a plurality of feminist projects, we can say that one goal of feminism is to fight against the sexual subordination that constitutes these categories of men and women."[57]

A fundamental dispute within the various types of feminist counterstrategies emerges: Is it possible to use notions of objectivity and aperspectival rationality to vindicate feminist projects? Is it possible to endorse traditional epistemological standards while simultaneously striving to unsettle the existing social hierarchy?[58]

Moreover, even if such a strategy is prudentially possible, is it intellectually honest? Naomi Scheman argues, instead, for acknowledgement of the partiality of epistemological perspectives:

> The only way to take diversity of perspectives seriously is to be robustly realistic, both about the world viewed and about the material locations of those doing the viewing. Archimedean, difference-denying epistemology ought to be seen as incompatible with such a robust realism: How could there possibly be one account of a world

shaped in interaction with subjects so diversely constituted and with such diverse interests in constructing and knowing it? . . . The real world is not the world of our best physics but the world that defeats any physics that would be final, that would desire to be the last word.[59]

MacKinnon dissects thoroughly the problems associated with traditional standards of rationality. She insists that allegedly universal rules masquerade as neutral and pretend to emanate from the demands of logic and objective reality, but that in fact these rules project the aspirations of those males powerful enough to make the decisions relevant to their recognition and acceptance. The notions of "value-free" and "aperspectivity" are therefore political and regressive.[60]

In this manner, through male ideological assumptions and the disingenuous selection of relevant differences and similarities and through the connivance of the patriarchal myth of objectivity, women are kept in their place by normative means. Their hold on power allows males to set the terms for notions such as "knowledge" and "truth" and, through objectification, to establish a viewpoint as "reality." Although such notions are socially constructed from the situation of male domination and female subjugation, sex differences come to be viewed as the justification for male power rather than the result of it. MacKinnon echoes this observation: "Men *create* the world from their own point of view, which then *becomes* the truth to be described. This is a closed system, not anyone's confusion. *Power to create the world from one's point of view is power in its male form.*"[61]

Moreover, by measuring rationality in terms of alleged aperspectivity, "what counts as reason will be that which corresponds to the way things are."[62] The failure of women to meet male standards and the relegation of women to carefully circumscribed inferior positions is accounted for and justified by their differences from men. Furthermore, a successful objectification project enlists the aid of the subordinate classes in their own continued subjugation. The method of detached justification and scientific explanation of the social order can secure a powerful stranglehold on the underclasses.

MacKinnon views the injustice of sexism as not merely error—a few mistakes made at the margins of legal and moral doctrine—but an integral part of an entire social system geared for the advantage of one sex at the expense of the other. Regardless of whether the imposition of male standards is conscious sex discrimination or "merely" an unintended side effect of the shared male point of view, the effects on women are devastating. At best, women must suppress their differences in order to meet male standards and become equally "male"; at worst, women who refuse to submit are tyrannized further by a system that proclaims its objectivity and universality.[63]

Feminist visions such as MacKinnon's, which critique the possibility of objectivity and neutrality so emphatically and indefatigably, and which mock so easily the alleged pretensions of patriarchally based knowledge, inevitably elicit charges of "nihilism" from centrist epistemologists and political theorists.

Scales's response to this charge has four parts. First, she renounces the common epistemological and normative assumptions that underlie the charge, and she reiterates the role these assumptions play in the continued systematic subordination of women. Second, she suggests that even if objectivity is viewed as desirable by some (males?), it is simply unavailable to us: "The business of living and progressing within our disciplines requires that we give up on 'objective' verification at various critical moments, such as when we rely on gravity, or upon the existence of others, or upon the principle of verification itself . . . [we] will forever be stuck in a post-realist battle of subjectivities . . . until we confront the distinction between knowing subject and known object."[64] Third, she maintains that feminism unmodified does not sever "the observer from the observed"[65] and is thus a prime example of the required confrontation of the distinction between the knower and the known. This method, she continues, has natural analogues: "The physics of relativity and quantum mechanics demonstrate that nature is on our side: Nature itself has begun to evince a less hierarchical structure, a multidirectional flow of authority which corroborates our description of perception. We warmly embrace the uncertainty inherent in that perceptual model."[66] Fourth, she denies that justificatory foundations require adherence to the myths of objectivity and neutrality: "There must be something reliable somewhere, there must be indicia of fairness in the system, but neither depends on objectivity . . . we need standards to help us make connections among norms, and to help us see 'family resemblances' among instances of domination. Standards, however, are not means without ends: They never have and never can be more than working hypotheses."[67]

Supporters of feminism unmodified, then, contend that the metaphysical and epistemological underpinnings of belief in objectivity, neutrality, and strict classification are fatally flawed, from a theoretical standpoint, and are instruments in ensuring the further marginalization of subordinate classes, from a practical standpoint.

Proponents of the theory, however, may be dragons without fire. In fact, their more general attacks on the metaphysics of presence, objectivity, the correspondence theory of truth, methodological neutrality, and single slices of reality are prefigured in the work of numerous males – the Sophists, Nietzsche, Pierce, James, Dewey, Heidegger, Wittgenstein, Kuhn, Quine, Sellars, Rorty, to name only a few. Given that these philosophers, taken as a group, hardly constitute a vanguard of feminism, it is doubtful that repudiating the presuppositions of metaphysical realism is necessarily connected with enlightened views on gender equality. By the same token, it is conceivable that one could embrace the "metaphysics of presence" yet decry the excesses of male-dominated society.

Appreciation and Acceptance of Paradox

Supporters of feminism unmodified acknowledge candidly that their description of the current subordination of women and their prescription for change generate paradoxes and manifest tensions internal to feminism. One such difficulty concerns the claims of the theory to veridical perception and its ability to stigmatize the perceptions of politically centrist women as illusory or as emanating from the noxious socialization of male hegemony.[68]

A related puzzle emerges when we ask how feminism can castigate the "male totality"[69] with such confidence, while simultaneously denying that it does so from a neutral or aperspectival vantage point. At times, MacKinnon denies that this puzzle is a paradox at all.

> Feminism criticizes this male totality without an account of our capacity to do so or to imagine or realize a more whole truth. Feminism affirms women's point of view by revealing, criticizing, and explaining its impossibility. This is not a dialectical paradox. It is a methodological expression of women's situation, in which the struggle for consciousness is a struggle for world: for a sexuality, a history, a culture, a community, a form of power, an experience of the sacred.[70]

At other times, MacKinnon denies that her conclusions are merely "partial" truths.

> Although feminism emerges from women's particular experience, it is not subjective or partial, for no interior ground and few if any aspects of life are free of male power . . . feminism unmodified claims no external ground or unsexed sphere of

generalization or abstraction beyond male power, nor transcendence of the specific-
ity of each of its manifestations. How is it possible to have an engaged truth that does
not simply reiterate its determinations? *Disengaged* truth only reiterates *its* determinations. Choice of method is choice of determinants—a choice which, for women
as such, has been unavailable because of the subordination of women.[71]

It seems that this brand of feminism often flaunts contradictions and paradoxes, self-consciously and proudly. It attributes to women a keen sensitivity
and veridical vision of the way things really are—the conditions of male
oppression and domination—even while portraying them as possessing "an
infinite capacity to be duped."[72]

Moreover, proponents of feminism unmodified often use what they take to be
social practice and manipulate the facts of that practice to support whatever they
are momentarily trying to establish. One example of this language of convenience is the alleged prevalence of sexual harassment of women by men as both
the explanation of its recognition by society—cases are too numerous to discount or ignore—and its nonrecognition—the frequency of sexual harassment
obscures the identification of abuse because it makes harassment seem commonplace and thus less offensive.[73] Furthermore, these theorists are convinced
that the liberal notion of women's consent being a prime factor in analysis of
various disputes is a fraud because women have not been allowed to form
themselves in male-dominated society; yet they demand that women in such a
society have their voices taken more seriously. Likewise, MacKinnon and others
counsel pluralism—urging that alternate ideologies be heard and that we
empathize with visions other than their own; yet it is likely that disciples of
feminism unmodified would sneer at, for example, female judges—"collaborators"[74]—who empathized with male litigants asserting claims antagonistic to
this particular feminist theory.

The theory, however, is unlikely to be unsettled by such remarks, for it takes
these very tensions and contradictions as descriptive of women's condition:
"Integral to women's experience is knowing one thing on one level, and a
different, inconsistent thing on another . . . [k]nowledge can occur on different
levels and in different parts of ourselves. Is not our ambivalence real? Might this
ambivalence even be further evidence of men's fraud against women?[75]

Although MacKinnon does not claim that feminism unmodified is universal,
she denies that it reduces to relativism and shuns efforts to make it a science of

sexism or an abstract theory seeking "generalities that subsume its particulars."[76] Rather, the theory prizes contextualism, refusal of polarity, tolerance of ambiguity, and even contradiction: "Feminism unmodified does not begin with the premise that it is unpremised. It does not aspire to persuade an unpremised audience because there is no such audience. Its project is to uncover and claim as valid the experience of women, the major content of which is the devalidation of women's experience."[77]

General criticisms of methodology could focus on the following set of questions: Do proponents of the theory, despite their avowed commitment to pluralistic interpretations, ignore the socioeconomic divisions among women? Are their arguments no more than the musings of a special interest group: privileged, educated, upper middle-class women? Can these reflections truly constitute "women's perspective"? Or are they, rather, class-based and thus unrepresentative of an entire sex? More to the point: Does feminism unmodified manifest the very urges that it otherwise stigmatizes as pernicious exemplars of the male (power) mindset – tidy classifications, a single, simple interpretation of reality?[78]

MacKinnon and other like-minded feminists arrive at a classic dilemma. On the one hand, they have a powerful point: the preferences of a subordinate class are, at least partly, the result of established social rules and practices. Thus those rules and practices cannot be justified noncircularly by appeals to those very preferences. On the other hand, their theory is guilty of philosophical imperialism if it automatically stigmatizes all who dissent from its prescriptions as unwitting victims of the dominant consciousness. This dilemma is not insurmountable, but "unmodified" feminists must advance a more refined analysis of the problem than they have to date.[79]

Does MacKinnon's theory, despite its refusal to accept reality as a single slice, posit both men and women as undifferentiated classes? Are these classifications based on question-begging definitions: "To be dominant is to be male and to be subordinate is to be female. Who is male? Anyone who is dominant? What is dominance? Whatever males do."?[80]

Beyond the call for more power and the critique of male-dominated society, MacKinnon is content to wait until women are no longer oppressed. But it is not clear that women can throw off the yoke of male oppression without a more complete prescriptive vision. Finally, MacKinnon seems to accept too easily the doctrine that we cannot assess the values articulated by women in a male-dominated society because such women are not speaking in their "authentic voices."[81] It is not clear that we cannot, at least to a significant extent, separate one's values from one's authentic voice and appraise those values.[82]

By identifying male hegemony as the perpetrator of women's oppression has MacKinnon ignored analysis of the economic structure of society? That is, does feminism unmodified lack an account or full explanation of women's oppression?[83] Does it merely charge "male domination" at all occasions of perceived disadvantage without any deeper account of the source of that domination other than males' (innate?) desire for "sexual access to women"?[84]

Moreover, the theory's metaphilosophical attacks on aperspectivity and metaphysical realism have numerous antecedents in philosophical literature; indeed, such a perspective partially constitutes one of the more traditional strains of epistemology: skepticism. Likewise, MacKinnon's emphasis on the role of power and the dominance of the ruling class treads a well-worn path. It would appear that the only truly distinctive feminist contribution to the debate is the primacy it places on patriarchal domination and the centrality of sexuality. Rather than identifying class, economic, or racial oppression, the theory designates males as the perpetrators of social inequality. It would seem that feminist unmodified is merely a form of Marxism that substitutes the oppression of women for the oppression of the working class and that does not necessarily call for the downfall of capitalist economics.

The suggestion that the theory is little more than a warmed-over variation of other (male-based) theories, however, would infuriate the authors of feminism unmodified and confirm in their minds classic patriarchal strategies. They would be firmly convinced that my remarks are a rather pedestrian attempt to defang their theory, assimilate it to male discourse, and thus trivialize it as derived and parasitic.[85]

What is New? What is Valuable?

A number of paradoxes and questions emerge from feminist critiques of mainstream epistemological traditions. First, it is sometimes unclear whether feminists criticize these traditions because the standards are biased and partial – as they allegedly exclude feminist experiences and ways of knowing – or because the standards mask their partiality by claims of objectivity. The former criticism is problematic: How can feminists who otherwise celebrate situatedness as legitimate and necessary contend with a straight face that mainstream standards fail because they are merely partial? The latter criticism is more to the point: By shrouding their partiality in claims of objectivity, mainstream standards insulate themselves from ideological disputation and arrogate to themselves an undeserved aura of inevitability. Mainstream standards can thus be attacked not for their partiality but for their denial of their own partiality.

Still, a deeper problem results: How can we distinguish positive partiality from negative partiality? That is, if mainstream standards relinquished their alleged claim of objectivity would they thereby redeem themselves in feminist eyes? Not likely. Or, more likely, would feminists still regard them as negatively partial because of the substantive conclusions they embody? If so, how can feminists judge the relative merits of competing (partial) standards without assuming a common measure of comparison? Would not this common measure itself constitute at least a mini-objective standard? And if no such measure is invoked, how is any legitimate rational comparison available? Are we not left with competing incommensurable partial viewpoints each of which can claim no more than circular self-validation? Would not this degenerate into a modern-day Tower of Babel?

Second, feminists are fond of underscoring the connection between mainstream epistemological standards and continued reinforcement of prescribed social roles for men and women. But the strength of this connection is never made clear. Are mainstream epistemological standards necessary conditions for the maintenance of traditional role differentiation? Are they sufficient conditions? Or are they contributing causes?

It is extremely difficult to argue that mainstream epistemological standards are sufficient for the maintenance of traditional role differentiation. These standards could generate specific social prescriptions different from the prescriptions supporting traditional role differentiation. Given that such alternate prescriptions would not necessarily compromise the alleged objectivity of the standards, it is wrong to conclude that the standards themselves guarantee a priori any particular pattern. Moreover, even if such standards could legitimate only one particular social order, the continued vitality of that order would depend on a host of economic and political conditions outside the control of epistemological standards.

Likewise, it is extremely difficult to argue that mainstream epistemological standards are necessary to maintain traditional role differentiation. Renouncing objectivity and impartiality cannot of itself augur the fall of patriarchy. Put differently: there is nothing inherent to the embrace of partiality and perspectivism, which are themselves mere abstractions, that necessarily demands the end of any particular social order. Entrenched social conditions could well be sustained by other measures where the will to do so exists.

Accordingly, the most reasonable interpretation of the feminist position is that, as a contingent matter, mainstream epistemological standards have served the ideological function of contributing to the maintenance of traditional gender-role differentiation. This view is sound because of the generally conservative (status quo – preserving) effects of social institutions – unless destabilizing mechanisms are deliberately built into the social system, most institutions, including prevalent views on knowledge, tend to legitimate the status quo. These social institutions obviously cannot guarantee the continued vitality of the social order they reinforce, because that vitality is dependent on a nest of relatively independent economic and political conditions, but they nevertheless are part of a socialization process designed to facilitate stability and acceptance of the bulk of received opinion. This view, however, lacks the panache many feminists seek because it merely identifies one contingent contributing factor to the existence of traditional gender-role differentiation. The precise efficacy of this factor, moreover, remains contestable.[86]

The third and most important question that arises from the feminist critique concerns the make-up of mainstream epistemological standards. The answer is far from clear. The critical attack launched by feminists hits the mark only against a certain strain of mainstream thought: one committed inexorably to the tenets of metaphysical realism and epistemological foundationalism.[87] But this branch of mainstream thought does not define the tradition. In the history of analytic philosophy there is no shortage of (male) thinkers who deny the persuasiveness of impartiality, objectivity, and Archimedean vantage points. MacKinnon's epistemological observations can be legitimately viewed as a contemporary formulation of a strain of mainstream thought that has existed at least from the time of the Greek sophists.

Louise Antony locates a prime source of MacKinnon's insights in the modern period, especially in the work of the rationalists and the empiricists:

First, there is the essentially rationalist insight that perfect objectivity is not only impossible but undesirable, that certain kinds of 'bias' or 'partiality' are necessary to make our epistemic tasks tractable. Second, there is Hume's realization that external-ism won't work, that we can never manage to offer a justification of epistemic norms without somehow presupposing the very norms we wish to justify. See this . . . as the beginning of the postmodern recognition that theory proceeds from an 'embedded' location, that there is no transcendent spot from which we can inspect our own theorizing.[88]

Especially after the work of Kuhn and Feyerabend in the philosophy of science,[89] many, probably most, philosophers today are convinced that per-sonal goals, hunches, intuitions, and normative commitments are necessary for theoretical advance.[90] The strongest pretensions of metaphysical realism and epistemological foundationalism were crumbling long before MacKinnon's criti-cal attack.[91]

The following hypothetical dialogue between an advocate of feminism un-modified *("A")* and a mainstream analytic philosopher *("B")* reveals some of the conceptual difficulties each side faces as it tries to rationally engage the other.

A: You cannot live up to your own standards. Your view rests on epistemologi-cal foundationalism and/or metaphysical realism, which are unconvincing be-cause of the indeterminacy of language, the fragility of classical two-valued logic, and/or the impossibility of an 'Archimedean point'.

B: We don't claim that reasoning is mechanical or that universal agreement is required to establish rational claims. You attack a strawperson. Moreover, your rule skepticism is self-referentially false, it degenerates into a nihilism that cannot be lived, and it disables you for constructing a positive program. Yet you are the ones who claim to "fuse theory and practice"! [A less frequent response would be a defense of foundationalism and realism.]

A: We merely hold you to your own pretensions, standards that are not only theoretically bankrupt, but worse, politically noxious because they mask the fact that the terms of knowledge and moral correctness ultimately stem from power, not disinterested reason.

B: It is your method of critique, not our conception of reason and morality, that results in disabling skepticism. Also, our formal requirements of reason do not imply substantive political results.

A: We reject the neat separation of process and result. Furthermore, our methods suggest nothing disabling. One does not give up one's beliefs or ability to assert claims just because one recognizes that those beliefs and claims are not founded on epistemological foundationalism and metaphysical realism. Just because our ideological disputes are not justified by God or Nature does not imply that they are trivial. Making explicit the contingent source of our beliefs does not contaminate their content. Thus, we are hardly disabled!

B: Such beliefs and claims reduce to nothing more than expressions of preference and taste.

A: We are all antecedently situated in social practices that form a context for our discussions. Our discussions are not arbitrary or mere expressions of preferences.

B: That response reflects ironically the crudest (status quo – preserving) conventionalism . . . from you, the apostles of radical change!

A: You accept the phony dilemmas that we repudiate: either objectivism or relativism; either foundationalism and realism, or nihilism. Reject those dualisms and you eliminate your apparitions and fears of nihilism. Nihilism is impossible, and there is no need to combat or fear the impossible.

B: Your romance with paradox is a trendy attempt to gloss over your disabling contradictions. You have no constructive program.

A: Our constructive program will emerge from democratic dialogue once we pierce the mystification of the dominant discourse.

B: The very "situation" and "context" you previously extolled!

A: You are straightjacketed by the principles of bivalence and stability, which blind you to the fluidity and dialectical tensions of life and in things.

B: Your claims are not innovative. Skeptics, relativists, and pragmatists have inhabited the minority strains of Western philosophy from the start. Moreover, the pragmatic strain is fast becoming dominant, at least among philosophers in the United States.

A: What a transparent rhetorical move! You try to assimilate, domesticate, and co-opt our position to the dominant discourse in order to soften our political threat. Thus you stigmatize our radical programs as "Utopian," and thus unrealizable, and ridicule our less radical programs as "assimilable to the dominant discourse," and thus mere reformism that makes our theoretical assertions unnecessary.

B: We only report the way things are.

A: Because you fail to understand our need to transcend the dominant discourse, which we take to be an accomplice in the silencing of politically radical voices, you fail to understand our need not to play by the usual rules of your language games.

B: You haven't transcended anything. As soon as you make any positive claim you reveal yourselves as either hopelessly incoherent thinkers or expounders of merely personal preferences.

A: We reject grand theory and, instead, advocate a more situational and pragmatic analysis. [Less frequently: acceptance of grand theory accompanied by invocation of a "new method" of analysis.] Remember that we do not share your belief that "correspondence with reality" or, in your less grandiose moments, intersubjective agreement defines "truth" and "rationality." Disagreement can itself be a sign of and part of rationality, whereas consensus is often a mask for crude majoritarianism and power.

B: We both agree that the dilemma of objectivism/relativism is a false polarity. [Less frequently: a defense of the dilemma, accompanied by a defense of realism and, even less frequently, foundationalism.] But there is still a need to attend to rational methods of justification.

A: Choice of method is choice of determinants. Neither you nor we can transcend our particular manifestations, and, in an important sense, we are both reduced to reiterating our determinants. But that is all that is available. Thus, there is no reason to despair!

B: There is at least one large problem with all that: your choice of method is grounded only on certain passionate commitments, which themselves will seem either arbitrary or conventionalist. All you seem to have left is "assuming responsibility for self-conscious value choices." Are we starting to hear whispers of "authenticity" from your existentialist chorus?

A: We have no need of foundationalist methods or presuppositions, which themselves are myths. Again, the lack of such foundations as the source of our beliefs does not force us to give up our beliefs about values or mute our expressions of them. You claim to renounce metaphysical realism and epistemological foundationalism, yet their vestiges remain in your attacks on our constructive programs. It is you who use the language of convenience, employing or denouncing metaphysical realism and epistemological foundationalism according to which strategy is more rhetorically effective at the moment.

B: Ironically, you accuse us of using one of your favorite maneuvers: using or rejecting metaphysical realism and epistemological foundationalism in unprincipled fashion. Your methods, however, force you to employ this strategy because of their failure to attend to strategies of rational justification after explicit rejection of metaphysical realism and epistemological foundationalism.

A: In order to give your criticisms currency, you once again resort to the very presuppositions that we reject. That is, you beg the question against us by evaluating our claims and methods by precisely those standards from which we have self-consciously distanced ourselves. The alleged maladies of our view, which you so confidently cite, are virulent only if foundational presuppositions are themselves possible and discernible. But they are not. Accordingly, we don't pretend that our views will be acceptable to your outmoded conceptual tools. We are glad they are not! Your criticisms merely restate our claims, contrast them with the dominant discourse, and describe the chasm as our weaknesses.

B: By trying to immunize your position from critical attack you trivialize yourselves. You respond to any criticism by claiming that it merely shows the strength of your position as opposition to the dominant discourse. Accordingly, it is you who beg the question!

This dialogue presents several charges the theory of unmodified feminism must encounter. First, although the gist of its critical attack on metaphysical realism and epistemological foundationalism is sound, it hardly constitutes the grand discovery that MacKinnon considers it to be. Second, feminism unmodified gives the mistaken impression that this version of mainstream epistemology is false because it has allegedly deleterious political effects. But this strategy inverts the causal process: it is more reasonable to assume that the mainstream version has harmful political effects in part because it is false.[92] Third, feminism unmodified either leaves obscure or vastly overrates the strength of connection between acceptance of the mainstream version of epistemology and the continued oppression of women. Fourth, it fails to grapple adequately with the reconstruction of normative debate: once we explicitly abrogate metaphysical realism and epistemological foundationalism, how should our explanatory and justificatory enterprises proceed? What standards, if any, can reasonably be adopted by interlocutors with different political agendas? Are we left only with conflicting assertions of will and a babble of incommensurable voices?

Although it is relatively easy to unsettle the strongest claims of metaphysical realism and epistemological foundationalism, it is more difficult to reconstruct normative enterprises without tacitly relying on the very standards that have been impugned. Certainly, invocations of slogans such as "validating women's perspective(s)," "consciousness raising," and "taking women's experiences seriously" are insufficient. Although actualizing these slogans can serve as an antidote to the politics of women's exclusion, more is needed where, as here, there is no obviously veridical women's perspective or experience. Moreover, even if there were such a perspective or experience, it is unclear whether its normative status could rest on anything more than self-validation. Thus, resolving its clash with men's perspectives and men's experiences would remain thoroughly problematic.

But all this criticism should not shroud the insights that MacKinnon underscores: the actual construction of knowledge is not politically benign; those people bearing the antecedent power to have disproportionate say in that construction too often, consciously or not, develop standards and institutions that further solidify that power; and the illusions of pure objectivity and impartiality are often complicitous in immunizing received opinion from robust political disputation. Antony, recognizing the frailties of feminism unmodified, offers a clearer conclusion: "The real problem with the ruling-class worldview is not that it is biased; it's that it is false. The epistemic problem with ruling-class people is not that they are closed-minded; it's that they hold too much power. The recipe for radical epistemological action then becomes simple: Tell the truth and get enough power so that people have to listen."[93]

Reconciliation?

I have assessed several aspects of MacKinnon's theory, but I must add a disclaimer. My criticisms flow from a background of analytic philosophy, which proponents of feminism unmodified would stigmatize as an accomplice in the perpetration of a variety of theoretical myths, and from the acceptance of several epistemological assumptions, which feminists would identify as the very assumptions from which they aspire to divorce themselves. Supporters of feminism unmodified will not, therefore, view my protestations as revealing embarrassing implications of their theory, but merely as restating its position and contrasting it with the dominant male discourse.

There is a temptation to throw up one's hands and conclude that analytic philosophers, given their predilection for coherence and disdain for contradiction, and feminists of MacKinnon's camp, given their appreciation of paradox and abhorrence of abstraction, can but talk around each other. Lacking enough common ground to engage in genuine dialogue, each merely recasts the other's central aspirations as criticisms, while the other sneers back, "So what!"

Perhaps things are not quite so bleak, however. Although it is probably true that "there can be no escape from plurality – a plurality of traditions, perspectives, philosophic orientations,"[94] we – Anglo-American philosophers and feminists – share a larger situated framework that makes it most unlikely that our "conceptual schemes are so self-enclosed that there is no possibility of reciprocal translation, understanding, and argumentation."[95] Rather than approaching contrasting views as philosophic opponents to be confronted and reduced gleefully to absurdity, Richard Bernstein advises us to "begin with the assumption that the other has something to say to us and to contribute to our understanding. The initial task is to grasp the other's position in the strongest possible light . . . understanding does not entail agreement. On the contrary, it is the way to clarify our disagreements."[96] If analytic philosophers and feminists have reached an impasse it is because they have shared an adversarial style of confrontation that precludes the type of "engaged fallibilistic pluralism" that Bernstein exhorts.

[Engaged fallibilistic pluralism] means taking our own fallibility seriously – resolving that however much we are committed to our own styles of thinking, we are willing to listen to others without denying or suppressing the otherness of the other. It means being vigilant against the dual temptations of simply dismissing what others are saying by falling back on one of those standards defensive ploys where we condemn it as obscure, woolly, or trivial, or thinking we can always easily translate what is alien into our own entrenched vocabularies.[97]

In order to break dialogical impasse, feminists must restrain their inclinations to portray contemporary normative analysis in so cynical and one-sided a fashion, to disdain analytic philosophy as merely the conceptual henchman of male domination, to ridicule the quest for consistency and coherence as either psychological error or aggressive male weaponry, and to castigate critics of their views as male oppressors or their collaborators. For if feminism unmodified deflects and disables all criticism as flowing necessarily from malevolent despots or their sycophants, then it trivializes itself. Likewise, analytic philosophers must curb their tendency to assault the perceived doctrinal weaknesses of feminism, for such tactics blind them to the undeniable insights of feminism: the law's complicity in the historical disenfranchisement of women, the subtle ways in which women's views are marginalized and trivialized in social life, the dangers of a blind justice that further oppresses the already disadvantaged, the blatant prejudices and biases built into our language and reflected in our experience, and the inadequacy of a gender-neutral approach in a society that has historically nurtured so much gender oppression.

Finally, feminism reminds us that much of what we know cannot be independently verified and that epistemic communities, like so many other social relationships, are susceptible to, even dependent upon, established structures of power and privilege.

INTERPRETATIONS OF ITALIAN IMMIGRANT WOMEN AND FEMINIST THEORY

I began with problems associated with interpreting the Italian immigrant woman's experiences. The three dominant interpretations in the literature — women as stablizers, as cultural transformers, and as matriarchs — overlap, but do remain distinct in important respects.

The examination of contemporary feminist thought, especially its critique of certain mainstream versions of epistemology, adds to our understanding of the interpretive enterprise. Although feminists are not the first to undermine uncompromising forms of metaphysical realism and epistemological foundationalism, they convincingly underscore the conceptual difficulties endemic to these forms and connect traditional standards of knowledge to power politics. Moreover, the feminist critique is especially relevant where, as here, we are struggling to sort out conflicting historical interpretations of women's experiences.

The feminist critique reminds us that data underdetermine theory: there are numerous, mutually antagonistic hypotheses compatible with any given series of data. Moreover, social data do not present themselves in raw, theory-free fashion: interpreters have considerable leeway to adjust data to fit particular hypotheses. Under such circumstances, formal logic and empirical observation are insufficient to generate theoretical insight and practical understanding. Thus, our hunches, intuitions, and antecedent normative commitments become paramount in the interpretive enterprise.

This phenomenon becomes more acute in the case of Italian immigrant women because of the scarcity of sociological data. Thus, areas of interpretive choice widen and it becomes more difficult to develop compelling paradigms that might command overwhelming acceptance. One should therefore be suspicious of dogmatic, overly confident answers to questions about the Italian immigrant woman's experience. Answers can emerge only after complicated interpretive processes that necessarily fall short of the aspirations embodied by strict deductive certainty.

Accordingly, interpretations of the Italian immigrant woman's experience must subject themselves to wider dialogue that includes discourse about competing descriptive and prescriptive world visions. Such dialogue will invoke a host of internally justificatory measures—human skill in mundane linguistic exchange, cooperative strategies conducive to psychological well-being, even appeal to transcendental conditions that legitimate human discourse—but these measures, however insightful, cannot establish the last word.

There is, however, no reason to despair. Once we renounce inflated epistemological expectations and nihilistic despondency, both of which depend on the false dualism of "either objectivism or relativism" for their vitality,[98] we experience liberating opportunities for theoretical advances. It is in this vein that much contemporary philosophy, including versions of feminist thought, seeks to expose the polarity of objectivism and relativism as inadequate and transformable.

I return then to the questions surrounding the experiences of Italian immigrant women: Which of the three main interpretations is most accurate? Which best captures the reality of Italian immigrant women and family life? The answer is surprisingly simple: they all capture aspects of the truth; they all give us a glance of the immigrants' reality.

The southern Italian family was a nest of paradoxes and puzzles: at once inflexible and resilient, suffocating and invigorating, restrictive and empowering. Advocates of the images sketched in this chapter choose to emphasize different portions of the Italian family mosaic: Gambino's effusive sentimentality and commendable sense of gratitude incline him to construct a sanguine tale of immigrants surviving and eventually prospering because of the stability of *la via vecchia;* Vezzosi's feminist consciousness impels her to highlight burgeoning solidarity among women, the precursor to required social change as an old-world culture transports itself to the New World; Orsi's realism and keen sense of individualism bring him to a consciously unsentimental rendering of the unliberating aspects of fixed community. We register a deeper understanding: just as humans confront and grapple with the continuum between individual and community, so too do we as interpreters of the past encounter that same continuum: Gambino's image celebrates the undeniable merits of intimacy and connection; Vezzosi's interpretation glorifies the salutary effects of the orderly rebellion of a hitherto disenfranchised part of the community; Orsi's vision reminds us of the preciousness of robust individualism.

Each image operates from necessary but limited data. For example, Orsi's picture is based on anecdotal information gathered from the residents of one predominantly Italian area of New York City; Vezzosi and Tirabassi base their work on even fewer anecdotal accounts and note that in fact fewer than one thousand Italian immigrant women had significant contact with the New York City social workers they describe; Gambino's image is based mainly on his personal interpretations of his Brooklyn neighborhood, supplemented by a few historical and sociological sources.[99]

None of these authors provides, or purports to provide, the definitive explanation of the experience of Italian immigrant women. Instead, they favor us with nuanced glimpses of part of that experience, revealing somewhat different partial truths about immigrant women's burdens and glories. Again, we must remember that there was no unitary immigrant experience for Italian men and women. Because of differences in urban and rural settings, occupations, class, age, gender and so on, each immigrant's narrative will add to a mosaic that we can label the Italian immigrant experience. We must also always remember that the experience remains a mosaic and can never legitimately transform itself into an unambiguous, singular reflection.

Important themes do emerge, however. First, we cannot begin to understand Italian immigrant women without examining family roles, for interpreters agree that such roles defined their personal identity. Second, the family itself cannot be legitimately understood as a simple reality; it was neither an unambiguous benefit nor a total burden. Instead, it embodied a complex host of existential implications for the immigrants and their children, implications that triggered profound fears and hopes along the individual-community continuum. Third, contemporary interpretations of the immigrant family will necessarily be colored by the interpreter's own life struggles along the individual-community continuum. This fact is no cause for regret. Lacking an accessible Archimedean perspective from which to judge neutrally events in the world, our normative assessment could not be otherwise. Fourth, when striving to understanding the immigrant woman and her family, we should guard against two common distortions: retrospective falsification that begins with the certitude that somewhere in the past the best human arrangements existed and flourished and proceeds to assert that if we could only recapture such relationships current social problems would evaporate; and anachronistic attributions that start with the firm conviction that the past is thoroughly contaminated when measured by contemporary normative standards and that our current sense of social possibility is a legitimate, veridical mechanism to reveal the excesses of earlier times.

I have argued that the three images of Italian immigrant women are different in degree but not in kind. Nevertheless, feminist interpreters of the past are more likely than others to be sternly critical of patriarchal excesses and to stand ready to invoke contemporary normative standards to castigate earlier times. Thus, such interpreters are more inclined to deny the existence of the patriarchy ("the immigrant woman as matriarch") or to highlight social change ("the immigrant woman as cultural transformer"). Other interpreters, particularly those who perceive themselves as clear beneficiaries of the earlier immigrant experience, are more likely to sentimentalize the immigrant family ("the immigrant woman as stabilizer") and to fall prey to the allure of retrospective falsification. Again, each of the resulting explanations nevertheless provides part of the mosaic that constitutes the Italian immigrant experience.

But my original questions remain: Was my mother a victim of the legacy of the pernicious southern Italian patriarchy? An illustration of the stolid virtues of a better time? A feminist hero? The answer to such questions is that she was all of these things in part, but none of these things completely.

My mother was, indeed, a victim of the pernicious southern Italian patriarchy: denied formal education because of economic necessity and gender; regarded by her generation as valuable mainly insofar as she ably fulfilled reproductive and domestic functions; viewed by the earlier immigrant generation as less inherently valuable than men; and prevented by familial and societal circumstances from sampling a healthy portion of the individual-community continuum.

She was also, however, an inspiring example of virtues less prevalent today. She harbored no illusions as to the prospects of her upward socioeconomic mobility or of her personal, as opposed to familial, happiness. Instead, she perceived herself as part of a wider subjectivity, as a link in a generational chain that stretched from Sicily to America. She understood clearly that her generation would never be fully American, but she enthusiastically accepted the challenge of guaranteeing that the next generation, her children, would fully enjoy the bounty of the New World. This guarantee, however, could be realized only through her enormous personal sacrifices and unwavering commitments. My mother accepted, even relished, the challenge. She persevered during a period when the call for "family values" was not merely a hackneyed political slogan but instead defined a way of life.

She was also a feminist hero. Once her children began school, she ventured into the public arena and secured a job. Given her ersatz formal education and limited work experience, it was unsurprising that the position she obtained required merely repetitive clerical tasks conducted in the cellar of a local tree nursery. From all reports, however, she performed these tasks with distinction. Thus, she combined job and family, without compromising on the demands of either. My mother did this, and more, without complaint and without resort to support groups or psychological counseling. She was a cultural transformer without public renown. More important, throughout her life she steadfastly refused to embody the moods and demeanors typically assigned to women: passivity, submission, social invisibility. On the contrary, she energetically, even fiercely, resisted patriarchal authority, especially when that authority jeopardized the family's well-being.

When my mother died in 1980 at the age of 62, her daughter was a tenured teacher of mathematics and her son was a student at Harvard Law School. The generational challenge had been vanquished, the dream had been realized.

CHAPTER 3

THE INDIVIDUAL RESISTS
THE STATE

Anarchy, Italian Style, and Political Theory

My father told me a story: a well-meaning civil servant arrived at the destitute immigrant's door and proclaimed cheerfully, "I'm from the government and I'm here to help." The immigrant peered back sternly and slammed the door after retorting, *"Essere poveru e una sfurtuna accettare elemosina e una vergogna"* ("To be poor is unfortunate, to accept charity is shameful.").

I got the point. The woman declined the state's tender mercies for a number of reasons: to accept charity from *stranieri* would have been tacit admission that the family network had failed; the immigrant may well have suspected that accepting the government's beneficence would saddle her with additional reciprocal obligations; she may have feared a general curtailing of her freedom by her new benefactor; and she may have been exhibiting a touch of the arrogance of the poor. In any event, the immigrant responded from a harsh background of generations of oppressive relations with the state that had finely sharpened her abiding distrust of government.

I was born and raised in a small village of about forty-five hundred residents, most of whom were Republican. My parents distrusted government and politicians, but they were crafty enough to ensure that at least one of them would be on the winning side of each election. The scheme was simple: one of them would register as a Republican, the other as a Democrat. To add a little spice, they often simultaneously switched their official affiliations. In reality, although they were personally conservative in their approach to life, they rarely voted for Republican candidates because they were firmly convinced that these politicians advanced too readily the interests of the wealthy and had historically supported discriminatory measures that had curtailed the immigration of southern Europeans to the United States. The moral of the story: government was untrustworthy and the wise citizen must be ever diligent in recognizing its traps and tricks.

In this chapter, I sketch Italian and Italian-American anarchical experiences in the late nineteenth and early twentieth centuries, discuss several versions of anarchist theory, and analyze the anarchical instincts of contemporary social philosopher Roberto Unger. My thesis is that although anarchism, as a developed political theory and prescription, has at best limited practical application, its animating spirit and distinctive moral posture maintain robust vitality today. When suspicion of government is radically heightened, when the pernicious effects of vast disparities in social power are most keenly felt, and when individual freedom seems most in jeopardy, the incantations of anarchism are enchanting.

ANARCHISM, ITALIAN STYLE

Two events gave rise to anarchism in Italy.[1] First, in 1864 Mikhail Bakunin visited Italy. Although he initially attracted only a few hundred followers, his appearance embodied great symbolic value. Second, in 1871 the Paris Commune[2] rekindled the revolutionary fervor of Italian radicals disenchanted with the outcome of the *Risorgimento*.[3]

The Decade of Beginning

The 1870s saw the beginning of the anarchist struggle in Italy. By 1872 the Italian Federation of the International Workingmen's Association was created at the Congress of Rimini. The Italian Federation adopted an ideology allied closely with Bakunin: anarchist, atheist, collectivist, anti–private property, anti–hierarchical institutions. At the Bologna Congress of 1873, the ideological alliance between the Italian Federation and Bakunin's collectivism, which stressed revolutionary action, the public ownership of land, and the extension of women's social franchise, became even clearer: the anarchists rejected the Marxist belief in the political conquest of state power to be followed by a dictatorship of the proletariat. The "People's State" was still a state that threatened personal and collective freedoms.[4] Moreover, the Italian Federation, seeking an eclectic membership, refused to identify the working class as the necessary vanguard of revolution: the federation itself would serve as instigator and facilitator of struggle. Finally, Italian anarchists shunned trade unionism on grounds similar to their abhorrence of reformist politics. Thus, the leadership of the anarchist movement such as Errico Malatesta, Carlo Cafiero, Andrea Costa, Francesco Merlino, and Luigi Galleani, were men of bourgeois birth who had abandoned their class and the conventional wisdom it had presumably nurtured.

The price of political purity was stiff: only violent revolution could uproot pernicious state power. The uncompromising, romantic belligerence of Italian anarchism, although an allure to the disenfranchised, would ultimately doom the movement.

By 1874 the Italian Federation boasted over 32,000 members, about 8,500 of which hailed from the *Mezzogiorno*.[5] That year marked the first anarchist attempt at insurrection: one thousand Internationalists were to attack Bologna straightaway, while two thousand comrades joined them from other parts of the Romagna. The capture of Bologna would then trigger additional uprisings in Tuscany, the Marches, Puglia, and Rome.[6] The plan dissolved feebly when the "two thousand comrades" appeared as only two hundred. Local police easily squashed these rebellions in each city, often capturing rebels before their revolts.

By 1876 the Italian movement had nudged toward anarchist-communism and away from Bakuninian collectivism. Led by Malatesta, it adopted the position that collectivism, although harboring antihierarchical and antiauthoritarian values, tended to reproduce social inequalities.

The anarchist movement in 1877, recognizing that its previous revolutionary ambitions had been drastically inflated, sought comrades from a hitherto untapped source: the destitute peasants of the *Mezzogiorno*. Convinced that insurrectionary acts, not stylized rhetoric, would be most likely to move these peasants, anarchists led by Malatesta and Cafiero conspired to wage guerrilla war in the Matese mountain range (between Campania and Molise). However, the *Banda del Matese*, twenty-five strong, were betrayed by a police informant and attacked by local *carabinieri*. Undaunted, the band emerged from the hills and descended upon the tiny village of Letino. In the words of Nunzio Pernicone:

> The peasants stared in amazement as these strangers entered the village waving red and black banners. Without further ado, they deposed King Victor Emmanuel and declared the village occupied in the name of the social revolution. The local tax records were then burned and the people declared sovereign . . . Before departing, the anarchists distributed arms and money confiscated from the local treasury, and Cafiero and Malatesta . . . urged the peasants to follow their example and revolt. Virtually the same scenes were enacted at Gallo, the next village they visited. But these gallant efforts proved barren. The peasants knew from bitter experience that rebellion would be answered with repression. In fact, a large detachment of soldiers was already hot on the heels of the insurgents. Forced to retreat to the mountains, the anarchists trekked about in the freezing rain and snow for several days before finally surrendering.[7]

Ironically, Italian anarchists, although repelled by the social outcomes of the *Risorgimento*, were inspired by its passionate faith in revolutionary might. They admired especially the military hero of the *Risorgimento*, Giuseppe Garibaldi (1807–1882), who would earn the sobriquet the "Lion of Caprera." This admiration, combined with an ideology that insisted on the necessity of non-political means, impelled the anarchists to insurgency. The newly formed national government, however, soon increased its repressive measures.

When a failed assassination attempt (not precipitated by anarchists) on King Umberto occurred in 1878, the government assumed it had a clear reason for harsh reprisal and soon applied policies of *ammonizione* ("reprimand"): "The successive waves of mass arrests, the many months spent in prison awaiting trial, and the steady diaspora of prominent leaders into exile all combined to destroy the International beyond hope of resurrection."[8]

The Decade of Retreat

The late 1870s and early 1880s found the anarchist movement in Italy in chaos: the authorities widened their employment of *ammonizione;* Andrea Costa, then the most eminent figure in the movement, defected from the movement; and members of the Italian Federation of the International tended to ally themselves on the basis of personalities rather than according to distinct programmatic ideals.[9] In an ideological backlash, the cult of personalities was replaced by radical antiauthoritarianism: any organizational efforts were perceived as inherently pernicious. The previously solid anarchist-communism of the movement was unsettled by powerful individualistic passions. As a result, the movement became more abstract – characterized by vague yearnings for radical transformation and liberation from oppressive government – and, because of its revulsion of organization, virtually incapable of concerted, practical action.

In 1881 the International Revolutionary Socialist Congress gathered in London. There, Malatesta, always a firm believer in the necessity of organization for social change, argued that Italian anarchists should join in revitalizing the International or in creating a new association. But the anarchists in Italy strongly rejected institutions, mandates, programs, and leaders they feared would jeopardize the prerogatives of individuals.[10] The result was a disaggregated anarchism that replicated at the group level the worst excesses of atomistic individualism: isolation, estrangement, and alienation.

Beyond a few scattered demonstrations and strikes,[11] the anarchist movement confined itself mainly to ideological dissemination in newspapers. During this period, about thirty anarchist newspapers, some enduring for only a few issues, were created. These newspapers gave government authorities occasional evidence of an anarchist conspiracy, and both Merlino and Malatesta were thereby convicted on vague charges. Merlino fled to London and Malatesta found refuge in Argentina. The loss of Malatesta disheartened the anarchist movement in Italy. Although impressive figures such as Luigi Galleani and Pietro Gori stepped up, no one was quite able to replicate the panache and inspiration embodied by Malatesta.[12]

The Decade of Romanticism

Malatesta returned to Europe in 1889, arguing, as always, in favor of organization and collective volitional acts.[13] In 1891 about one hundred Italian anarchists constituted the Capolago Congress, formed a Revolutionary Anarcho-Socialist Party, and advocated a general strike on May Day. When May 1 arrived in Rome, the insurgents were badly outnumbered. Limited to general rioting, the strike produced the worst outcome: resistance too feeble to accomplish any significant goal, yet tangible enough to invite another round of government repression of anarchists. Moreover, the debacle reinforced in the minds of numerous Italian anarchists the dangers of organization,[14] causing a split in the Revolutionary Anarcho-Socialist Party which culminated in the founding of the Socialist Party in 1892. The tilt toward individualism and against organization, when combined with a lack of effective leadership and explicit governmental repression, disabled most concerted practical action against the state. As a result, some anarchists were drawn to discrete acts of terrorism and assassination.

The indefatigable Malatesta regrouped, however, for he viewed the rise of the *Fasci dei Lavoratori* ("Bands of Workers")[15] in Sicily as emblematic of a regional rebelliousness toward government. Although not inspired by anarchism, the work of the *Fasci* seemed to embody the type of popular discontent that might inspire greater insurrection against the state. But the anarchist movement was still influenced by anti–political action contingents, and Malatesta found only limited support for his plan to journey to Sicily. Malatesta was not easily discouraged and, with the support of Merlino and a few other notables, still planned his trip.[16] The government, meanwhile, in the person of Prime Minister Francesco Crispi, reacted strongly against the *Fasci* and against a spontaneous, anarchist-led sympathy revolt in northwestern Tuscany. He placed both areas under a state of siege in 1894.[17]

Malatesta, acting decisively if not wisely, concocted a tripartite insurrection with Merlino and a French anarchist, Charles Malato. Merlino was to operate in Naples, Malatesta in Romagna, and Malato in Piedmont and Lombardy. The outcome was grimly predictable: undermanned, overly ambitious, and betrayed by police informants, the three anarchists accomplished nothing and were forced to retreat. Merlino was arrested; Malatesta and Malato fled to London.

The anarchist threat in Italy consisted, at best, of smoke and mirrors. The most able anarchists exalted organizational strategies and concerted insurrection, but they were fewest in number. Others who called themselves "anarchists" would more accurately have been labeled "atomistic individualists," believers in a radical personal freedom that rejected antecedent obligations and attachments not founded on the individual's voluntary choice. Moreover, state repression had anarchism generally on the run. And in June 1894, two events shook the fragile remnants of the anarchist movement in Italy: a solitary assassin, Paolo Lega, shot at Prime Minister Crispi, and another anarchist, Sante Caserio, who was a better marksman than Lega, killed the president of France.

The Italian Parliament immediately enacted emergency legislation designed to wipe out the anarchist menace: all anarchists were sentenced to *domicilio coatto* ("house arrest"). These laws remained in effect through 1895 and condemned all prominent anarchists to two choices: surreptitious flight from Italy or house arrest on one of the islands near the mainland.[18]

By 1897, however, the ubiquitous Malatesta, under the pseudonym "Giuseppe Rinaldi," had returned and established secret headquarters in Ancona.[19] He gave lectures, advocated the founding of workers' organizations, and published a journal. Due largely to his influence and efforts, a brief resurgence of anarchism occurred in north and central Italy. Once again, however, the specter of the assassin emerged: Pietro Acciarito tried to kill King Umberto.[20] And again the authorities rounded up the usual suspects for *domicilio coatto*.

Greater social calamities soon befell Italy. In 1898 severe weather contributed to poor harvests, which, combined with high import duties and freight charges, greatly increased the price of bread. Hungry Italians in all parts of the country responded with demonstrations, looting of granaries, and land seizures.[21]

The government moved to quell the disturbances and were finally able to indict and sentence Malatesta to a short prison term for "inciting class hatred."[22] But the crisis deepened with the *Fatti di Maggio* (May Events) in Milan. To crush a series of street demonstrations and barricades, the authorities declared martial law and sent soldiers. When the dust and blood had settled, somewhere from 118 to 600 Milanese workers were dead and hundreds more were wounded.[23] The emergency laws of 1894 targeting anarchists were reinstated and as many as three thousand anarchists were incarcerated in the penal islands. This police strategy, however, was not a clear success: The incarceration actually nourished and desensitized the rebellious anarchists it was designed to destroy, and the penal islands became training grounds for the next generation of the anarchist movement.[24]

Finally, in 1900, yet another anarchist assassin, the New Jersey resident Gaetano Bresci, proclaiming revenge for the state's reaction to *Fatti di Maggio*, killed King Umberto.

Anarchism and the Contadini

The leaders of the anarchist movement in Italy were predominantly defectors from the middle and upper social classes. Rejecting Marx's belief in the inexorable laws of history and economics, these leaders understood the need for mass action. Moreover, rejecting Marx's belief in the proletariat as the inevitable engine of social change, they acknowledged that the proletariat class in Italy was insufficient for mass action. They therefore sought to persuade the disenfranchised peasants to rally to their cause.

At first blush, the peasants of the *Mezzogiorno* seemed to offer fertile ground for anarchism. Heirs to centuries of government oppression and foreign invasion, witnesses to unremitting insurgency and rebellion, victims of usurious economic policies, the *contadini* had little stake in maintaining and defending existing social institutions. Peter Ciano argues that

> Anarchism was uniquely rooted in Italy's peculiar feudal heritage. In southern Italy radicalism grew out of extreme economic and cultural backwardness. Such conditions (along with the savagery of land owners and their clerical supporters) promoted anarchism rather than politically-based labor socialism, and the repeated flaring up of rebellions which were repressed with great bloodshed.[25]

Yet first appearances reveal only part of the picture. Many peasants were plagued by a *fatalismo* ("fatalism") that drained their sense of robust possibility: their social context seemed inherent, inevitable, and even necessary. Moreover, because they understood far better than the anarchist leaders the history and effects of governmental *ammonizione*, the peasants were not easily led to seemingly fruitless rebellion, especially not when smooth-talking *stranieri* from the north were the main instigators.

Also, anarchism, with its conglomeration of cosmopolitanism, anticlericalism, and collectivism, seemed a peculiar hybrid. The *contadini* were hard put to view themselves as citizens of Italy, much less to perceive themselves as citizens of the world. Although the liberating sense of transformation that animated anarchism might have rekindled hope, it also carried an unsettling threat to the security and preservation of *l'ordine della famiglia*. In the social context that enveloped the *contadini* for centuries, a citizen of the entire world was a citizen of no world. Because, as I have argued previously, the family order and wider social institutions shared a mutually constitutive relationship, the call for thorough social transformation bore ambiguous possibilities. The visceral, if not rational, recognition of this threat militated against massive number of peasants swarming to anarchist colors and sharpened the antiorganizational instincts of those who did. Anarchist action undertaken by peasants was more likely to be personal, partial, and vengeful rather than impersonal, general, and motivated by abstract principle: concrete acts of romantic heroism were more prevalent than ideologically-based concerted action.

Accordingly, anarchists, although capable of murdering particular public officials and of generating sporadic obstreperous activities, never embodied a serious threat to dominant social institutions. Moreover, although not inherently contradictory, the ideology of anarchy, with its simultaneous veneration of both individualism and collectivism; its distrust of hierarchy, organization, and long-term strategy; and its inspirational but hazy prescription for the future, ensures this result in most social contexts.

Italian Anarchism in the United States

The Italian immigrants to the Americas were drawn predominantly from the *Mezzogiorno*, a region of Italy that, contrary to Ciano's suggestions, was not influenced greatly by anarchist ideas.[26] But among these immigrants were indeed a disproportionate number of anarchists fleeing from Italy's *ammonizione*. Moreover, contrary to popular belief, the immigrants were predominantly from the penultimate, not lowest, social class. By the fact of immigration itself, they manifested a degree of adventure that loosened the limits of *fatalismo*.

The Haymarket events of 1886 and 1887,[27] when four German immigrants were executed and three imprisoned after a labor demonstration in which a bomb killed seven policemen, spurred national interest in anarchist ideology and personalities. By the 1890s small Italian anarchist colonies were located in New York City and Paterson, New Jersey.[28] At least four anarchist journals were started, and visits by anarchist leaders, including Merlino, Pietro Gori, Malatesta, and, most importantly, Luigi Galleani, intellectually nourished the colonies.[29] The colonies, however, remained insular and relatively obscure until Bresci's assassination of King Umberto.

Early anarchist activity included a strike by Paterson silk workers in 1902, and a Barre, Vermont, stone- and marble-cutters' strike in 1908.[30] But Italian-American anarchism did not merely replicate Italian anarchism. The evidence suggests that the growth of anarchism in the United States during the first two decades of this century resulted from the social and economic conditions that confronted the immigrant upon arrival. Few Italian immigrants had been anarchists before their arrival in the United States.[31] Strains of anarchist

individualism, anarchist communism, anarchosyndicalism, and anarchism unmodified characterized the immigrants' new world.

Galleani, born in Piedmont in 1861, was the most prominent advocate of
anarchist communism. His rhetoric demanded nothing less than the overthrow
of capitalism and government by whatever means necessary. He scorned all
reforms as corruptions and betrayals, insisting instead on complete destruction
of the established order.[32]

Carlo Tresca, born in Abruzzo in 1879, was the most prominent Italian-
American figure in anarchosyndicalism. He rejected the idea of social transformation through political conquest of state power. Instead, he advocated the full
development of workers' own revolutionary organizations, especially industrial
unions, as the way to unsettle capitalism.[33]

Because the other strains of anarchism suffered from lack of organization,
anarchist-communism and anarchosyndicalism became dominant. With the
rise in labor consciousness, many Italian-American anarchists, like their Italian
counterparts, embraced anarchosyndicalism.[34] Advocating the industrial union
as the engine of social change, the International Workers of the World (IWW)
proved attractive because, in Ciano's words:

> IWW disavowed political solutions, embraced all ethnic groups, and tried to under-
> stand the needs of the most downtrodden unskilled labor . . . the IWW attempted to
> stir them from their lethargy by teaching these outcasts of society that power is gained
> through solidarity and that only power moves men and societies.[35]

Leadership in the Italian-American immigrant community was provided by
Joseph Ettor, Arturo Giovannitti, and Tresca, who together fueled much of the mil-
itancy and passion of the IWW.[36] For example, one or more of the three was involved in the Lawrence, Massachusetts, textile strike of 1912, a strike of cigar-
makers in Tampa, and labor activism among miners in Minnesota. These leaders
attracted support not primarily on the basis of abstract ideological appeal, but for
pragmatic reasons: they held out the possibility of better working conditions and
exemplified ethnic solidarity. Italian-American workers, most of whom were personally conservative in their outlook on life, accepted anarchistic and socialistic
leadership without embracing the accompanying radical political convictions.[37]

Advocating the overthrow of capitalism by social revolution and, in 1917, by
noncompliance with a government mandate that demanded the registration of

all aliens of military age,[38] the anarchists were eventually targeted by a governmental antiradical campaign that was begun before the United States entered World War I.[39] Spurred by increased radical activity in the United States[40] and by the Bolshevik Revolution in Russia, Attorney General Palmer, under the authority of the Espionage Act, began proceedings against thousands of suspected anarchists, socialists, communists, and antiwar advocates. In October 1917, for example, Ettor, Giovannitti, and Tresca, among others, were indicted after a raid on IWW offices. In 1918 alone, over one hundred IWWs were indicted, convicted, and sentenced to terms ranging from two to twenty years.[41]

The year 1920 marked the most famous anarchist episode. Two disciples of Galleani, Nicola Sacco, a shoemaker, and Bartolomeo Vanzetti, a fish peddler, were charged with the murder of a shoe factory paymaster and a guard during a robbery in South Braintree, Massachusetts. They were tried, found guilty, and sentenced to death. In 1927, after almost seven years on death row and worldwide attention generated by explicit procedural irregularities in the trial and a general perception that the two were victimized by their ethnicity and their anarchist convictions, the two men were executed.[42]

In the words of Jerre Mangione and Ben Morreale:

> The case was tried before a prejudiced judge, with an aggressive prosecutor who played to all the prevailing antipathies of the time, and before a jury chosen from a population that largely shared the judge's viewpoint. When Sacco and Vanzetti were executed, on August 22, 1927, there was good reason to believe that the case was just as much a lynching as that of the more than thirty Italians lynched elsewhere in the nation.[43]

Italian-American and Italian anarchism lost much vitality during and after the 1930s. The rise of Mussolini, the failure of the Spanish anarchist revolution, the emergence of more politically conservative labor unions, the ramifications of the Palmer raids, and the partial assimilation of immigrants to American life all contributed to the attenuation of anarchism on both continents.[44] Moreover, activists who remained politically radical chose more explicitly socialist or communist ideology.

The Italian-American radical movement was itself never purely anarchistic. For example, Tresca referred to himself at various times as a socialist, a syndicalist, and an anarchist. Laborers were not drawn to carefully crafted ideologies but to demands for equitable material distribution, limits on government power, heroic acts of rebellion, and promises of a higher overall quality of life.[45] Animated perhaps by the disparity between their inflated expectations and the reality of their everyday existence, and oscillating between romantic visions of a better world and desperate cynicism in the face of inexpugnable governmental power, many Italian-American radicals vented their frustration in strikes, boycotts, and sabotage. Like most radicals, they struggled mightily with the conflict of employing violent means to accomplish nonviolent ends: to extinguish human evil by presumably turning the dark side against itself. Like its counterpart in Italy, Italian-American anarchism never seriously threatened entrenched power. Instead, anarchism burst forth in militant action that raised the specter of social danger, revealed the vast disparities between classes, challenged the industrial world to fulfill its own promises, and took seriously the human genius to reimagine the terms of existence.

THE ROOTS OF ANARCHISM

"Anarchism" derives from the Greek word *anarkhia,* and it bears both positive — the salutary absence of government — and negative — a stage of confusion and chaos — connotations. Numerous intramural debates focus on what constitutes "genuine" anarchism: Must anarchists oppose all government? Or is anarchism merely a special form of government? Must anarchists resist all authority? Or may anarchists accept nonhierarchical or noncoercive authority? Must anarchism be radically individualistic? Or is anarchism, although nonauthoritarian, necessarily communitarian? Is anarchism best portrayed as psychological and moral resistance to social hierarchy and division? Or must it translate to specific prescriptions for social, economic, and political organization?[46]

Rather than concentrating on resolving such questions, which suggest that "anarchism" has a discernible essence or absolute defining character that once discovered can truncate internal ideological disputes, I touch upon some of these questions while exploring several versions of anarchism.

Although I accept the robust pluralism embodied in different versions of anarchism, at least one common theme does emerge: hostility to sovereign governments, which by their very nature translate into harmful social hierarchy and division. The renowned Russian anarchist, Petr Kropotkin (1842–1921), captured this sentiment when he described anarchism as a principle or theory of life and conduct under which society is conceived without government—harmony in such a society being obtained, not by submission to law or by obedience to any authority, but by free agreements concluded between the various groups, territorial and professional, freely constituted for the sake of production and consumption, and also for the satisfaction of the infinite variety of needs and aspirations of a civilized being.[47]

This rejection of government is dialectically related[48] to a host of other propositions widely shared by anarchists: celebration of individual sovereignty and freedom, disdain for and resistance to all coercive authority that transgresses individual sovereignty and freedom, acceptance of the inseparability of the individual and society, and firm conviction that mutual aid and interdependent voluntarism are the social foundation of society. Although anarchism can conceivably be based on the atomistic individualism that fuels political libertarianism—the belief that the individual is logically and empirically prior to society; that individuals bear natural negative duties toward others that morally prohibit them only from defrauding, harming, or coercing others; and that only a minimum government limited to enforcing general compliance with individuals' natural negative rights is permissible[49]—most anarchists venerate human solidarity, look fondly upon society, contrast its egalitarian authority with the hierarchical authority of government, accept that robust development of human agency requires extensive social interaction, but reject even minimum government.

Moreover, anarchists' scorn is not limited to government but usually encompasses the other important socializing institutions in modern nation-states: family, church, schools, and law. Accordingly, significant practical questions emerge: Would anarchism truly herald a peaceful, noncoercive, nonhierarchical society? Or would the negative connotation of "anarchism" be realized: chaos and confusion? The answer to such questions depends heavily on whether anarchists can transcend relentless critique of the social and political status quo and construct a persuasive prescriptive vision of society redeemed.

Anarchist principles are informed by the assumptions that power is inherently a corrupting influence, that humans are capable of structuring their activities without instruction from governmental hierarchies, and that individuals' voluntarism and mutual aid, based on acceptance of human solidarity, can facilitate better structures than those fashioned by hierarchical authority.

The recurrent anarchist themes are summed up by the Russian anarchist Mikhail Bakunin (1814–1876):

> On our banner, the social-revolutionary banner . . . are inscribed in fiery and bloody letters: the destruction of all States, the annihilation of bourgeois civilization, free and spontaneous organization from below upward, by means of free associations, the organization of the unbridled rabble of toilers, of all emancipated humanity, and the creation of a new universally human world.[50]

Many of these themes are also found in Marxist thought, and some anarchists, such as Kropotkin and the Italians Carlo Cafiero (1846–1892) and Errico Malatesta (1850–1932), allied themselves explicitly with communism. At least one major difference, however, separates the two perspectives: communists are willing to accept a period of transition from the fall of advanced capitalism to the blossoming of the final stage of communism during which state socialism is firmly in place, expelling the vestiges of capitalist-bourgeois thinking and nurturing the social consciousness that is one of the preconditions of the final stage. Most anarchists, however, reject the period of the political transition and insist that once solidly entrenched a state, regardless of its avowed ultimate purposes, is unlikely to facilitate its own "withering away." Thus, they argue that after the fall of nation-states anarchical society should commence unencumbered by government.

Furthermore, anarchists rarely embrace the values of democratic procedures and institutions. Such values presuppose the validity of majority rule or other delegation of social responsibility that, from the anarchist perspective, individuals themselves should cherish and exercise. Likewise, anarchists impugn Plato and other philosophers who conjure ideal visions of government that purport to capture absolute political truths. Anarchists are much more likely to view truth as part of an emerging social process that, at least in certain paramount respects, resists final determination.[51]

In another antidote to bourgeois consciousness, anarchism often adopts an international perspective that aspires to eventual worldwide community. Thus Bakunin held that nationalism and patriotism were bourgeois creations, formed to preserve the state that in turn secured the privileges of dominant classes.[52]

Although broad categorizations are fraught with oversimplification and distortion, they also serve the important purpose of efficient reference. I classify the striking variety of anarchist perspectives as follows: *individualistic anarchism* comes closest to political libertarianism. Here the absolute independence of the individual is prized to the exclusion of antecedent social connections. Individualistic anarchists scorn not only government but society as well. Sensing the eradicable antinomy of freedom and equality, individualistic anarchists embrace negative freedom—freedom from coercion, harm, and deception wrongly caused by others—and its image of egoists choosing and acting in a context of mutual respect. Given factual inequalities among humans, individualistic anarchists accept that the outcomes of choice within that context will undoubtedly produce social inequalities, but they console themselves with the alleged equality of opportunity individual freedom nurtures.

Individualistic anarchists argue against collective ownership of goods, but they differ on the desirability of capitalist economic systems. Those who champion capitalism and who enthusiastically accept the imperatives of natural negative duties become indistinguishable from political libertarians: given contingent national and international conditions, they may feel compelled to accept, albeit reluctantly, the minimal state.

Those individualistic anarchists who reject both capitalism and socialism offer few specific prescriptions; instead, they trust the outcomes produced by a radically empowered individualism. This brand of anarchism is associated most closely with the German thinker Johann Kaspar Schmidt (1806–1856), who wrote under the name Max Stirner. Although Stirner was aware that social cooperation is often essential to the fulfillment of human needs, he refused to perceive such cooperation as inherently valuable. Rather, he viewed voluntary associations as, at best, instrumentally valuable and dependent upon the antecedent existence of radically empowered individuals. Accordingly, in a literary style that serves as a philosophical precursor to Nietzsche's individualism, Stirner wrote:

> Do not seek in self-renunciation a freedom which denies your very selves, but seek your own selves . . . Let each of you be an all-powerful 'I.' There is no freedom but that which the individual conquers for himself. Freedom given or conceded is not freedom but 'stolen goods.' There is no judge but myself who can decide whether I am right or wrong. The only things I have no right to do are those I do not do with a free mind. You have the right to be whatever you have the strength to be. Whatever you accomplish you accomplish as a unique individual: Neither the State, society, nor humanity can master this devil.[53]

Part of Stirner's program is to desanctify the bourgeois moral and political consciousness that embodies stultifying tendencies toward conformity and repression. In fact, he invokes the metaphor of the mediocre "herd" decades before Nietzsche: "The young are sent to school in herds to learn the old saws and when they know the verbiage of the old by heart they are said to have come of age . . . God, conscience, duties, and laws are all errors which have been stuffed into our minds and hearts."[54]

Stirner, true to his individualistic spirit, distinguished revolution from rebellion. Revolution is a sociopolitical act to overthrow the established order and replace it with another. At its heart, then, lurks a faith in centralized institutions. Rebellion, by contrast, is the action of individuals to forever destroy the state and the collective consciousness that sustains it. It seeks a "dynamic balance of power between men aware of their own might."[55]

Stirner's rendition is at once the purest, most stimulating, and least plausible version of individualistic anarchism. It is pure because it absolutely refuses to compromise with individual freedom: neither coercion from superiors in governmental hierarchies nor benign authority from social equals is morally acceptable. It is stimulating because of the sheer audacity of its nihilistic moment, during which empowered individuals, self-authorized and ratifying only their own subjective evaluations, liberate themselves from the leveling and mediocrity of equality of result. It is implausible, finally, because it conjures the pejorative images of anarchism: an everything-up-for-grabs chaos, a Hobbesian war of "each against every," in which might is the immediate determiner of right. Stirner hopes to destroy the tensions of the individualism – community continuum by denying one of its poles. It is no surprise that Stirner's radical individualism is considered today a marginal form of anarchism.

A second form of anarchism is *mutualism*, most closely associated with the French writer Pierre Joseph Proudhon (1809–1865). Although his views changed, Proudhon is known for his highly social conception of anarchism, his rejection of revolutionary violence and even more benign forms of political action, and his hope that federal organizations emerging from local communes could replace national governments. Thus, in contrast to individualistic anarchism, his was a deeply communitarian form of anarchy.

Although emphasizing peaceful dispersion of workers' associations as a prime agent of reform, mutualists rejected large-scale collectivization as a danger to freedom. Instead, they based their economic program on individual possession of the means of production by peasants and small craftsmen united in a framework of exchange and credit arrangements.[56] Under this view, workers should shun the temptations of representative democracy and universal suffrage, the twin idols of bourgeois consciousness. Mutualists held that the social revolution is significantly contaminated if it results from political devices. Instead, workers must radically separate themselves from the illusions of bourgeois democracy by refusing to collaborate with inherently oppressive government. Mutualists claimed that if the masses were truly sovereign, government and thus the distinction between governed and governor would disappear. The state, lacking its essential function, would be identical with society and disappear into industrial organization.[57]

Proudhon conceived the essentials of workers' self-management in this way: every member of a local workers' commune must have an indivisible share of the commune's property; every worker must assume a fair share of the heavy and unattractive jobs, and gain the widest training possible in the range of work operations and activities; commune offices will be gained by election, and all workers' regulations will be submitted to the associates for ratification; every associate will receive profit dividends commensurate with service rendered and salary in proportion to the nature of position held and degree of skill and responsibility borne; each worker will set his own hours, discharge his duties, and depart the association at will.[58]

Mutualism was explicitly internationalist and federalist in character. Proudhon's federalism, which he contrasted to government centralization, revolved around a pact transacted among the various territorial workers' organization. Federalist centralization must be created from the bottom up, with all functions independent and self-governing.[59] This federalist aspiration embodied international ambitions: an organization of nations constituting a union of mankind.

Despite the apparent rigidity of his prescriptions, Proudhon was an explicitly antisystematic philosopher. This stance is especially apparent in his notion of progress as "the affirmation of universal movement and in consequence the negation of all immutable forms and formulae, of all doctrines of eternity, permanence, and impeccability, and of every subject, object, spiritual or transcendental, that does not change."[60]

Nonanarchists deride Proudhon's mutualism as based on a utopian view of workers as less corruptible and inherently more communal than governmental elites; as grounded in a romanticized illusion of workers' capacities and willingness for self-government; as naively socialistic and ahistorical in its pretensions to federalism and internationalism; and as hopelessly naive in its conviction that the peaceful spread of workers' associations could overcome massive inherent coordination problems. These critics would insist that workers are no different from the hated bureaucrats: we should therefore expect workers' structures, regardless of their animating spirit, to replicate the hierarchy and division endemic to bourgeois governments. Moreover, Proudhon's prescriptions for workers' self-management, depending as they do on elections and salary differentiations among workers, betray his own avowed goal to eviscerate bourgeois ideology.

A third form of anarchism is *collectivism*. Associated most closely with Bakunin, collectivism differed most clearly from mutualism in several respects: its emphasis on revolutionary activity to destroy the state; its belief in public ownership of land, services, and the means of production; and its thorough rejection of the vestiges of individualism still implicit in mutualism. Bakunin also explicitly extends anarchist principles to women.[61]

Bakunin accepted mutualism's position on the connection between work and consumer rights—one's claim to goods should be proportional to the quantity and quality of one's labor—but he rejected mutualism's conviction that peasants and craftsmen must retain possession of land and instruments of production as security against loss of independence.

Best known as a rival of Marx, Bakunin and his fellow collectivists challenged Marx's authority within the International Workingmen's Association. Marxists insisted that the workers, upon facilitating the fall of capitalism, must assume power, create a "dictatorship of the proletariat," and begin the process by which the state will eventually "wither away." The collectivists, however, brandished their anarchist colors and argued for the earliest possible dismantling of the state. They viewed state power as inherently evil and were gravely suspicious that any state apparatus could aspire sincerely to its own obsolescence. As a result of this confrontation, Bakukin and his collectivists were expelled from the International in 1872.[62]

The collectivists' disdain for the state extended to the ballot box, which they viewed as the paradigm of noxious bourgeois politics. Universal suffrage is not a liberating antidote to oppression; indeed it constitutes the complicity of the masses in their own oppression: voting results only in a government aristocracy against the people. His abhorrence of suffrage and of a dictatorship of the proletariat led Bakunin to accept spontaneous and continuous mass action as the locus of social revolution.

Although Bakunin's overall position is refreshingly coherent, its purity exacts a steep price. Like all spontaneity theorists, Bakunin must confront the overwhelming conservatism (in the sense of "status quo preserving") of the masses. Having been deeply socialized into an allegedly false consciousness and having little prior public empowerment, workers are highly unlikely to be the vanguard of social revolution even if they are urged by the invisible hand of history. As a result, elite ideologues are undoubtedly required to create and stimulate revolutionary sentiment. Under collectivism's own precepts, however, such elites, once entrenched, are unlikely to disaggregate themselves: power is inherently intoxicating and self-sustaining. Thus, collectivists confront a pitiless dilemma: inertia, or hierarchy and division.

Bakunin was aware of this problem and claimed to solve it through the creation of internal vanguards and trade union efforts: "The vanguard must be neither the benefactor nor the dictatorial leader of the people but simply the midwife to its self-liberation. It can achieve nothing more than to spread among the masses ideas which correspond with their instincts."[63] Moreover, trade unions could provide workers with experiences in self-management and public empowerment and herald the age when the state apparatus would be replaced by councils of workers' associations.

Bakunin's response is less than convincing. We should be suspicious when people insist they are not swaying our opinion but merely eliciting latent political views. Too often this assertion is grounded in the notion that explicit political views emanate from a false consciousness nurtured, consciously or not, by the politically powerful. In turn, this notion is used to discount opposing views by automatically stigmatizing them as flowing from the pernicious ideologies of dominant groups.

Undoubtedly, the preferences of subordinate classes are at least partly the result of established social rules and practices. Thus, those rules and practices cannot be justified noncircularly by appeals to those very preferences. But neither can the preferences of subordinate classes be discounted automatically simply because they vary from a revolutionary's political prescriptions. If I am a vanguard ideologue and you agree with my proffered political prescriptions then I have performed my midwife chores well and have succeeded in extracting your authentic judgment; if you disagree, however, that merely demonstrates the power of dominant ideologies to mystify and hypnotize the masses: heads I win, tails you lose. Of course, the game only works if we can antecedently establish that my political prescriptions are themselves sound and in the best social interest, and that the masses suffer from a collective narcolepsy that prevents awareness of those interests. Vanguard ideologues, however, do not independently establish such conclusions; instead, they assume them as axioms of the game. Accordingly, the distinctions between "midwives," "benefactors," and "dictatorial leaders" becomes less and less clear, and we again journey between the Charybdis of inertia and the Scylla of hierarchy and division.

A fourth form of anarchism is *anarchist-communism*. Most closely associated with Kropotkin, this version of anarchism explicitly adopts the communist slogan "from each according to his abilities, to each according to his needs." Departing from mutualist and collectivist visions of compensation based on quantity and quality of labor, anarchist-communists "envisaged open warehouses from which any man could have what he wanted."[64] They thereby accepted other dogmas of communism: humans are most fulfilled and closest to their species-being when they perform unalienated labor; under such conditions material abundance will occur; and, once liberated from material scarcity, humans can be trusted to confine their demands to their true needs and most essential wants.

Anarchist-communists differed from communists mainly in their portrayal of the transition between the overthrow of the bourgeois state and the rise of communism. Here they accepted much of the mutualist and collectivist vision: state power is inherently damaging, there should be no temporary dictatorship of the proletariat, and local workers' association should be the immediate locus of decision making as a prelude to wider federations.

But what about the potential tension between anarchy, with its deep veneration of personal liberty, and communism, with its equally deep appreciation of social equality? Some anarchist-communists, such as Carlo Cafiero, deny potential tension: "*Anarchy and communism,* far from howling at being found together, howl at not being found together, because these two terms, synonyms of *liberty* and *equality,* are the two necessary and indivisible terms of the revolution."[65] Here lies a clue to why some anarchists would be drawn to communism: communists can hatch a revolutionary plan, prophesy a time when conditions of material scarcity disappear, and define when the felt conflicts between individualism and community evaporate. Cafiero rightly points out that individual liberty and social equality are both essential for the anarchist impulse, and he implicitly suggests what is necessary for their successful marriage.

Underlying these conclusions is the assumption that material scarcity is the ultimate reason for the state, for scarcity prevents humans from transcending the polarization of individual and community. This plausible assumption is often accepted by nonanarchist thinkers. Niccolo Machiavelli (1469–1527), for example, centuries prior to the flowering of anarchist movements, accepted the assumption but arrived at different conclusions: material scarcity is part of the human condition and the underlying reason why the world is a competitive battleground. Viewing international relations as a zero-sum enterprise in which the overall amount of political greatness is constant but the amount possessed by particular countries variable, Machiavelli encouraged the state to lessen the tensions of the individualist-communitarian polarities by facilitating national identity, and to strengthen the nation as a prerequisite for victory in the inevitable international competition for political greatness. Where anarchist-communists posit the withering away of scarcity and the state, Machiavelli champions their inevitability.

Most contemporary thinkers are closer to accepting Machiavellianism than anarchist-communism on the question of scarcity. Unless we assume falsely that human needs and wants are fixed and that once we achieve a level of production equal to that fixed amount we eliminate scarcity, establishing conditions of material abundance strikes most of us as fanciful. Alternately, we may ground the elimination of scarcity in the transformation of human personality once liberated from alienating conditions of labor. But although such a transformation may well permit workers to better fulfill their inherent creative urges and even to be more productive, it will not necessarily alter their consumptive and acquisitive drives. Unless we insist, with many communists and anarchist-communists, that our consumptive and acquisitive drives are invidiously nurtured by the requirements of capitalist economics, or that they are ersatz substitutes for unfulfilled creative expressions, no necessary connection links increased material production and complete reconciliation of human desires. The kernel of truth in the anarchist-communist critique of capitalism's role in creating acquisitive drives should not lead us to wrongly reduce the complex phenomenon of consumerism to only one of its elements. There are numerous reasons why the world's demand for goods and services outstrips world supply, including climate, distribution of natural resources, and population. It is wrongly reductionist to attribute all contributing factors to evils perpetrated by one omnipotent economic or political force, whether capitalism or the state itself. Scarcity is less a matter of satisfying fixed quantities and more a function of unfixed human ambitions and self-assertions. If anarchist-communism is explicitly dependent on material abundance, its plausibility, not the state, is likely to wither away.

Furthermore, we may reasonably reject both Machiavellianism and communism and declare that the source of the tension between the individualism and communitarian polarities is not grounded merely or mainly in conditions of material scarcity. Instead, those tensions may stem at least in part from our basic biological construction. Felt experiences belie the claim that once material abundance and nonalienating labor appear humans can transcend the tension between the yearning to assert specialness and uniqueness and the longing for intimate connection with others. If anarchism assumes that the elimination of the state is dependent on (or will help produce) human transcendence of the polarities between individualism and communitarianism, and if it assumes that such transcendence is dependent only on achieving material abundance, establishing the conditions of unalienated labor, and eliminating hierarchical coercion, then it may be fatally flawed from the outset. Thus anarchism would embody an impoverished notion of the self: a notion that is grounded too ponderously in work as constitutive of self, too naively in the human capacity to transcend its own conflicts and contradictions, and too artlessly in the role of material scarcity as the sole or main producer of human conflict and contradiction.

Fortunately, anarchism need not be so desperate. Most anarchists place little or no faith in the miracle of material abundance. They espouse, instead, a frugal sufficiency as the basis for life.[66] Thus, with the exception of a few anarchist-communists, anarchism is not wedded to the redeeming effects of material abundance. Moreover, anarchism need not depend on the complete transcendence of human conflict and contradiction. Instead, it need claim only that the elimination of hierarchical coercion and the establishment of conditions conducive for unalienated labor permit the transformation of the individualism-communitarian and freedom-equality polarities. Accordingly, anarchists can argue plausibly that social struggle will continue because even under anarchism administrative perfection is beyond human reach. Once we have eliminated the major forms of alienated social discord, however, we can experience less intense personal conflicts and achieve the maximum possible reconciliation between individual freedom and communal equality. It may in fact be unfair to saddle anarchism with the seemingly impossible task of completely reconciling polarities that are aspects of the human condition. The more modest anarchism sketched here is still problematic, especially in terms of practical implementation, but at least it does not rest on assumptions that are fatally flawed from the start.

A fifth form of anarchy is *anarchosyndicalism*. In the late 1880s many anarchists entered the French trade unions, or syndicates. Two proletarian journalists, Fernand Pelloutier (1867 – 1901) and Emile Pouget (1860 – 1931), were among the early theoreticians of French anarchosyndicalism. They focused on the syndicates as instruments of solidarity and education: through joint work and struggle workers could come together as a class and learn the art of self-management and wider social administration. Anarchosyndicalists aspire to fuse theory and practice by preparing workers' collectives to be from the outset the actual basis of wider social organization. The common struggle must employ direct action, such as boycotts, sabotage, and, especially, general industrial strikes. Possessing latent social power because of their essential placement as industrial producers, workers could bring both capitalist economics and the state to a stunning halt: after general industrial strikes paralyzed the state, workers' syndicates would become the basic units of the free society as the workers assumed control over their factories and federated by industries.[67]

Unlike anarchist-communists, the anarchosyndicalists refocus anarchism on the producers, rather than the consumers. Three basic principles united anarchosyndicalists: each industry must be organized into a federation of independent communes, each industry must be controlled by its own workers, and intercommune policies and relations should be resolved by coordinating councils. Modern anarchosyndicalists, however, are more suspicious of trade unions, seeing them as inherently conservative, too cooperative with management, and not inclined sufficiently toward workers' control. All anarchosyndicalists, however, recognize that a small commune or industry is insufficient for modern life and that a high level of cooperation among industries is required for the sufficient production of diverse goods. The acknowledgment of this natural interdependence among workers in various industries is the first step toward the general administration of society.

Critique of Anarchism

Underlying all anarchist frameworks are two imposing and potentially devastating antinomies: individual versus community, and freedom versus egalitarianism. The first antinomy can be summed up as follows: On the one hand, anarchists exalt the authority of the individual and deride collectivist government; on the other hand, most anarchists refuse the allure of atomistic individualism and, instead, insist on collectivist social movements. How is this consistent?

The answer has three parts. First, the authority of collectivist government— hierarchical, and, at best, representative and detached—differs from the authority of collectivist society that aspires to nonhierarchical and participatory decision making. Second, anarchists reject the "individual versus community" formulation on philosophical grounds: they perceive humans as essentially social animals and thus view society as a precondition of robust individuality. Third, anarchists can perceive the formulation of the first antinomy as question begging: they may argue that the formulation itself presupposes the same atomistic individualism that anarchists reject. Rather than conceiving individualism versus community as an ahistorical, biological component of enduring human nature, anarchists may argue that the antinomy itself emanates from a flawed and pernicious bourgeois ideology that accepts the false axiom that the individual is logically and empirically prior to society. With a philosophical strategy reminiscent of Marxist thought, anarchists can argue that once we liberate ourselves from the oppressive features of the modern nation-state, humans will transcend the individual versus community antinomy and the consciousness from which it arose.

The second antinomy can be formulated in this fashion: to the extent a society celebrates freedom, it jeopardizes equality. Maximum individual choice combined with clear factual differences among humans are unlikely to result in social and economic equality. As political libertarians are fond of reminding us, people differ considerably in their natural and nurtured inclinations toward commerce, interpersonal persuasion, intellectualism, physicality, and ultimate ends. Left unfettered by allegedly injurious government interference, significant social inequalities can be expected. Such inequalities, libertarians insist, are morally justified so long as they arise through processes that respect individuals' voluntary choices and do not violate anyone's natural negative rights, which prohibit harm, fraud, and coercion. Accordingly, the many anarchists who are not explicitly libertarians must struggle to reconcile or at least prioritize the often competing values of freedom and equality.

An anarchist might take numerous routes. First, there is the strategy of denial: the dilemma of either freedom or equality (but not both) is false because once people liberate themselves from the vicious throes of bourgeois government they will collectively choose, from a newly free and equal starting point, social arrangements that facilitate enduring equality. Thus, such anarchists may argue, the felt tension between freedom and equality is most acute in the hierarchical governments that anarchists excoriate; once the governments vanish then freedom and equality can manifest their vital interdependence.

This response is plausible but too facile: it suggests that people will choose, freely and equally, a strategy that actually reconciles freedom and equality. In fact, this strategy appears implicitly only to prioritize equality over freedom. This ordering may be an acceptable solution from a moral standpoint but it fails to illustrate the falseness of the original dilemma. Instead, it seems ultimately to embrace one horn of that dilemma rather than the other.

Second, there is the strategy of transformation: the dilemma of either freedom or equality (but not both) is real only where we conceive freedom in libertarian terms — as the negative freedom to be free from harm, fraud, and coercion. In fact, anarchists may argue, a more robust conception of freedom, dependent on and not in conflict with equality, is available: a positive notion that stresses the empowerment inherent in collective action and heightened mutual vulnerability. Thus, Bakunin writes: "The only liberty that is truly worthy of the name, the liberty that consists in the full development of all the powers, material, intellectual, and moral, that are latent in everyone . . . I mean the illimitable liberty of each through the liberty of all, liberty by solidarity, liberty in equality."[68] Malatesta adds that "freedom is not an abstract right but the possibility of acting . . . it is by cooperation with his fellows that man finds the means to express his activity and his power of initiative."[69] Anna Goldman observes more explicitly that "real freedom, true liberty, is *positive:* it is freedom *to* something; it is the liberty to be, to do; in short, the liberty of actual and active opportunity."[70] By transforming the conception of freedom, these anarchists aspire to resolve the dilemma between equality and freedom.

This strategy is promising but it finesses the tensions that often develop between negative and positive freedoms when collective activity is possible only through (at least the limited) coercion of some individuals. Thus, a critic may contend that even if fully successful the strategy of transformation does not address the question posed but instead solves a problem of its own contrivance. Even if negative freedom is not the whole of freedom it still is a part. Unless they wish to reject completely negative freedom, anarchists still must reconcile equality with that aspect of liberty.

Third, there is the strategy of explicit prioritization coupled with limited transformation: the evaporation of oppressive governments will loosen the limits on collective deliberation and action, thus transforming society's notion of freedom. There will still of course be occasions, as libertarians suspected all along, where equality will conflict with freedom. In such circumstances, anarchists might well choose equality over freedom; but they would also emphasize that lateral coercion of an individual, which flows among social equals, is much less pernicious than hierarchical coercion, which is imposed by superiors upon subordinates. In fact, lateral coercion may not be coercion at all, but merely a benign form of authority.[71]

This third strategy, then, softens the harshness of lateral authority and suggests that under certain circumstances individual freedom, at least in its negative form, must yield to the wisdom of the collective deliberation of social equals. This conclusion might be seen as anarchism's philosophical capitulation – its admission that full social equality, positive freedom, and negative freedom are not always mutually compatible – but a more charitable reading would point out that this conceptual conflict is not unique to anarchism but is shared by all political and social theories. Moreover, anarchists, while admitting that they cannot completely resolve the discord internal to equality and freedom, might still highlight that they can best soften the negative effects of the occasional disharmony by insisting that authority devolve from the collective deliberation of social equals rather than from inherently coercive hierarchical institutions.

Beyond the conceptual antinomies described above, anarchism confronts several practical difficulties. First, there is the problem of the revolution: How will anarchism secure enough acceptance to constitute a mass movement? On the one hand, if it amounts only to the feverish discontent of a few, anarchism threatens to replicate government's alleged tyranny over individuals. On the other hand, securing mass acceptance creates enormous coordination problems: grave systemic pressures incline the bulk of workers towards inertia and against spontaneous revolt, yet a vanguard movement by intellectual elites strikes a decidedly antianarchistic chord. The compromise solution, which weaves a precarious path between spontaneity and vanguardism, aspires to develop gradually workers' instincts for social transformation and capacities for self-rule through immediate empowerment in the workplace. But this "organic group" model is ripe for co-optation by the dominant forces of the status quo. For example, one of the reasons that trade unions are now perceived as inherently conservative is that even moderately crafty managers and politicians have devised policies that facilitate nonthreatening incremental changes, thus forestalling serious social transformation yet permitting dominant classes to retain their disproportionate power.

Second, even if an anarchist revolution occurs, there remains the problem of transition: How do we arrive at an adequately functioning anarchic society after the defeat of government? Under anarchy, everyone governs and rules of unanimity are prized, making decision making both difficult and disingenuous. Calls for consensus and unanimity too often mask power differentials within groups and too often foster a false orthodoxy of perspective. Moreover, absent political authority, only attenuated pressures exist to ensure general compliance with societal decisions. The dual problems of decision making and compliance contribute to the general perception of anarchism as ineffective and unstable. The possibilities of anarchism seem most vibrant in small, informal, heterogeneous contexts, a most inapt description of modern nation-states. What begins by luxuriating in individual empowerment possibly ends in insipid conformity.[72]

Third, although it is inaccurate and uncharitable to claim that anarchism is grounded in a contradictory notion of the self that requires one to be energetically individualistic yet thoroughly involved in community, it is fair to reiterate that the antinomies of self are inadequately resolved by anarchist theory. It may well be possible to achieve a heightened individuality through community solidarity, but anarchists have been more likely to assert this achievement than to explain the necessary social prerequisites and to describe fully the resulting social phenomena.

Fourth, although many anarchists regard all violence as self-defeating and brutalizing, there have been a disturbing number of episodes of seemingly mindless destruction performed under anarchist colors. Anarchism's romantic calls for individual empowerment, spontaneous uprising, and suffocation of governmental oppression too often nurture violence as heroic expression and emotional necessity.

CONTEMPORARY POLITICAL THEORY

Many themes that animated anarchism and other radical philosophies — distrust of political hierarchy and social division, concern for economic equality, zeal for transcending existing social contexts, attraction to heroic and romantic action, and infatuation with utopian social visions — resound in the work of contemporary social theorist Roberto Unger. Unger's work is arguably the best example of the modern transformation of anarchist themes: he retains the spirit of anarchism while purging anarchist theory of some of its most unpersuasive elements (such as the belief that the state is unnecessary and inherently harmful). I examine Unger's work here to further understand the human psychological inclinations that fueled Italian and Italian-American anarchist experiences and to illustrate that anarchist themes, albeit in altered forms, exude vitality today.

A Theory of Persons, Existential Dilemma, and Human Passions

Unger argues that the animating drive of human passion is to transcend the cultural contexts that structure established forms of personal relations, intellectual inquiry, and social arrangements. We face, however, an existential dilemma: a simultaneous yearning and fear when in the presence of others. Human passions thus center on the duality of our undeniable need for others and our felt danger at their approach. Moreover, there is only one noncontingent fact of human personality: contingency itself — the capacity of human personality to transcend the limits of the culturally determined possible and impossible.[73] Although we cannot transcend all contexts at once and experience contextlessness itself, we can transcend any particular context at any particular time. Unger concludes that to advance self-understanding and to mediate our existential dilemma, we must open ourselves to a full life of personal encounter, thereby giving complete expression to our need while accepting the accompanying danger. Unger tells us that we all experience the "problem of contextuality": ambivalent feelings of being necessarily embedded in a thick cultural and social context that seemingly defines the limits of the possible and impossible, and able to transcend cultural contexts and limits as we experience modes of thought and being that cannot be translated adequately by the logic and language of current norms. For Unger, we are most truly ourselves when engaging in activity in which we deny the false necessities generated by the structures of social life, for during such activity we celebrate the possibilities of our infinite personalities. The human drive to self-assertion includes the yearning not to be limited to any particular social role; it is the need to undertake experiments in self-knowledge and self-redefinition.[74]

Unger acknowledges that the act of context smashing creates a new context: we are never unencumbered and unsituated. We do, however, progress as we ascend to looser contextual structures that encourage their own destabilization, thereby giving currency to human personality. Although we never ascend to an Archimedean point that might arrest all future context smashing and we never create a nontranscendable context that is indisputably superior to all competitors, certain conditional contexts are superior to others based on their flexibility and acceptance of destabilization.

Unger poses three rhetorical questions to provide additional support for his plasticity and empowerment theses: Do his conceptions suggest "more readily verifiable or falsifiable ideas"? Are his theses compatible with a persuasive and potent social theory? Are his theses validated by the "qualified introspection" of humans?[75]

To avoid the charge of contentlessness — for what can truly follow from claims about the plasticity of human nature? — Unger seeks a normative conception of human personality that fuses description and prescription but does not fall prey to skepticism or abject relativism.

Images of Personality and Convergence

According to Unger, the four main images of personality as reflected in literature and philosophy are: the heroic ethic, fusion with an impersonal absolute, Confucianism, and the Christian-Romantic ideal.[76] Unger argues that if we take these four images and cleanse them of aspects that deny the infinite quality of personality, then the remaining theoretical ideas converge and produce similar answers to our most important normative questions. From the first two images of personality, Unger discerns the importance of authoritative principles that transcend the mundane, equivocal sphere of human interaction.[77] Yet both the hero and the speculative monist manifest unattractive features: efforts "to become invulnerable to others and to the disappointments that may result from not being in charge."[78] Thus, the heroic ethic and the ethic of fusion with an impersonal absolute rightly venerate the transcendent qualities of human personality but wrongly disengage from heightened mutual vulnerability. From Confucianism, Unger identifies the importance of contextuality and the intimate connection between human passions and societal structure. Confucianism, however, wrongly insists on freezing the terms of social debate and on rigid social hierarchies. Finally, from the Christian-Romantic ideal, Unger recognizes a commitment to concrete persons and to the search for human empowerment: a conviction of the primacy of the personal encounter with love as its redemptive moment, accompanied by an iconoclastic attitude toward particular social arrangements.[79] Love and iconoclasm are necessarily bound: the world must be transformed, contexts and hierarchies must be unsettled so that human openness and vulnerability to love may flourish. From a "modernist criticism and restatement of the Christian-Romantic image of man that forms the central tradition of reflection about human nature in the West,"[80] Unger fashions a theory of human identity that does not depend on religious commitment.

Unger insists that the concept of infinite personality permits us to avoid abject relativism, whereas the phenomenon of convergence provides a substantive conception of human personality. The resulting conception of human personality includes the primacy of personal encounter and love, and a commitment to social iconoclasm. Heightened mutual vulnerability is a prerequisite for advancing self-understanding, and, according to Unger, we are most empowered and most truly ourselves when we engage in context-transcending activity informed by faith, hope, and love.[81]

Methodological Criticisms

Unger has been taken to task for allegedly adopting the classical method of logically deriving normative conclusions from a particular view of human nature.[82] Critics have argued that it seems puzzling to derive anything from claims about the plasticity of human nature.[83] Such claims appear to be an admission that we cannot discern who or what humans are. Thus, to begin from conditionality and indeterminacy and to purport to derive substantive conclusions seems preposterous.

Because Unger's efforts can be viewed as just another failed attempt to deduce by means of classical logical categories substantive (and ahistorical) moral and political conclusions, some political radicals can plausibly charge him with intellectual treason. By his apparent acceptance of the standards of proof, truth, and argument that, from critics' perspective, emanate from the false consciousness of the dominant centrist regimes, Unger may be viewed as trying to play the other guy's game while adding only one more rule or assumption—his one unconditional fact of human personality. The charge is that all Unger has done is to change the initial premise of a tired and disreputable centrist political argument, and in so doing to merely amend that argument by moving from a closed theory of human nature to an open theory. Despite the breadth of his thought and the originality of his political program, he is doomed to failure by his very acceptance of mainstream philosophical categories and ways of carving up and describing the world. By accepting such categories, Unger may be revealing an objectivist impulse that would repel many political radicals.

In defense of Unger it must be noted that in contrast to such classical thinkers as Plato and Hobbes, who derived substantive normative conclusions from fixed theories of human nature, Unger contends that fixed theories of human nature are too often merely projections of the current social and political order, not the discoveries of ahistorical truths about human personality. Fixed theories of human nature artificially restrain thought and action, and Unger, in fact, is less a prisoner than a liberator of classical method.

This defense of Unger, although true, does not meet the critics' point. For critics here do not necessarily dispute the type of theory about human nature that Unger advances, but the very method of trying to derive moral conclusions from a theory about human nature.

A stronger defense of Unger does however exist. He does not derive moral conclusions from a theory about human nature. There is no antecedent, determinate theory of human nature that might set the boundaries of normative disputes; it is in fact one of the tasks of moral theory to help form the most acceptable nature for which persons should strive. Unger posits only one noncontingent fact about human personality: its ultimate plasticity. But he recognizes clearly that no substantive conclusions can follow from his starting point. To avoid the charge of contentlessness, he provides a more substantive view of human personality informed by the convergence of the four main available images purged of those aspects that deny plasticity. Even here he does not pretend to derive deductively his programmatic vision from his substantive view of human personality.

Unger would agree that we cannot appeal to an antecedent and disembodied theory of persons as an axiomatic starting point in our quest for moral theory. Rather, a theory of persons partly constitutes particular versions of moral theory, and the acceptability of a moral theory helps determine the acceptability of its component theory of persons. The notion of "acceptability" used here is much looser and contestable—appealing to concrete experiences of human personality more than to formal categories—and this looseness suggests strongly that Unger is not trying to meet the strict standards of deductive proof. Hence, the critics' charge is misplaced.[84]

His critics here are the "ultra-theorists,"[85] to use his own phrase. Renouncing attempts to develop general explanations and comprehensive plans for political transformation, they mercilessly thrash the conclusions and justifications of the dominant ideology and often conjure images of a more desirable social life—but they do not formulate deep theoretical justifications for their favored practices. At their most radical, they ridicule all normative discourse and revel explicitly in arbitrariness and nihilism.

For Unger, ultra-theorists cripple effective and liberating theory and practice by obliterating the links between normative discourse, theoretical insight, explanatory power, and practical action.[86] Lacking an underlying explanation of the respective roles of contexts and context smashing in human flourishing and empowerment, ultra-theory collapses into a nominalistic form of standard social science or degenerates into relentless existential rebellion for its own sake.

Critics have also argued that Unger's program merely restates and does not solve the problem of our existential dilemma.[87] Although promising to liberate social conflict from its marginalized place in centrist politics, Unger ends by creating yet another structure—his "structure of no structure"—that is immune from destabilization. Thus, Unger merely relocates the point at which social conflict is prohibited.

Given that he believes that there is one objective nonconditional fact of human personality, Unger cannot go all the way and claim that everything is always up for grabs. To do so would court a philosophical nihilism that he denies. But he does more than merely relocate the point of conflict, for he provides a structure designed to allow the fullest amount of social conflict consistent with his commitment to honor and facilitate the infinite human personality. Apparently, once he denies that everything is contingent, he must build from what is objective.

Unger's notion of progress seems puzzling, however. He tells us that, despite our inability to transcend all conditionality, progress is possible as we "loosen the limits" of conditionality. If progress means that some conditional forms are less conditional than others, or that some conditional forms are better than others, Unger may be presupposing a standard by which to evaluate conditional forms that itself is not conditional. Alternatively, if progress acknowledges that all forms are equally conditional – a democracy of conditionality – then it is not clear how progress adds up. Is it simply the explicit recognition that our modes of discourse are conditional and the appreciation of the freedom we exercise when we continually recombine and reimagine contexts? Or is progress simply the process of recombination and reimagination itself? Finally, it is not clear that the prescription to accelerate revision follows from the assumption that all forms of social life and all modes of discourse are conditional. We might well decide that, given the fact of conditional forms and modes, we should not accept any established structure as ultimate truth; although we might well allow a reasoned process of change in our structures and modes, why choose to *accelerate* revision? Lacking evidence that such a change would be an improvement – a higher form of conditionality? a closer approximation to a nonconditional standard? a realization of freedom? – why advocate change for change's sake?

Unger would probably reply that his model is based on a modern view of science, a progression from the Euclidean paradigm. The best science is viewed as capable of accelerating self-revision, recognizing and absorbing anomalies and incongruous perceptions without destroying itself or repressing the facts it has found. Science might be viewed by Unger as transforming the fact of conditionality into an intellectual advantage and theoretical method.[88]

More fundamentally, progress can be defined in terms of Unger's one unconditional fact of human nature: its ultimate plasticity. Unger acknowledges that the act of context smashing creates a new context. However, we progress as we ascend to looser contextual structures that encourage their own destabilization, thereby giving currency to human personality. We are not engaged in a self-defeating rebellion for its own sake, but we transform contexts for a purpose: to liberate human personality so that its one objective aspect can flourish. We never create a nontranscendable context that is indisputably superior to its competition, but neither are we trapped by a democracy of conditionality. There is a nonconditional standard by which to evaluate various conditional contexts: the one objective feature of human personality. Certain conditional contexts are superior to others by virtue of their flexibility and acceptance of destabilization. The contrast here is between rigid structures that resist attempts at destabilization and flexible structures that facilitate their own transformation.[89] In rigid contexts, the distinction between context-preserving and context-transforming activities is relatively clear, whereas in plastic contexts there is no firm distinction between the two activities.[90] Presumably, context smashing itself does not turn into yet another routine because the process is not ceaseless and monotonous; progress, in the senses noted earlier, can be made.

Unger tries to document how plasticity has been paramount in military, economic, and social triumphs throughout history.[91] Accordingly, we should accelerate revision in order to precipitate an understanding of ourselves and to achieve worldly success. It must be noted, however, that Unger is not seduced into extolling a condition of permanent indefinition, a ceaseless flux of conflict and transformation. Instead, he acknowledges the need for relatively tranquil periods of stability: "What should the moment of rest be like? To a greater or lesser extent it may keep the qualities that distinguish the moment of transformation."[92]

Doubts nonetheless linger about the overriding value of context smashing. In the words of Ernest Weinrib: "What Unger ignores is that the capacity to negate context does not immediately tell us how we are to act but only what it is to act. Through this feature of action normativity becomes intelligible, and it is therefore not a feature to which normative force can simply be ascribed."[93]

Moreover, we must question whether Unger ultimately overrates the human need for context-smashing activity and underrates the human need for context-preserving activity. These two types of activity correspond to the human needs for adventure and security, and it should be clear that the relative attraction of these needs differs radically among people of varying education, age, gender, socioeconomic class, and aggressiveness. Offering no guarantees and exhilarated by the promise of empowerment, Unger also heightens social risks: heroism and tragedy may be inextricably joined. Will "everyday people" be attracted to such a vision? Will the many people who are less politically inclined than Unger truly be empowered by the activity he and other intellectuals cherish? Does Unger demand too much of us when he insists that we risk mutual vulnerability and gamble with our deepest fears? Can humans achieve much the same benefits with less risk by smashing contexts that are local and personal and thus less intractable than Unger's grand institutions?

Crucial questions emerge: Is Unger's vision truly a general account of human personality? Or is it the highly stylized projection of an academic who himself is closely bound by particular contexts that impel him to universalize his own real or fantasized proclivities? Unger has a seemingly boundless faith in the liberating capacity of ideas and the heroic potential of purposive context smashing. This faith is both his glory – for it accounts for the breathtaking imagination and brio of his work – and his betrayal – for it suggests an isolation from the aspirations of common people.

Programmatic Vision

Unger's perceptions of human personality trigger his legal and political prescriptions. Social arrangements should incorporate destabilization mechanisms, rather than being depicted classically as a set of concrete social institutions defining a fixed and closed structure. The mechanisms must undermine existing social arrangements and unsettle hierarchical relations before they solidify into entrenched power. Unger's goal is to recognize the contingency of our institutional and social arrangements, and open them to transformation. Unger therefore places no faith in communitarian arguments that presuppose citizens sharing fundamental ends. Acceptance of these arguments too often leads to "paralysis of the power to innovate" and "self-conscious austerity."[94]

Thus, rather than advancing a particular, substantive political situation such as socialism, communism, liberalism, republicanism to which all societies should aspire, Unger concentrates on the process and necessity of recurring social change.[95] His project can be viewed as grafting the framework of radical contingency onto the classical method of arriving at normative conclusions from a conception of human nature.

Unger's project thus realizes two immediate theoretical advantages over other radical philosophies: he can easily engage the dominant political discourses while seemingly retaining the radical implications of his main theses, and, unlike several versions of Marxism and feminism, he can avoid the elusive subtleties embodied by the notion of "false consciousness."[96] He can thus act as an insider but preserve an outsider's transformative panache.

Political Vision

For Unger, political change cannot be achieved by advocating violent revolution, by abrogating law or democracy, by vilifying the policies of the United States, or by fantasizing a new abstract idea of society. Political change is achieved by the internal development of existing legal doctrine, social relations, and political institutions. Social change is fueled by alterations in the relative functionality and transformation of existing formative contexts, not by comprehensive alien ideologies.

Internal development is animated by two themes: no one scheme of political association has conclusive and everlasting authority, and the mutual correction of abstract political ideals and their specific institutional embodiments offers the best chance of significant political change.[97] Internal development is the process by which we create new institutional embodiments for our ideals and alter our ideals and the spheres of their domain.[98]

Social power must no longer be viewed, as it is by the disciples of false necessity, as antecedently right or necessary; instead it is exposed as laden with contestable political presuppositions. Here the distinction between laypersons and officials such as judges and lawyers becomes less clear as deviationist doctrine and internal development employ looser, more contestable standards of rationality and produce tentative conclusions.

Institutional Structures

Unger advocates a particular system of rights, a central economic principle, and an organization of government. Although he leaves their specific embodiments to the collective deliberations of the people, he does provide the following general outline.

He begins by affirming that we must radicalize the available conceptions of rights to avoid solidifying forms of privilege and hierarchy. A scheme of rights should not reify a particular version of social life, for such a sanctification is yet another manifestation of false necessity. The internal development of existing ideals of rights and democracy combined with respect for our infinite personalities will afford us humans a measure of security without concomitant domination. Unger describes an altered scheme of rights as important for its own sake and "also for its encouragement to a systematic shift in the character of direct personal relations and, above all, in the available forms of community."[99]

The central economic principle is the establishment of a rotating capital fund. Agencies of government would set outer limits to disparities of income and authority within work organizations and to the distribution of profit as income. Capital would be made available, temporarily and at a rate of interest, to teams of workers. The fund, which would disaggregate the control of capital into several tiers of capital takers and givers, would maintain a constant flow of new entrants into the economy and ensure that no economic enterprise could use legal devices to seclude itself from market instabilities.[100] The long-range aim of the fund might include more decentralization and economic experimentation.

Critics will wonder whether Unger's program will result in perennial economic insecurity. His heralding of long-range decentralization, a rotating capital fund, and disaggregated property rights will strike many as anathema to traditional entrepreneurial incentives and destructive of citizens' confidence in business enterprise. Moreover, his programs may seem hopelessly indeterminate and vague.

To counter such criticism, Unger advises constitutionalizing some of the procedures and rules of the rotating capital fund, thereby shielding them from radical instability. But given his view of the judicial role, the importance of deviationist doctrine, and general proclivity against freezing the terms of social life, it is doubtful whether this maneuver would be desirable or effective. He is more likely to subject the issue of the relative amount of economic security to recurring public conflict. His economic program gambles that constraints on individual and family capital will be outweighed by the greater mobility of and access to capital made possible by the rotating capital fund.

Unger's economic program must be viewed in light of his other prescriptions for the reorganization of work. Rejecting public ownership of the means of production, Unger also denies the rigid distinction between task-definers (employers and managers) and task-executors (workers).[101] He strives instead to accelerate interaction between the two work sectors and to insulate no component of the workplace from politics and the logic of recombination.

Although his program remains indefinite, Unger feels the problem besets any programmatic vision that tries to avoid transcendental appeals without lapsing into abject skepticism. Viewing his program as a contestable proposal that is itself subject to political conflict, Unger prefers it to the illusions of current democratic-centrist practice, which gives large-scale investors explicit monetary incentives and which insulates managers and owners from the possible destabilizing effects of mass democracy. Unger suggests that current centrist practice falsely extrapolates from one possible economic predicament: underconsumption during periods of economic growth. Unger decries present practice, in which a relatively small group of investors has disproportionate voice in the market, and he places his faith in the greater mobility of and increased access to capital by more groups of entrepreneurs.

At bottom, Unger has no clear retort to the critics' charge. His firm conviction is that current democratic-centrist practice rests on the illusion that our particular form of the market is necessary and that this illusion nourishes economic rigidity that can only end in long-term economic inefficiency. Centralized-communist attempts to maneuver macroeconomic aggregates by a combination of public ownership and the authority of technical experts have also failed. His alternative is vague and indeterminate, but his stance is unwavering: increased mobility of and access to capital, when combined with restructuring of workplace relations and recurrent political conflict, will result in greater long-term efficiency than current practice and will serve to invigorate and transform our market.

More generally, critics have charged that Unger's preferences for context smashing and destabilization, though lauded by modernist intellectuals, are not representative of ordinary people.[102] Most humans, it is claimed, yearn for increased security and experience upheaval and radical change as unwelcome threats. Thus, Unger's call for increased human empowerment through the transcendence of fixed structures is in fact an elitist's self-indulgent fantasy. The masses of people, who are denied the material comforts that upper-class intellectuals take for granted, appreciate the security of a fundamental structure susceptible only to marginal adjustment.

Unger's response to this criticism would undoubtedly point to the stabilizing aspects of his own program: immunity and solidarity rights, constitutionalization, and the right to remove oneself from political conflict or leave the state entirely. He might reiterate that the fear of context smashing is simply another manifestation of the paralyzing effects of the illusion of necessity communicated by centrist ideology. Rather than accepting the alleged longing of the masses for security as a basic independent fact of human nature, Unger would perceive it as damning evidence that dominant ideology has retarded the flourishing of our infinite personalities. Accordingly, the critics' charge is further proof of the need to liberate the masses from the political status quo, not a demonstration of any presumed inadequacy in Unger's account.

To adjudicate this dispute we would have to deal more fundamentally with Unger's claim that there is only one noncontingent fact of human personality. Is the masses' craving for security a sign of a deeper fact about human nature or is it merely further evidence of the corrupting influence of dominant politics?

Moreover, some radicals will insist that Unger's vision is romantic and ultimately impotent.[103] Buoyed by the assumption that rational argument can raise social consciousness and liberate us from the chains of dominant ideology, Unger renounces violent revolution as the instrument of social change. Yet, some critics will argue, true and lasting fundamental change is not produced by better rational demonstrations nor by more comprehensive social theories; instead, it springs from widespread alterations in the way humans perceive their daily activities. Such sweeping upheavals, they will argue, only follow class struggles and successful violent revolution.

This criticism undercuts the practicality of Unger's "superliberalism" and its prospects for implementation. Unger's predicament here is clear: if he advocates violent revolution he can be attacked as utopian, for the prospects for successful revolution in the major centrist-capitalist regimes are worse than dim; if he advocates consciousness raising and exalts the role of theory as the engine of social change he can also be attacked as utopian, because many believe that theoretical vision plays at best a minor role in the restructuring of fundamental politics. This predicament may, however, merely underscore the present power of dominant centrist ideology in the West.

To escape the charge that his program is impossible to implement and doomed to remain mere theory, Unger could cite the advances made by feminists. It is undeniable that by raising social consciousness without threats of violent revolution feminists have succeeded in leading significant change. Although one might respond that feminism has in fact been coopted and assimilated by centrist-capitalist regimes, Unger can still maintain that the necessary link between violence and political conversion is breakable. At worst, the prospects of success for meaningful political change in the West seem no dimmer for consciousness raising than for violent revolution.

Meanwhile, however, centrist critics will be tempted to inquire whether Unger's program of recurrent conflict and incessant appeals to conditionality will invite the rise of overtly authoritarian regimes. Without objectively true moral and political standards, Unger's program may seem to encourage relentless instability. Under such conditions, critics fear that totalitarian regimes will eventually be embraced as a way of providing security and order in the face of political anarchy.

Unger, however, has a plausible response to this criticism. He could claim that the rise of totalitarian regimes is not implied by the fact of conditionality nor by the presence of recurrent political conflict, but is instead generated by the depoliticized character of large segments of unorganized and manipulable citizens. If he is correct, his program constitutes an antidote to totalitarianism because its central aspiration is to extend the political franchise to more citizens in more areas of their everyday existence. Moreover, Unger's program is not a celebration of permanent, overt revolution. Unger aspires only to efface the distinction between full-blown revolution and total stagnation. Thus, he would strive to dissociate conflict from fundamental, nonnegotiable issues and confine it to concrete, compromisable proposals. For Unger, our political choices are not confined to "chaos or totalitarianism or centrism."

THE INDIVIDUALISM-COMMUNITY CONTINUUM

The Italian and Italian-American anarchist experiences do not reveal unique, unalterable features of Italian ethnicity. Instead, they point to certain aspects of human personality, such as our need to transcend our social contexts, that are most sharply felt during economic crises. Certainly, Italian anarchist experiences, especially those in the *Mezzogiorno*, must be viewed against the background of centuries of ineffective, oppressive government. Furthermore, the social and economic hardships of the New World that confronted Italian immigrants reinforced their deep distrust of government. But were Italian peasants and workers more attracted to anarchism than their counterparts in other European countries? Were Italian immigrant workers in the United States more persuaded by anarchist appeals than other immigrant workers here? The answers are "no." Perhaps because Italians and Italian immigrants to the United States embodied intense family affiliation as their primary allegiance, they also harbored deep distrust for grand social movements. Their fervent suspicion of government, one necessary component for the enthusiastic acceptance of anarchism, was not generally complemented by joyous appreciation of society, another necessary component of anarchism. Accordingly, Italian and Italian immigrant anarchist affiliations were inherently fragile and sustained more by harsh socioeconomic conditions and transient labor movements than by reliable ideological bonds.

Although anarchism everywhere failed in its specific professed aspirations, it exemplified the spirit of social possibility and the unbridled enthusiasm for transcending the social and political status quo. Roberto Unger's social theory, although highly problematic, accepts and transforms the radical political legacy partially attributable to anarchists: distrust of political hierarchy and social division, concern for economic equality, zeal for transforming existing social contexts, and attraction to heroic and romantic action. As the world develops greater technological and communicative capacities it grows, at least potentially, closer, and calls for anarchy become more and more attenuated, less serious, and less convincing. The animating spirit of the anarchists endures, however, compelling us to reimagine our social world and measure ourselves and our institutions by what we and they might become.

CHAPTER 4

THE NATION ENCOUNTERS THE WORLD

Garibaldi and the Philosophy of War

After graduating from college in 1970, I was conscripted into military service during the Vietnamese War. I was ideologically opposed to that war for all the usual reasons offered at the time. So what was I to do? Refuse to take the dramatic step forward that signaled acquiescence to military service and subject myself to criminal prosecution and a likely stretch in the slammer? Disavow military service, leave the country, and adopt the persona of a lightweight fugitive? Remain in the country but go underground to escape prosecution? Or bite the bullet, accept induction, and cope with intense internal conflict between deeply held ideology and practical behavior?

In pondering these options, I was not the least concerned about the prudential prospects of killing or being killed. I knew that if I entered the armed forces I would enlist and, given my education and my academic skills, would be relatively safely ensconced in a non-infantry role. Even at the age of twenty-two, I understood that three years, the minimum term of enlistment, could be experienced as shorter than two years, the term of conscription.

But I decided that my ideological convictions were too constitutive of my self to compromise: I would disavow military service, enter a graduate program in Canada, and apply for landed immigrant status there.

My father howled. We had the worst arguments of our lives. Although we never came to physical blows, their effects would have been more merciful than what we suffered in our verbal confrontations. My father's opposition stemmed not from ideology or morality—he thought the war rather stupid and pointless—but from strict prudence: if I left the country I could never return without being subject to capture and criminal prosecution. Weaned on too many original episodes of *The Fugitive,* I was convinced that I could easily outwit the authorities and come and go as I pleased, whereas my father was equally convinced that someone in our small town would enthusiastically give me up. The problem was compounded by the failing health of my mother that would seemingly impair her and, by extension, my father's ability to visit me in Canada. And so my father and I viciously and continually bickered.

Just before my departure, however, my father came into my bedroom, threw a set of keys on my bed, and growled: "You'll need these for your trip." That is all he said. The keys attached to an automobile, a Cutlass, he had purchased for me. This gesture was typical of my father's instinctive generosity in the face of unresolvable conflict. I cried that day. I think he might have too.

I went to Canada and, aided by an uncommonly professional and compassionate border authority, applied for landed immigrant status. I enrolled into the graduate program in philosophy to which I had been accepted and began the unsettling process of learning a new, but not radically different, culture and the vagaries of Canadian football.

Events were soon to conspire against me. My mother's health degenerated, and it became clear that any appreciable travel was out of the question for her. I learned this not from my parents, who were now, as usual, solidly behind my decision, but from other sources.

After only a few weeks in Canada, I returned to the United States. I enlisted in the army and was deemed qualified for military intelligence. I served almost three years, most of which were spent in Washington, D.C., and Korea. I have never regretted my original decision to go to Canada, nor my later decision to return and serve in the military. Even ideological commitment must surrender to the vehemence of blood ties: concreteness trumps abstraction.

In this chapter, the nation-state confronts the world. First, I describe and analyze the unique place Giuseppe Garibaldi won in the hearts of southern Italians. Garibaldi was an unabashed supporter of the nation-state and was firmly convinced that sustained military action was necessary to establish and to maintain it. But Garibaldi was also that rarest of nineteenth-century military men: a dreamer who conjured ideals of international unity. As such, Garibaldi tacitly understood an aspect of the individual–community continuum, the antinomies generated by the meeting of nation-state and world, and aspired to overwhelm it by force, if necessary. Second, I explain and examine the philosophy of war of contemporary philosopher Robert Holmes. Holmes argues that all modern wars are presumptively immoral. He, like Garibaldi, implicitly recognizes the antinomies produced by the confrontation of nation-state and world, but hopes to "underwhelm" these antinomies by passive resistance, if necessary. Finally, I draw lessons about war from both men and tie these lessons to the wider themes of this book.

THE BRIO OF GIUSEPPE GARIBALDI

Few historical figures in the Anglo-European world have experienced the kind of intense devotion lavished upon Giuseppe Garibaldi in the nineteenth century. A skilled guerrilla warrior who advanced protest movements in several areas of Europe and South America, Garibaldi embodied a uniquely international outlook, eschewing the intense parochialism of nationalism.

Garibaldi was born in 1807. His birthplace, Nice, had been seized from the kingdom of Piedmont by Napoleon ten years earlier. His father and mother were wholly "Italian," having been born and raised in Chiavari and Loano, respectively. Garibaldi's first stage of postadolescent development spanned the years 1824 to 1833, when he lived as a sailor in the Mediterranean and Black seas. In 1833 he came into contact with the Saint-Simonians, self-proclaimed interpreters of the gospel of the Comte de Saint-Simon, and with Giuseppe Mazzini's *La Giovine Italia* ("Young Italy"), a patriotic organization committed to Italian unification. It was at this point that Garibaldi was exposed to the unusual ideologies that were to influence him thereafter: the obligation of the state to ameliorate the moral and material conditions of the underclasses; the need for the state to be organized hierarchically and ruled by an ascetic, simple, selfless leader; the right of women to full social equality with men; and the joys of physical pleasures, particularly sex.[1]

In 1834, as a member of the Piedmontese navy, he took part in a mutiny for the republican cause. After escaping to France, he was sentenced to death by default. During his second stage of development, from 1836 to 1847, he sailed for Rio de Janeiro, fought for the province of Rio Grande in its attempt at liberation from the Brazilian Empire, commanded a small Uruguayan fleet against Argentina, and formed and commanded the "Italian Legion" at Montevideo. It achieved several successes, including victory at the battle of St. Antonio.[2] In this period, Garibaldi, buoyed by Mazzini's burgeoning public relations efforts on his behalf, gained considerable renown in Europe.[3]

Perhaps Garibaldi's greatest political oscillations occurred during his third stage, roughly 1848 to 1857. At the start of this period, he led eighty of his legionnaires back to Italy, offering his services to the king of Piedmont. His offer was rejected, but he soon thereafter led a volunteer unit at Milan against the Austrians. In 1849 he was elected a deputy in the Roman Assembly and undertook a series of military adventures: he commanded a brigade that repelled a French attack in Rome; defeated a Neapolitan army at Velletri; led a few thousand men from Italy through central Italy in flight from French and Austrian armies; disbanded his men in San Marino, only to be chased by the Austrians; and arrived in Piedmont where he was promptly arrested and deported as an undesirable.

From 1850 to 1851 Garibaldi stayed in New York, working in a candle factory on Staten Island. From there he embarked for Peru and led a clipper on cargo missions to a variety of countries. During these travels he purchased part of the island of Caprera, north of Sardinia. By 1856 he was in England, hatching a failed conspiracy to buy a ship and lead a mission to liberate political prisoners in Naples.

He enjoyed his greatest military glories during his fourth stage, from 1858 to 1860. Having been summoned by the prime minister of Piedmont, the crafty Count Camillo Benso Cavour,[4] Garibaldi organized volunteers, a corps known as *Cacciatori delle Alpi*, in readiness for a war with Austria. While the main Franco-Piedmontese forces were fighting in Lombardy, he won battles at Varese and Como. An armistice was soon declared, and Garibaldi was placed in command of the army of Tuscany. His aspirations to march into the Papal States were overruled, however, and he returned briefly to civilian life.

Garibaldi's highwater point occurred in 1860. As a deputy for Nice in the Piedmontese parliament, he vilified Cavour for ceding Nice, which had been returned to Piedmont in 1815, to the French in consideration of its acceptance of the annexation of Tuscany and Emilia to Piedmont. He then organized "the Thousand" to engage in guerrilla attacks against the Neapolitan Bourbons.

Composed of volunteers, the Thousand were drawn from a strikingly diverse membership: "Students, workingmen, vagabonds and ruffians, tradesmen, civil servants, journalists, authors, university lecturers, barbers, cobblers, gentlemen of leisure, painters, sculptors, ships' captains, chemists, adventurers, businessmen, engineers, a hundred doctors, a hundred and fifty lawyers, and one woman . . . of peasant stock who worked as washerwoman and cook. They were of all ages – the youngest not yet twelve."[5]

After a battle at Calatafimi, he captured Palermo. He soon won the battle of Milazzo, crossed the straits of Messina, pressed a bold campaign in Calabria, and captured Naples. After seizing both Palermo and Naples, Garibaldi proclaimed himself "Dictator of the Two Sicilies." He held plebiscites in Sicily and Naples, which permitted him to present the whole of southern Italy to Piedmont and to proclaim Victor Emmanuel of the House of Savoy as king of a united nation. Garibaldi's military triumphs combined with Cavour's stunning political intrigues had forged *il Risorgimento:* there was now an "Italy," at least in name. Only the Papal States and a few cities remained unjoined. Garibaldi returned to Caprera, which was by now his permanent home.

The Anglo-European world took notice. In 1861 Abraham Lincoln offered him a command of a federal army corps in the U.S. Civil War. Garibaldi demanded supreme command and the formal abolishment of slavery. Negotiations fell through. In 1862 he revived his longstanding aspiration to march on Rome and was seriously wounded in a clash with Italian troops at Aspromonte.[6] He was briefly imprisoned until the king granted him amnesty. In 1864 he enjoyed a majestic reception in England.

Garibaldi led another army of volunteers against Austria in 1866, after which Venice joined Italy; and in 1867 he again marched on Rome but was repelled at Mentana by papal and French forces. In 1870, sixty-three years old and suffering from several infirmities, he joined republican France in the Franco-Prussian War and commanded an army in the Vosges that enjoyed a series of partial successes. Meanwhile, because of that war, nearly all French troops were withdrawn from Rome, and Victor Emmanuel's Italian forces were able to enter. *Il Risorgimento* was complete.[7] Garibaldi returned home at the end of 1871. The "Lion of Caprera" died on June 2, 1882.

As noted in Chapter 1, the southern Italian immigrants to the United States had few heroes. The immigrants cast a gravely suspicious eye on their fellow humans, alive or dead, with the exception of their saints who allegedly had the power to rectify certain social wrongs. Yet Garibaldi was widely venerated among them. Why? He was a Piedmontese, a *straniero*, who spoke of an abstraction called *Italia* that easily eluded most disenfranchised sons and daughters of the *Mezzogiorno*.[8] He embodied an idealistic, romantic socialism, at great variance with the practical orientation of most southern Italians, that often issued in blatantly contradictory political recommendations.[9] He espoused a united Europe, even a united world order, views that would strike southern Italians as freakish and ludicrous. Nevertheless, pictures and relics of Garibaldi were common in southern Italian immigrant homes.

Part of the veneration resulted from Garibaldi's personal appearance and charisma. He was

> rather bow-legged and stocky—less than 5 ft. 7 in.—with broad shoulders and hips and a narrow waist, he had a round face, a fresh complexion and fair, reddish hair. His small brown eyes deeply set and rather close together were divided by a long, aquiline nose, with a very high bridge, so that it seemed on occasions that he had a slight squint. He had well-defined eyebrows and long, fine lashes, and a friendly, charming smile.[10]

He also cultivated sartorial flair, complete with red shirt, flowing cape or poncho, and carefully groomed long hair and beard.

Garibaldi reportedly was always brave and self-reliant. He retained the childlike qualities of being easily flattered and impressed. He was a serious man who lacked a refined sense of humor, but he deeply enjoyed the pleasures of the flesh. Like all great leaders, he exemplified extraordinary abilities to remain calm and concentrate on the task at hand during apparent pending disasters. He inspired his men through his example: resolute, courageous, able to swallow self-doubts in times of crisis.

Deeply sensitive to criticism and unwilling to accept guidance, Garibaldi was often stubborn and resentful.[11] He sparked hostilities with equally strong-willed men such as Mazzini and Cavour. But he embodied a certain purity of spirit— whether a result of his hazy political philosophy, his firm conviction of the moral appropriateness of his own military actions, his typical indifference to material aggrandizement, or his instinctive understanding that his frequent displays of generosity and inspiration transcended the events that occasioned them—that resonated throughout his followers: "He appeared as the ideal patriarch, tolerant yet commanding, whose benign features, soft voice and air of unemphatic authority inspired immediate and lasting devotion. He could disappoint [his followers] on occasions, but he rarely disillusioned them."[12]

Garibaldi, then, was a unique blend of naivety,[13] honesty, and singular conviction: "A hero not afraid to act outside the law, a man of courage and ability, of determination and passion, a simple man given to grandiloquent and apocalyptic announcements, but a man of shining sincerity in a murky and selfish world."[14] Although he evidently was often irritating, he was rarely materially self-aggrandizing.[15] His high ideal of a united Italy, even if hopelessly romantic, echoed with warmth and unadulterated passion.

Moreover, Garibaldi stirred the passions of the peasants in the *Mezzogiorno*. Many southern Italians embraced him as their avenging angel, "the incarnation of their ancient myth of a mighty warrior come to restore justice."[16] His simplicity of spirit and his understanding of their hopes and sorrows, combined with his special military virtues and personal power, permitted Garibaldi at once to transcend yet affirm the common people of the *Mezzogiorno*. It was also clear that Garibaldi's empathy for the South was unfeigned. Throughout his career as a soldier and political deputy, he wrote about the wrongful slighting of Sardinia and the south, the problems of vast disparities of wealth and substandard education, the causes and remedies of brigandage, and the enormous sums wasted on imperialistic ambitions and armaments instead of on the internal needs of Italy.[17]

Perhaps most important, Garibaldi understood and manifested the deeply entrenched southern Italian ritual of *rispetto* ("respect"):

> Garibaldi understood both Mazzini and the south better than Cavour ever did, for the same reason that he had much more knowledge of and sympathy with the common people. Instead of assuming that southerners were idle and corrupt, and instead of trying to impose a cut-and-dried system upon them, he had worked by appealing to their good nature; and this had evoked a far more positive response than greeted his more technically efficient successors. What he gave them was enthusiasm, faith in a cause, and a fine example of self-sacrifice and courage.[18]

Accordingly, through his personal charisma, personification of righteous vengeance, embodiment of military virtue, and instinctive displays of *rispetto*, and through the connivance of political circumstances, Garibaldi achieved the status of secular saint among numerous residents of the *Mezzogiorno*, despite their general lack of zeal for the *Risorgimento* as a whole.[19] Even after crossing the ocean to America, many of these people retained their allegiance to Giuseppe Garibaldi.

Ironically, in the purest sense, Garibaldi was not a great general. As a guerrilla leader, however, he was an inspiring visionary. He retained a keen sense of honor regarding a particular version of the war convention, that set of normative rules and principles that define proper military conduct during war: "Garibaldi's rules were few but they were known and they were respected. Looting church property was, within limits, tolerated, but violence was not; and while a man might go into a convent and come out with a pocketful of candles, he could not go into a house and come out with a bottle of wine."[20] In fact, one of his most memorable outbursts occurred when he recounted a particularly grievous violation of the war convention: the treacheries of foreign mercenaries who, while under a flag of truce, had attacked his forces.[21]

Clearly, however, Garibaldi never questioned the necessity and efficacy of military retaliation in the world that he knew. The advocation of nonviolent resistance and a pacifist way of life would have struck him as dangerously deranged, a failure of the spirit, and an inexcusable timidity of the will.

ARE ALL MODERN WARS MORALLY WRONG?

Robert Holmes has advanced an interesting argument that concludes that all modern wars are morally wrong and that nonviolent resistance and pacifism are prescribed ways of life. Holmes's work is, in my judgment, the best contemporary rendering of the pacifist position. I contrast his work here with Garibaldi's firm conviction in the inevitability of war, drawing insights from both men to clarify an aspect of the individual – community continuum.

Holmes's conclusion is not the banal claim that wars necessarily and inherently involve wrongful aggression – that it is impossible for both sides to act simultaneously in self-defense and thus it is impossible for both sides to act justly.[22] He argues instead that modern warfare will inevitably kill some, usually numerous, innocent people. Because the killing of innocents is morally wrong, modern war is morally wrong. Holmes then proposes the positive case for pacifism as a strategy of resistance to aggression.

Means and Ends

To analyze and evaluate Holmes's argument we must first acknowledge a host of traditional assumptions in the philosophy of war. For example, there is the distinction between *jus ad bellum*, the justice of initiating or entering war, and *jus in bello*, the justice of the means, tactics, and strategies employed in war. Conventional wisdom construes judgments about *jus ad bellum* and *jus in bello* as logically independent: a warring party that is morally justified in entering the fray is not necessarily morally justified in the methods it uses in conducting the war; a warring party that is a wrongful aggressor is not necessarily morally unjustified in the methods it employs during the war. Conventional wisdom, then, recognizes a relatively sharp distinction between moral assessments of wrongful aggression and permissible self-defense, and assessments of violation and observance of the moral conventions of engagement.

The traditional distinction thus rejects the Principle of Righteous Retaliation, which claims that the horrors of war are the sole responsibility of wrongful aggressors and that soldiers repelling aggression are therefore morally blameless for whatever means they use to facilitate victory.[23] The Principle of Righteous Retaliation conflates moral judgments of *jus ad bellum* and *jus in bello*, in effect endorsing the view that people morally justified in entering a war are completely immunized against moral criticism for the means they use. Accordingly, this principle adopts an end-justifies-the-means posture that permits the killing of innocents, the infliction of more injuries than necessary, and disproportionate retaliation as long as the perpetrator has a morally justified cause. All moral blame affixes to the wrongful aggressor.

There is a certain appeal to this principle—"If the wrongful aggressor had not started things then no wrongs would have occurred"—but the traditional distinction is correct to reject it. To use the principle would be to disregard several indispensable moral factors: the inherent immorality of certain means; the principle of proportionate response that demands we achieve a good that outweighs the injuries and devastation of war; and the need to approach war with a rightful intention that excludes, among other things, atrocities and cruelties. Thus, the wrongs of another do not confer automatically a moral imprimatur on the actions of respondents.

Holmes rejects the Principle of Righteous Retaliation, but he is also unconvinced of the traditional distinction between *jus ad bellum* and *jus in bello*. He claims that we cannot morally assess *jus ad bellum* in isolation from the inevitable means of waging modern war: "Unless one can justify the actions necessary to waging war, he cannot justify the conduct of war and the pursuit of its objectives; and if he cannot do this, he cannot justify going to war."[24] Rather than first assessing the morality of cause and justification in entering the war, as the traditional distinction suggests, then fashioning morally appropriate methods of engagement, Holmes claims that

> justice in the waging of war (by which I mean the justifiability of the violence and killing and destruction that are part of the nature of warfare) is a necessary condition of both justice in the conduct of war *(jus in bello)* and justice in the resort to war *(jus ad bellum)* . . . [thus] *jus ad bellum* and *jus in bello* cannot be separated.[25]

Holmes's view depends on a highly persuasive moral proposition: an activity is justified only if the necessary means and constitutive acts inherent to it are themselves morally justified. Thus, the moral bankruptcy of war can be demonstrated if it is true that modern warfare's necessary means and constitutive acts are morally unjustified. Holmes identifies the killing of innocents as the inherently wrongful act constitutive of modern warfare that demonstrates war's immorality.

Killing Innocent Persons

To unpack Holmes's argument we must first examine the wrongfulness of killing innocents. Conventional wisdom typically describes this problem as the killing of noncombatants. The moral impermissibility of killing noncombatants presumably follows from a host of observations: noncombatants are nonparticipants who do not undertake or cooperate closely in the violence of war, and they thus resemble more closely unthreatening bystanders than attacking assailants; it is morally impermissible to treat people as a mere means to our ends; we cannot ignore the choices of others when we pursue our ends; the unthreatening bystander has not consented to the situation of war, and if others force violence upon him or her they thereby treat the unthreatening bystander as a mere means to their ends.[26]

The conventional argument depends on premises that are, at least initially, quite persuasive: the distinction between combatants and noncombatants, the Kantian prohibition against objectifying and exploiting others, the primacy of consent in moral judgments, and the underlying understanding that the conduct of war is subject to deeply engrained principles of moral assessment.

Not all these premises are mutually compatible, however. For example, the distinction between combatants and noncombatants is not obviously coextensive with the dichotomy between consent and nonconsent. Do all combatants truly consent to their military service? Do all noncombatants truly withhold consent to war? Can it be plausibly argued that all citizens, at least in a democracy, bear some responsibility for the warlike activities of their government regardless of whether those citizens wear military uniforms?

The answers to such questions are not obvious, nor do they obviously support the conventional argument for the moral impermissibility of killing noncombatants. Moreover, the Kantian prohibition against wrongful objectification and exploitation must confront a common utilitarian rejoinder: if directly killing a relatively small number of noncombatants results in a speedier resolution of the war in favor of the otherwise morally justified side, and if such a resolution lessens the overall number of war casualties for both combatants and noncombatants, is it not moral fanaticism to cling desperately to the Kantian prohibition?

Holmes senses the frailty of the conventional argument and rejects straightaway the moral soundness of the distinction between combatant and noncombatant. Instead, he presses the distinction between innocent and noninnocent and emphasizes the notion of responsibility for wrongful aggression.

> Members of a nation that is justly warred against will fall roughly into one or more of six categories: (a) initiators of wrongdoing (government leaders); (b) agents of wrongdoing (military commanders and combat soldiers); (c) contributors to the war effort (munitions workers, military researchers, taxpayers, etc.); (d) those who approve of the war without contributing in any significant way; and (e) noncontributors and nonsupporters (e.g., young children, some active opponents of the war who refuse to pay taxes, the insane, etc.).[27]

In his view, most people in the first category and probably some in the second category are morally responsible for wrongful aggression and thus are noninnocents, whereas those in the final category are uninvolved and thus innocent. The third and fourth categories constitute potpourris: some members of these categories bear responsibility for wrongful aggression in attenuated ways, others may contribute essentially against their will, still others may deeply approve of the aggression but be unable by circumstances to contribute to it.[28] In assessing all categories we must pay special attention to the enormous social pressures that contaminate assumptions of pure consent: the habit of obedience to government, the psychological force of patriotism, the moral investment of the typical citizen in his or her state, the misinformation and limitations on information provided by government, and the fears that opposition to official policies will engender governmental and social reprisals all cloud citizens' judgment and call into question the moral force of claims that citizens truly consented to the war effort.

The point of this exercise for Holmes is to demonstrate that even the wrongful aggressor, the side that conventional analysts would declare deficient from the standpoint of *jus ad bellum*, contains numerous innocent people. More strikingly, at least some of these people will necessarily be killed during modern warfare, regardless of the intentions and conduct of the other side, because, among other reasons, the morally righteous party will be unable to distinguish adequately "innocent" from "noninnocent" members of the wrongfully aggressive nation.

Moreover, Holmes describes *all* the killing done by the wrongfully aggressive nation as the killing of innocents: "If at least one side acts unjustly (it may easily be the case that both sides act unjustly, of course), then *all* of the killing done by that side, whether of soldiers or civilians, will be wrongful . . . The killing of *anyone* who has done no wrong relative to the war in question is, in the relevant sense, the killing of an innocent person."[29]

Thus, Holmes's understanding of "innocence" becomes clearer: all members of the morally righteous side—the nation(s) satisfying the judgments typically embodied by *jus ad bellum*—and many members of the wrongfully aggressive side—those who bear no or very little personal responsibility for the wrongfully aggressive policies. Here Holmes implicitly rejects the Principle of Righteous Retaliation: the wrongful aggression of one side does not confer boundless moral license on the actions of the other side. Framed in this fashion, Holmes's distinction between innocent and noninnocent bears radically different implications from those of the traditional boundaries between combatant and noncombatant. Specifically, Holmes's distinction widens the category of impermissible killing by including numerous combatants and noncombatants on both sides.

This difference crystallizes when Holmes considers the possible combinations. First, he rejects the possibility that both sides in a war can be morally right: "If one side acts justly, it can only be because the other side acts unjustly, and vice versa, so to say that both sides are acting justly would be to say that both are acting rightly *and* wrongly, which is incomprehensible."[30] Second, and in apparent contradiction of this quotation, Holmes states that "it may easily be the case that both sides act unjustly, of course."[31] If both sides act unjustly, the killing of some innocents (those on both sides who bear little or no personal responsibility for the wrongfully aggressive policies) is inevitable. Third, it may be the case that one side is a wrongful aggressor and the other side is morally righteous. In such instances, there will be massive killing of innocents: all members of the morally righteous side killed by the wrongful aggressor, as well as some members (those who bear no or little personal responsibility for wrongful policies) of the wrongful aggressors killed by the morally righteous side. Accordingly, modern war is presumptively wrong because it inevitably destroys innocent lives.

Holmes's analysis begins by entertaining the distinction between *jus ad bellum* and *jus in bello*, for his categorization of wrongful aggressors and morally righteous defenders attends solely to judgments of *jus ad bellum;* but once he demonstrates the practical impossibility of satisfying the demands of *jus in bello*, as each side will inevitably destroy innocent lives regardless of the purity of their intentions and methods, the distinction between *jus ad bellum* and *jus in bello* evaporates. If the means used in conducting modern war are *inevitably* morally contaminated regardless of a side's antecedent intentions, and if we reject the proposition that the ends justify the means, we must conclude that antecedent awareness of the inevitable employment of morally impermissible means contaminates the justice of entering war: the impossibility of *jus in bello* consumes the moral possibility of *jus ad bellum*.

Holmes is careful to modify his conclusion: "If it is presumptively wrong to kill innocent persons, and if . . . war should *inevitably* involve such killing, then war itself is presumptively wrong. This also does not mean that war may not yet be justified. But it does mean that the presumption in question must be defeated and war's justification demonstrated if one proposes to engage in it."[32]

Holmes then entertains and rejects what he takes to be the main strategies for rebutting the presumption that modern war is morally wrong: an argument that killing innocent persons, at least on a small scale, does not necessarily render an entire war morally wrong; the positivistic realism that claims that wars are outside the parameters of conventional moral assessment; the doctrine of double effect; and utilitarian calculations.[33] Thus, Holmes concludes that

> What I consider the strongest arguments to defeat that presumption [that modern war is unjustified], by way of trying to defeat the presumption against the killing of innocent persons, also do not succeed. If that is the case, then war has not been shown to be justified, and if it has not been shown to be justified, then it is unjustified. This does not of itself mean that modern war *could* not be justified; to show that something has not been justified and that the main attempts to justify it are inadequate can never logically foreclose the possibility that a justification might someday be forthcoming. But that justification must be produced.[34]

Before assessing Holmes's arguments, I must highlight a few observations. First, Holmes is sometimes trapped by the philosopher's binary fantasy—for example, either a party to war has a just cause or it has an unjust cause—which falsely depicts reality in "black or white" and "either X or − X" terms. In fact, assessments of justness are better viewed as constituting a continuum that admits of various degrees: frequently neither party to a dispute is either totally in the right or totally in the wrong. Second, Holmes himself occasionally trips over his predilection for binary classification: for example, he tells us that on the one hand "if one side acts justly, it can only be because the other side acts unjustly, and vice versa,"[35] and on the other hand "it may easily be the case that both sides act unjustly, of course."[36] Here he seems at first to make the presence of a just party a necessary condition for properly attributing unjust action to the other party, but he then seems to renege on this commitment. Third, although Holmes's distinction between innocents and noninnocents, drawn on the basis of personal responsibility and support for wrongful aggression, constitutes a theoretical advantage, the traditional distinction between combatants and non-combatants remains of greater practical use. Lacking the complicated, often conflicting, information required to produce refined judgments of innocence and noninnocence in this sense, participants in a war are better served by the traditional distinction.

These observations, however, are not devastating and indeed do not even touch Holmes's main argument that modern war is presumptively unjust be-cause it inevitably involves the killing of innocent persons, none of the standard attempts to rebut that presumption have succeeded, and therefore war, insofar as we can presently discern, is unjustified.

Is Modern War Unjustified as Such?

There are at least two possible interpretations of Holmes's main claim. A weak interpretation would insist that modern war taken as a whole is unjustified. Under this view, when we morally assess all the actions embodied by any particular modern war we must conclude that the war was unjustified. This interpretation is not especially surprising or interesting: given that all wars stem from wrongful aggression or initiation and necessarily destroy innocent lives, they are morally wrong when viewed in toto. It would still seem, however, that a particular nation waging modern war might be justified on grounds of self-defense, permissible humanitarian intervention, acceptable preemptive action, or whatever. A strong interpretation would contend that not only is modern war taken as a whole unjustified but every participating nation is also unjustified. That is, given antecedently known facts such as the inevitability of each side's killing of innocent persons, appeals to *jus ad bellum* ring hollow: foreknowledge of the impossibility of adhering to the demands of *jus in bello* contaminates from the outset pious invocations of a nation's just cause. Under this view, every participating nation is morally wrong, although some, depending on their motives, intentions, and manner of conducting the war, may deserve more moral disapprobation than others.

I take Holmes to be asserting a version of the strong interpretation. One rejoinder to his view might run as follows. In moral philosophy, "ought implies can" is a well-accepted bromide: one necessary condition of moral obligation is that the action in question must be possible for the agent to perform. To put it a bit differently, if an action is impossible for an agent to perform then that action cannot be morally obligatory for that agent. In the present case, one could argue that if refraining from killing innocents is impossible, given the conditions of modern war and the manner in which Holmes defines "innocents," then we cannot properly insist that warring nations have a moral obligation to refrain from killing innocents. If warring nations have no such moral obligation, we cannot consistently claim that the killing of innocents renders such nations immoral.

Of course, this rejoinder is stated too crudely. It could be used disingenuously by nations seeking to evade moral responsibility for wanton acts of violence. Although it may be true that under conditions of modern warfare all participating nations will kill *some* innocent persons, it hardly follows that it is *always* impossible for these nations to prevent the killing of innocents. Surely, warring nations bear moral obligations to do everything possible to avoid the killing of innocent persons, even though they know from the outset that they cannot completely avoid killing some innocents. They can, however, succeed in "doing everything practically possible to avoid the killing of innocent persons," and this possibility is one of the necessary conditions of affixing the correlated moral obligation. Under this modified rendering of the rejoinder to Holmes, warring nations would have an obligation to perform the possible task of "doing everything practically possible to avoid the killing of innocent persons" but no obligation to perform the impossible task of "never killing an innocent person." Accordingly, a warring party that discharged its moral obligation to innocent persons, even though it killed some innocents, would deserve no moral disapprobation. If sound, this argument challenges the strong interpretation's contention that all warring nations are morally wrong because they all kill innocent persons.

Is the argument sound? Much ambiguity inheres in the prescription to "do everything practically possible." Appeals to "military necessity" resound early and often during war, and leaders of warring nations bear great psychological and social pressures to minimize their country's casualties and to hasten the day of victory. We can therefore expect wartime policy makers to interpret the prescription to "do everything practically possible" quite loosely. History confirms this expectation.

Analytically rigorous philosophers, however, can tighten the prescription by specifying conditions and activities that would satisfy the ambiguous phrase. Moreover, the fact that most warring nations have not in fact satisfied the prescription would not of itself demonstrate the unsoundness of the argument. Thus, the ambiguity of the prescription can be cured and compliance with the terms of the moral imperative would still be possible.

But Holmes's objection to the argument might go deeper. He could argue, for example, that the argument begs the question, for his greatest objection to war is the very fact the argument concedes: all warring nations must kill innocent persons. Regardless of whether we can legitimately *excuse* such conduct on the basis of warring nations' limited knowledge and imperfect ability to distinguish innocents from noninnocents, we cannot *justify* the conduct given our antecedent awareness that it must occur in modern war. Holmes could argue that the ballast of the ought-implies-can argument in this context is precisely what he denies: belief in the inevitability and general permissibility of modern war. Thus, Holmes could insist that the ought-implies-can argument in this context does not support the conclusion that warring nations can avoid moral disapprobation even after they have killed innocent persons, instead it presupposes that conclusion.

Of course, advocates of the ought-implies-can argument can lodge a parallel claim against Holmes: he assumes from the outset that any measure of foreseen killing of innocents morally delegitimates an activity, an assumption that precludes him from serious consideration of the ought-implies-can rejoinder.

We are left, as philosophers so often are, with an inconclusive debate that seems to lack sufficient common ground for adequate resolution. Much, if not everything, seems to turn on the moral stringency of the moral imperative to preserve, or at least not to destroy, the lives of innocent persons.

Reductionism and the Fallacy of Composition

There are, however, illuminating ways to examine that moral imperative. One challenge to Holmes's main argument might be to raise the specter of wrongful reductionism—in this context, the oversimplification of a complex moral question by myopic focus on only one of its components. In this vein, Holmes ably illustrates the inevitable and foreseeable killing of innocents in modern war; given the well-recognized moral imperative against such killing, modern war must be morally wrong.

But Holmes's analysis may be wrongfully reductionist, for it derives a substantive moral conclusion from only one aspect of modern warfare. This charge is especially serious in this context because Holmes also asserts that the inevitable and foreseeable killing of innocents contaminates morally the antecedent cause of a warring party. He thus precludes a nation's invocation of just cause on the same basis upon which he censures war as a whole. Accordingly, critics may argue that Holmes is permitting his commitment to one moral imperative to obscure a full analysis of the complexities of war. Once Holmes demonstrates that innocent persons will inevitably and foreseeably be killed by all warring parties, he is oblivious to the larger context. He may thereby be tacitly endorsing a fanatically absolutist rendering of his favored moral imperative: there are no circumstances under which the foreseen killing of innocents is morally permissible, and should such killing occur within a larger context or series of activities, they too automatically degenerate to morally bankruptcy.

Indeed, Holmes himself entertains an argument flowing from such sentiments: Richard Wasserstrom's suggestions that the foreseen killing of innocent persons in war does not necessarily morally impugn the killer-nation or the war as a whole.

> Given the number of criteria that are relevant to the moral assessment of any war and given the great number of persons involved in and the extended duration of most wars, it would be false to the complexity of the issues to suppose that so immediately simple a solution [as concluding that regardless of consequences the intentional killing of an innocent person is never justified in war] were possible.[37]

Holmes responds to this suggestion by claiming that Wasserstrom's remarks rest on one of the following grounds: either an allegation that Holmes has committed a fallacy of composition or the positivistic realist assumption that moral predicates cannot legitimately apply to war.

Holmes's response is extremely disappointing. Although he is correct in dismantling the positivistic realist assumption, this position surely does not characterize Wasserstrom nor the philosophers who would find Wasserstrom's remarks persuasive. Very few positivistic realists stalk the halls of philosophy departments, and Holmes's repudiation of positivistic realism is sound but largely irrelevant.

His other response highlights the fallacy of composition, a mistake of supposing that because a certain attribute can be assigned properly to a part of X, it can also be ascribed to the whole of X. Should a critic lodge such a charge in this context it would take the following form: although the foreseeable or knowing killing of an innocent person during war is morally impermissible, it does not follow that this war is or wars as a whole are morally impermissible because to assume otherwise is to commit the fallacy of composition.

Holmes clearly misunderstands the thrust of the charge against him. The wise critic is not indicting Holmes in the courtroom of formal logic—she is not accusing Holmes of committing a well-recognized informal fallacy. Instead, the critic is arguing that Holmes has taken a wrongly reductionist or absolutist stance on war. What is the difference in the two renderings? The charge of fallacy of composition could be successful only if Holmes's argument required the following premise to sustain its conclusion: if part of X is immoral, then X as a whole is immoral. But surely Holmes's argument does not require such a pedestrian and blatantly fallacious assumption. His argument requires only that he demonstrate that *in this case* the inevitable antecedently known killing of innocent persons destroys the moral legitimacy of war as a whole. This demonstration requires that Holmes attend to the distinction between *jus ad bellum* and *jus in bello* and between innocents and noninnocents, as well as to the normative connections between means and ends. Indeed, Holmes attends to precisely such matters. Holmes is not, however, required to adopt the general proposition that constitutes the fallacy of composition. That is, he does not need to assume that *in all cases* showing the immorality of a part of X logically entails the immorality of X taken as a whole. In fact, to address this general proposition would be fatuous because it is so patently unnecessary to his argument. Accordingly, any critic who would lodge allegations of fallacy of composition against Holmes would be stalking an apparition of her own imagination.

By the same token, however, Holmes conjures a straw person when he assumes that such criticism represents a powerful version of Wasserstrom's suggestions. In fact, Holmes finesses the entire problem badly. His invocation of the positivistic realist is largely irrelevant, for most of Holmes's critics would readily agree with Holmes's critique of positivistic realism, and his struggle with the imagined critic alleging fallacy of composition is a pitiful, manufactured conflict.

Reductionism Refined

A better rendering of Wasserstrom's suggestions takes Holmes's argument as a wrongly reductionist or absolutist stance on war. According to this strategy, a critic could argue as follows: Holmes wrongly reduces the morality of war to only one issue—the foreseen and knowing killing of innocent persons. By taking an absolutist position on this issue—there are no circumstances under which a moral agent is justified in knowingly killing an innocent person in wartime and no conditions under which it is morally preferable to kill rather than not kill an innocent person—he completely rejects the relevance of consequences in moral assessment. Moreover, he thereby wrongly embraces an absolutist position on the relationship of means and ends: the ends *never* justify the means. Furthermore, he addresses the notion of moral justification in isolation and not in the context of practical alternatives: if there is no practical, less violent alternative to war when confronting a wrongfully aggressive nation, then claims that the responding nation's conduct is morally impermissible because war necessarily involves the foreseen and knowing killing of innocent persons are misplaced. Thus, Holmes's argument, although it does not rely on a fallacy of composition, is nevertheless unsound because of its reductionist and absolutist convictions.

The Argument from Prevention

The affirmative side of this argument, which I call the Argument from Prevention, would follow this pattern: Although a person may be "innocent" in the sense of lacking personal responsibility for the wrongful aggression of her country, she still may be engaged in activities that threaten and inflict harm on persons whose nation is not engaged in wrongful aggression. Thus, despite its theoretical raggedness, the distinction between combatant and noncombatant is more practically useful than the distinction between innocent and noninnocent. As in criminal law, we must recognize moral distinctions between different states of mind that animate killing: intentional, knowing, reckless, negligent, and accidental killings constitute a spectrum of decreasing moral culpability; a difference also exists between foreseeing that particular antecedently identifiable innocent persons will be killed by a specific wartime action and being able to predict with great inductive confidence that over a period of time a certain number of innocent persons will be killed in war.[38] Taking such precepts into account, the knowing and foreseeable but merely incidental killing of noncombatant "innocent" members of the wrongfully aggressive nation may be justified only if doing so prevents the loss of a greater number of innocent lives, the killers-combatants undertake such action as a last resort, the killers-combatants minimize the evil involved (including the manner and number of killings), and they accept reasonable risks and costs to themselves in minimizing that evil.[39]

Although Holmes often gives the impression that he is an absolutist, in fact he explicitly distances himself from that perspective.

> If one takes the prohibition [against killing innocents] to rule out the killing of innocents in all conceivable circumstances, it is an absolute prohibition and can consistently be held only if one is prepared to defend the most absurd of moral judgments in wildly hypothetical cases. Absolutism of that sort borders on fanati-

cism. Those who subscribe to it usually have in mind a different principle, one that absolutely prohibits only the *intentional* killing of innocent persons.[40]

A quick reading of this passage might augur reconciliation between Holmes and my argument: my argument justifies only certain types of knowing and foreseen killings of innocents, whereas Holmes seems to be necessarily opposed only to the intentional killing of innocents. We might even conjure a warm philosophical embrace once mutually acceptable distinctions have been recognized. This blissful ending to this debate, however, is fantasy. Holmes explicitly distinguishes the morality of an agent from the morality of her actions and rejects the efficacy of the doctrine of double effect, which makes great use of distinctions between intentional and foreseen and between direct and indirect. Instead, he argues that even if intentions could be clearly discerned, they would be relevant only to assessments of moral agents, not to their actions: "If one prohibits the killing of innocents, he cannot then invoke good intentions to justify proceeding to kill them."[41] Thus, no felicitous reconciliation between Holmes's position and my argument is forthcoming. Moreover, it becomes unclear whether Holmes, although not an absolutist with regard to assessing the moral culpability of killers, might not remain an absolutist with regard to the action of killing innocents. The first quotation seems to distance him from the latter view, but the second quotation seems to reinstate that view. The ambiguity is deepened by the conditional mood of the second quotation: "*if* one prohibits the killing of innocents."

It is not necessary to resolve the presence of absolutism in Holmes's thought. Whether he regards all intentional killings of innocent persons as morally unjustified (as he apparently does) is secondary to his position on such killing during wars. Here his position is quite clear: "Modern war inevitably kills innocent persons. And this, I contend, makes modern war presumptively wrong."[42]

Holmes's reductionist tendencies, however, are clear: the killing of innocent persons in war sufficiently establishes the wrongness of war. Moreover, Holmes explicitly rejects utilitarian calculations when analyzing the moral justification of war: "Utilitarianism (and consequentialism generally) is inadequate as a basis for moral theory."[43] Finally, he seems to eviscerate the distinction between means and ends: for Holmes, not only do morally deficient means taint an agent's ends, they render the ends irredeemably evil. Although he rejects the radical separation of means from ends, Holmes seems to reinstate an equally unattractive alternative: the virtual indistinguishability of ends and means. Again, he registers his unwavering commitment to binary possibilities—either ends and means are radically distinct or they are fully merged. For Holmes the ends can never justify the means because there are not two entities to compare. A critic might well rejoin that although means are prefigured in ends—the two entities overlap—there is vital theoretical and practical sense in retaining, for example, the distinction between *jus ad bellum* and *jus in bello*.

Consequences and the Death of Innocents

It is unfair, however, to charge Holmes with failure to consider alternatives to war. The underlying theme of his work is that there does exist a practical, less violent alternative to war when confronting a wrongfully aggressive nation: concerted peaceful nonviolent resistance. Moreover, he explicitly considers part of the Argument from Prevention: "Sometimes [killing innocents in wartime] is the only way to prevent other innocent persons—perhaps in greater numbers—from being killed. Some aggressors will pursue their objectives at any cost."[44] Holmes elaborates:

> If a consequence of refusing to wage war would be to let innocent persons die, and if there is no moral distinction between 'killing' and 'letting die,' then the fact that one would inevitably be killing innocents by waging war is by itself an inconclusive reason not to do so. Innocents are going to die whatever you do. So better to resist evil as best you can than to maintain what is only the appearance of clean hands.[45]

He then examines thoroughly what he takes to be the two central assumptions animating the Argument from Prevention: "The first holds that there is no moral distinction between killing an innocent person and letting an innocent person die . . . the second holds that the consequence of refusing to fight is that innocents will be killed by the aggressor."[46]

Holmes addresses the second assumption by arguing that it is unclear whether the deaths of innocents would be among the consequences of our actions whatever we do. The responses of others are not always properly recognized among the mediated consequences of what we do; there is no neutral criteria for resolving what should and should not be viewed as a morally relevant mediated consequence of our actions; it is a moral question what to include among the consequences of actions, which implies that one cannot simply assume that preventable deaths of innocents through the agency of aggressors are among the consequences of the refusal of others to respond violently to the aggression. Although he refuses to conclude that one ought never to include such deaths among the consequences of our actions, Holmes insists that "it is an open question morally whether to do so."[47]

This bit of philosophical legerdemain is designed to demonstrate that it is not so obvious that the killing of innocent persons by wartime aggressors can be properly called a *consequence* of the pacific nation's refusal to engage in battle. But two points are relevant here: first, the Argument from Prevention need not rely on a technical notion of "consequence" at all; second, even if the Argument from Prevention does rely explicitly on such a notion, it need not subscribe to the general proposition that *all* mediated results must properly be called consequences of the omissions that might have prevented them.

The Argument from Prevention can be supplemented along these lines: but for the inactivity of the nonaggressor nation, fewer innocent lives would be lost; specifically, if that nation responds militarily it will lose X number of innocent lives and the aggressor nation will lose Y number of innocent lives, but if the nonaggressor nation fails to respond militarily it will lose X^4 innocent lives and the aggressor nation will lose few if any innocent lives; X^4 is much greater than $X + Y$. Moreover, the nonaggressor nation would undertake military action as a last resort, strive to minimize the evil involved (including the manner and number of killings of innocent persons), and its combatants would accept reasonable risks and costs to themselves in minimizing that evil.

To be sure, this argument makes a host of contestable empirical claims about what will in fact occur if the nonaggressive responds militarily or does not, about the nonexistence of alternative methods of resistance, about the overall number of innocent lives that might have been saved through military self-defense measures, and about the efficacy of a particular nation's military response. And indeed it includes numerous fuzzy phrases such as "reasonable risks and costs" and "last resort," but it need not be committed to a specific technical notion of "consequence" other than "what will happen if the pacific nation does nothing that would have been prevented had that nation counterattacked" and "what will happen if that nation responds militarily." In any event, the Argument from Prevention clearly need not subscribe to the general proposition that *all* mediated results must properly be called "consequences" of the omissions that might have prevented them.

Killing and Letting Die

Holmes is more forceful in attacking what he takes to be the first assumption of the Argument from Prevention, that there is no moral distinction between killing and letting die in general. In the context of war, he poses the question in this way: "When we ask about the comparative morality in wartime of allowing innocents to die as opposed to killing them, the question is whether we should kill some innocent persons so as not to let others die; whether we should alter the death-threatening conditions to some by ourselves killing others."[48] He rejects the view that in general killing and letting die are morally indistinguishable. Holmes grounds his view in a variety of moral observations. First, we judge it permissible to allow thousands to die daily from hunger, disease, exposure, and malnutrition. We could presumably prevent many such deaths by timely, systematic efforts. Partly because such efforts would undoubtedly require enormous sacrifices of our interests and might alter the entire structure of our own lives,[49] we do not judge such instances of letting people die as harshly as we would assess killing people straightaway.

Second, "if killing and letting die were indistinguishable, then they should be so in the case of the person sacrificing all for the suffering souls of the world."[50] But such is not the case. Those who sacrifice deeply for impoverished, needy people are lauded for their supererogatory acts, for going above and beyond the call of moral duty, but we nevertheless morally demand that impoverished, needy people not be killed. Thus, although letting such people die is judged unfortunate, killing them is assessed as one of the most serious moral wrongs. To not kill such people is merely to fulfill a basic moral duty, to save such people is to extend oneself beyond moral duty. Thus, killing and letting die are not parallel actions from a moral point of view.

Third, none of us has a *right* to the services and sacrifices of others when we are in need. We cannot legitimately "expect as a matter of obligation that [others] go out of their way, perhaps sacrificing their interests or even their lives, to preserve [us]."[51] But we all have a right not to be killed by others. Hence, Holmes is convinced that he has revealed yet another distinction between the moral gravities of killing and letting die.

Fourth, there are extensive differences between the phenomenologies of killing and letting die: "To kill someone (other than inadvertently or acciden-tally) requires doing something knowingly and, in the clearest cases, deliberately causing his death . . . Letting others die, on the other hand, may involve nothing more than going about one's everyday activities; it may even result from engagement in moral and self-sacrificing undertakings."[52]

Holmes concludes there are several moral distinctions between killing and letting die. Accordingly, the conviction of the Argument from Prevention that there is no moral distinction between killing and letting die is so seriously flawed that it undercuts the conclusion that waging war in self-defense, which presumably saves the lives of some innocents who would otherwise die at the hands of the aggressor nation, is morally permissible even though it would result in, at least, the knowing and foreseen killing by the nonaggressor nation of a number of innocents within the aggressor nation.

I strongly believe that Holmes's remarks prove much less than he suspects.[53] In fact, some of his observations can be used to unsettle, rather than to prove, his conclusion that there are moral distinctions between killing and letting die. Take, for example, his remarks on the differing phenomenologies of killing and letting die; they can be used to unsettle his conclusion in the following fashion: some philosophers fail to distinguish between the fact that most *actual* violations of a negative duty, such as the duty not to kill, are morally worse than violations of the correlated positive duty, such as the duty under certain circumstances to render aid to those in distress, and the understanding that there is something *intrinsic* to the relationship of these duties that this fact be so.

Usually we murder, rob, and harm—violations of negative duties—from malicious motives and in service of evil ends; but we fail to render aid—under certain circumstances, violations positive duties—from simple apathy or ignorance (as Holmes notes). Although apathy is hardly a praiseworthy attitude, it is reasonable to view it as less morally pernicious than malice. Thus most actual killings are morally worse than correlated instances of letting die because harming from malicious motives is morally worse than not rendering aid for apathetic reasons. Yet this moral difference is not something indigenous or necessary to the nature of violations of negative and positive duties. Once we equalize the intention, motivation, attitude toward victim, geographical proximity, and foreseen and actual consequences in two correlated cases of killing and letting die, and stipulate that the sacrifice required of the moral agent in complying with each duty be minimal, there may well be no moral difference between violators and violations of each.[54] Thus, to conclude that most actual killings are morally worse than cases of letting die does not imply that negative duties issue stronger moral imperatives than those prescribed by correlated positive duties.

Surely Holmes is correct when he observes that conventional morality does not require the same level of sacrifice to help those in need as it does to refrain from killing?[55] This observation, however, demonstrates only that the *scope* of the two duties may differ. That is, the scope of our duty to refrain from killing may be wider, including more people under more circumstances, than the scope of our duty to render aid to those in distress. This difference may in part be attributed to other dissimilarities we encounter when trying to fulfill these duties: for example, problems of knowledge and coordination, and the need for collective, rather than individual, action in performing the activities required for saving people in distant lands. Thus, Holmes's observations do not necessarily imply that killing, other things being equal, is morally worse than letting die, or that where there is a duty to render aid that duty is less morally stringent than the correlated duty to refrain from killing.

What philosophers mean by a morally relevant consideration is that it, of and by itself, constitutes a *reason* either for or against the performance (or nonperformance) of the action we are pondering. This reason may not be the only one we must consider, and it may even be contravened if there exist other stronger reasons contrary to it; but if this something is morally relevant, then it is always at least part of our moral calculations when we are attempting to determine the moral worth of various actions. Consider the following:

(C): Lying is a morally worse act than telling the truth.

What C means is that to say that one act is a case of truth telling and another act is a case of lying is to give one reason why the former is morally superior to the latter. C does not mean to say that one always ought to tell the truth and avoid lying, for there are circumstances in which the consequences of truth telling are so morally horrible that telling a lie is preferable. But C does state that one reason that counts in favor of one act and against another is that the former is a case of truth telling and the latter is a case of lying. Now consider the following:

(C1): All instances of lying are morally worse acts, other things being equal, than instances of telling the truth.

C1 implies that to say that one act is a case of truth telling and another act is a correlated case of lying, and all other moral factors are equal, is to accept that the latter is morally worse than the former. As all *other* morally relevant reasons for and against the two acts balance out, the only remaining reason morally to differentiate the two acts is that one is a case of truth telling and the other is a case of lying. In the absence of contravening reasons, we ought to prefer telling the truth to lying.

Accordingly, all other things being equal, if we have a choice of lying or telling the truth, we are firmly convinced that we ought to tell the truth because the distinction between lying and telling the truth is a morally relevant one. The distinction itself, grounded in the nature of the two acts, provides a reason to prefer truth telling to lying. If all other morally relevant factors were equal and we were confronted with the choice of lying or telling the truth, we would not just flip a coin to decide our course of action, because we firmly believe that the distinction between the two acts is morally relevant. Moreover, this distinction is morally relevant in *all* correlated cases of truth telling and lying: in every instance, the distinction provides a reason to prefer the former act to the latter.[56]

In the cases of killing and letting die we have two acts that logically entail the same consequence—someone dies. So the phrase "killing is worse than letting die" means that, of and by itself, to call one act an act of killing and the other an act of letting die furnishes one reasons to suppose that the former is morally worse than the latter. Thus, if the distinction between killing and letting die is morally relevant, then, all other things being equal, killing is worse than letting die.

In my judgment, however, there is no morally relevant distinction between killing and letting die. Unlike correlated cases of lying and truth telling, once we equalize all other morally relevant factors—once "all other things are equal"—there remains nothing intrinsic in the acts themselves to morally prefer one to the other. The other factors to be equalized include the intention, motivation, attitude toward victim, geographical proximity to potential victim, and foreseen and actual consequences of the respective acts. Of course, the cases of killing and letting die must be correlated, which means, among other things, that they both fall within the scope of moral duty. Accordingly, I am firmly convinced that one can subscribe consistently to all of the following propositions:

1. There is no morally relevant distinction, in the sense described above, between killing and letting die.
2. Most actual killings are worse than actual cases of letting others die.

3. The scope of our duty to refrain from killing is wider than the scope of our duty to render aid to those in need.

4. Accurately describing one act as a "killing" and another as a case of "letting die" of itself provides no reason to morally prefer the latter to the former, at least when both acts would violate moral duties.

I have argued extensively for these conclusions elsewhere and will not belabor them here.[57]

The Argument from Prevention Revisited

Here is the ironic twist to this inquiry: even if Holmes is correct that there is an important moral distinction between killing and letting die in general, this fact need not unsettle the claims of the Argument from Prevention, for that argument does not need to take *any* position on the moral distinction between killing and letting die *in general*. Instead, the Argument from Prevention takes a much more specific position on the relationship between killing and letting die: the knowing and foreseen killing of a certain number of innocent persons within an aggressor nation in wartime, when there are no less horrible means of prevention available, is morally preferable to permitting that aggressor nation to kill straightaway a larger number of innocent persons in the nonaggressor nation.

Regardless of whether one agrees or disagrees with the substance of this narrower claim, its persuasiveness clearly does not depend on a particular position on the moral distinction between killing and letting die in general. That is, one could hold, with Holmes, that there is a strong distinction between killing and letting die but agree with the Argument from Prevention that in this particular instance allowing the nonaggressor nation's innocent persons to die is morally worse than killing the aggressor nation's innocent persons. The latter position could be held on a variety of grounds consistent with belief in the general proposition.

In sum, Holmes may have fallen victim to the type of error he otherwise disparages when he conjures the critic hurling accusations of fallacy of composition at him. Recall that the charge of fallacy of composition could be successful only if Holmes's argument required the following premise to sustain its conclusion: if part of X is immoral then X as a whole is immoral. But Holmes's argument requires only that he demonstrate in the instant case that inevitable antecedently known killing of innocent persons destroys the moral legitimacy of war as a whole. The Argument from Prevention enjoys precisely this insulation in relation to Holmes's remarks about the alleged general moral distinction between killing and letting die.

Moreover, there is a problem of description here. When we are judging the situation from the perspective of the nonaggressor nation contemplating its response to an aggressor, we might pose the question in this way: "Is it morally preferable for our nation to respond militarily and knowingly kill X number of innocent persons within the aggressor nation or to make no such response and allow Y number of innocent persons to die at the hands of the aggressor nation?" When we are judging the situation from another, more abstract, perspective, we might pose the question in another way: "Is it morally prefer-able that the aggressor nation kill Y number of innocent persons within the nonaggressor nation or that the nonaggressor nation kill X number of innocent persons within the aggressor nation?" Posing the question in the latter fashion eliminates the entire question of the relationship between killing and letting die.

Of course, both of these descriptions are partial: they conceal a host of empirical assumptions, including the supposition that there are no alternatives to waging war. But the point is that, with sufficient ingenuity, the Argument from Prevention can even avoid localized references to the distinction between killing and letting die.

But let us accept Holmes's rendition of the argument as it emerges from the perspective of the nonaggressor nation contemplating its response to an aggres-sor. Assuming that I am correct in insisting that the Argument from Prevention, at most, needs to make only a localized appeal to the relative merits of killing and letting die, there are morally relevant factors that Holmes has obscured. First, the nonaggressor nation is not merely calculating whether to let innocents in the abstract die, but is actually contemplating letting its own people die. Surely a nation has special duties to prevent the slaughter of its own people; indeed, many thinkers would take the protection of its citizens to be the raison d'être of the state. In the face of such special obligations, the debate over the moral disapprobation, if any, that should accompany the general failure to render aid to those in distress in distant lands is fatuous. Regardless of whether we think such cases of letting die are morally serious, surely cases of a nation that through its policies permits its citizens to die at the hands of an aggressor *are* serious. Unless one holds a chillingly abstract position—lives are lives, we have equal responsibility for everyone, no special duties to anyone—the moral relevance for the nonaggressor nation that its own citizens may die from aggression is unmistakable. (The confusions inherent in overly abstract positions have already been exposed in Chapter 1.)

Second, Holmes identifies what he takes to be the two prime premises of the Argument from Prevention—that there is no moral distinction between killing an innocent person and letting an innocent person die, and that the 'consequence' of refusing to fight is that innocents will be killed by the aggressor—and strives to demonstrate their unpersuasiveness. In so doing, he displays the worst excesses of analytic philosophy: taking a specific argument and raising it to a series of highly general abstractions that mask the anguish of the dilemma faced by the nonaggressor nation and that obscure the social meaning of the refusal to defend militarily a way of life. Also, his rejoinder is defective by the standards of analytic philosophy themselves: as I have shown, the Argument from Prevention need not depend at all on the highly generalized two premises Holmes has identified.

Holmes does advance, however, some observations on a more localized version of the Argument from Prevention. First, he refuses to accept the view that national self-defense is a justification for the knowing killing by the nonaggressor nation of innocents within the aggressor nation: "The killing of innocents by an aggressor is no worse *as such* than the killing of innocents by those who would oppose him by waging war. Human beings have as much right to be spared destruction by good people as by bad."[58] Second, he refuses to embrace the view that the ends of the nonaggressor nation morally permit such killing: "If I choose to kill innocent persons in order to prevent the deaths of others at the hands of an aggressor, I, no less than and perhaps even more than he (if his killing of innocents is only incidental to his attaining his ends) am using innocent persons as a means to an end."[59]

These observations strike me as moral sloganism at its worst: the ends do not justify the means, killing of innocents is evil, one cannot use another person merely as a means to her ends. It is not that such slogans are necessarily wrong, but they are too often used to obscure the particularities and social realities of moral choice. Furthermore, they tend to categorize overinclusively a plethora of different acts, in this case killings of innocents, under the same rubric, then stigmatize the acts in one fell swoop without regard for the idiosyncrasies of situation and context. Thus, although the slogans embody important partial truths, they do not reveal the complexity of our moral judgments and often prevent nuanced descriptions of moral acts. As a result, their facile use misdescribes reality. For example, the description "using some innocents, indeed killing them, to alleviate the life-threatening situation of other innocents" fails to include a host of morally relevant features of the situation, such as the reasons why anyone is at risk in the first place, the differences between direct and incidental results of ends, the assumed lack of available options, distinctions between the stringency of duties owed those close to us and those owed to strangers, and the contrasting number of innocent lives likely to be lost if the respective alternatives are pursued.

For the moment, consider an illustration outside the context of war: the lives of five innocent persons who are close friends are threatened by a wrongful aggressor who attacks them. Typically, we would immediately agree that the five have a right of self-defense up to and including killing the aggressor if necessary. But there is a slight problem. The wrongful aggressor has strapped an innocent person to his back. The five have the weapons to destroy the aggressor, but doing so will also destroy the innocent person strapped to the aggressor's back. There are no ways to resolve the situation that will save all the lives at stake: either the five destroy the wrongful aggressor, thereby killing, as an incidental but nevertheless known and foreseen result of their ends, the innocent person strapped to his back; or the five let themselves die at the hands of the aggressor.

How would we judge the five if they destroyed the aggressor? Would we say, "You have used the strapped person as a mere means to your ends," "Your deaths at the hands of the aggressor would have been no worse than your killing the strapped person," "The strapped person had as much right to be spared destruction by you as you had to be spared destruction by the aggressor," "Your ends cannot justify your means," "You and your acts are no better than the aggressor and the acts he attempted," or "The number of lives saved is irrelevant, just another consequentialist trick"?

I hope that we are not so entrapped in general moral sloganism that we would levy such charges. Consider some of the situational nuances such slogans obscure: the reason the strapped person is at risk is due to the wrongful actions of the aggressor who strapped him; the death of the strapped person is incidental to the ends of the five innocents, although they undoubtedly foresaw the death; there are no other available alternatives; each of the five innocents may well have owed stronger moral duties to each other than to any stranger, including the strapped person; the five innocents had an antecedent right of self-defense; the ends of the aggressor were wrong on a number of counts, while the ends of the innocents were righteous; the saving of five innocent lives, other things being equal, is morally preferable to the saving of one innocent life and one wrongful aggressor's life; and so on.

Granted, the example itself is an arid, overly simplified hypothesis with artificially truncated alternatives and is thus far removed from everyday concerns. Moreover, it does not constitute a perfect parallel to situations of war. But it does help illustrate aspects of moral assessment that I suspect are marginalized by Holmes's account.

How might the Argument from Prevention describe these aspects in the context of war? It could point out that nations have special duties to prevent the wanton slaughter of their own people; the retaliatory actions of the nonaggressor nation presumably prevent the loss of a greater number of innocent lives overall; the nonaggressor nation undertakes such action as a last resort, after recognition that there is no less horrible, practical alternative; the nonaggressor nation must minimize the evil involved (including the manner and number of killings); the combatant-killers of that nation must accept reasonable risks and costs to themselves in minimizing that evil; and the knowing and foreseen killings of innocents perpetrated by the nonaggressor nation are incidental to that nation's ends.[60]

A critic might contend that the preservation of the nonaggressor state's particular governmental form is not, on balance, morally worth the destruction that massive retaliation by the nonaggressor nation will produce. But, despite its apparent reliance on a fragile analogy between the justified self-defense of individuals and that of states, the Argument from Prevention need not be directly concerned with preserving the specific political structures or government of the nonaggressor nation. That is, the underlying justification for retaliation, preemptive strikes, or third party interventions is not necessarily allegiance to a particular government or state.

Instead, the argument's core concern is to preserve the socially basic rights, including fundamental security and subsistence rights, of the people within nonaggressor nations. Such people form a political community based on their shared history, communal sentiments, and established social conventions. The political community, in turn, is a sphere of activity that can, under reasonably decent circumstances, facilitate individual fulfillment. If the specific political structures of the nonaggressor nation provide, in morally acceptable ways, political and civil liberties to the relevant communities, then they are worth preserving. But the paramount concern of the Argument from Prevention remains the preservation of the socially basic rights of the people who form the political community that defines the nonaggressor nation. Thus, the people within the nonaggressor nation need not surrender their political community merely because an aggressor nation has threatened or has undertaken military action against them. Moreover, one of the obligations of the state, the government of the nation, is to defend its people from the wrongful attacks of aggressor states, for the people of the nonaggressor nation have socially basic rights of self-defense.

Again, the Argument from Prevention makes a host of contestable empirical claims and includes numerous indeterminate phrases such as "reasonable risks and costs" and "last resort" that beg for clearer specification. In my judgment, however, it holds its ground forcefully against Holmes's critical attack, although it may still not be sound.

An Alternative to Retaliation?

Following conventional wisdom, I have defended the Argument from Prevention against Holmes's critical attack by relying, in part, on a strikingly pedestrian assumption: that at times a nonaggressor nation has no practical alternative to military retaliation when confronted by an aggressor. Holmes is at his best when he argues forcefully against this assumption.

Specifically, Holmes advocates a form of nonviolent resistance. He begins by softening his previous acceptance of strictly binary reasoning: "Approach disagreements not in the spirit of conviction that you are right and your opponent wrong but rather with an openness to the possibility that each of you may have hold of a part of the truth, and that only be taking seriously that possibility are either of you likely to make progress toward a completer truth."[61] We must also abandon our convictions that human nature is inherently corrupt and that war is thus inevitable.[62] Moreover, and most important, we must efface our commitment to the social institutions inextricably intertwined with the military values that preclude peaceful resolution of international disputes. To accomplish these goals requires nothing less than societal transformation.

We need to make peace education a priority; to make development of alternatives to violence a priority; to begin to take seriously the values we profess to cherish . . . economies need to be converted to peaceful ends. This would have to be gradual, and in a country like the United States would require the cooperation of government, industry, unions, and local communities. But there is no reason it cannot be done.[63]

Holmes recognizes that many people will warmly embrace nonviolence as an inspiring ideal but still insist that while "it would be fine if everyone renounced war in one grand gesture, the consequences could be grievous if only some do while others do not."[64] He is, however, unmoved by such observations. He distinguishes "$power_1$" as "ability to achieve one's ends" from "$power_2$," as "capacity to cause destruction." After registering his firm conviction that the ever increasing $power_2$ of the United States has not produced a commensurate $power_1$, he advocates nonviolent strategies of self-defense as a way of diffusing the $power_1$ of potential invaders:

Consider a population of 240 million persons committed to nonviolent resistance against an invading army bent upon ruling the country. A large industrialized society like ours cannot be run . . . without the cooperation of the population . . . Deny to an invading army that support—as one can through passive resistance, strikes, boycotts, civil disobedience, and other nonviolent techniques—and you render it virtually incapable of attaining its objectives.[65]

Moreover, nonviolent self-defense includes deep consideration for the invading soldiers as a way of unsettling their probable conviction that the nonaggressor nation deserves to be repressed: "A people committed to nonviolence may be deprived of their government, their liberties, their material wealth, even their lives. But they cannot be conquered."[66]

For Holmes, nonviolence must be a way of life rather than fashionable garb donned for special occasions: "To live nonviolently and to encourage others to do the same *is* the end, and the question is not whether nonviolence is effective . . . but whether this or that person or society is successful at living nonviolently."[67] Holmes acknowledges that all this end requires concerted action by large numbers of people but points out that the same can be said for war. Moreover, he cautions us not to compare "nonviolence with some ideal of conflict resolution in an ideal world but with our present methods in the actual world. And our present methods have brought us to the brink of disaster."[68]

Reiterating his disbelief in the inherent corruption of human nature, Holmes insists that

> the problem is with the misdirection of loyalties, with too much rather than too little willingness to sacrifice at the behest of others . . . the horrors nations perpetuate . . . [flow from] the dedication of functionaries who serve [the Hitlers of the world] and of the millions of ordinary persons like ourselves whose cooperation is essential to the success of their enterprises . . . What is needed is a new perspective that sees the people of the world as arrayed, not basically against one another, but against the deceit, ignorance, and arrogance of governments and the ways of thinking that have produced them.[69]

In sum, Holmes concludes that with the proper societal transformation and restructuring of common sense, we can come to see nonviolent resistance as part of an entire way of life far preferable, both day-to-day and as a response to aggression, to our current acceptance of violence as inevitable. Moreover, once nonviolent means of defense and the collective mindset needed to sustain them are in place, unilateral disarmament is reasonable.

My first reaction to this is ambivalence: deep admiration for the sheer audacity of Holmes's argument coalesces uneasily with sad recognition of the radical, and thus improbable, alterations in social meanings that its realization demands.

First, one might wonder why nonviolent resistance after a nation has been successfully invaded is incompatible with prior military retaliation. That is, why cannot a nonaggressor nation defend itself first militarily but then, if unsuccessful, fall back on nonviolent resistance—the complete lack of cooperation Holmes urges—once the aggressor nation has assumed control? One might see this strategy as a nonaggressor nation's attempt to maximize its opportunities to prevail. Holmes might respond that the incompatibility of violent and nonviolent tactics emanates from the radically conflicting sets of motivations, emotions, and arguments required to establish and sustain them. Thus, we cannot oscillate expediently between strategies of convenience: we either embrace the underlying consciousness of violence or that of nonviolence. Such a response is plausible, but it is far from obvious that once the proper distinctions have been made, ones that could morally and prudentially determine when violent and nonviolent responses are best, a nation could not maximize its opportunities in the fashion suggested.

Second, nonviolent resistance offers no barriers to an aggressor's wrongful military advance. Although it does constitute a strategy of noncooperation once the aggressor has arrived and, if applied relentlessly, does encourage an unconquerable mental toughness, it nevertheless may result, as Holmes admits, in the deprivation of the pacifists' "government, liberties, material wealth, and lives." But what does "unconquered" mean here? Refused to cooperate and admit defeat? Resisted giving allegiance to the invaders? Denied the aggressors certain fruits of victory? Retained nonviolent consciousness and ideological integrity? It is not unreasonable to reply, "Well, great, you did not 'cry Uncle' and bend your knee in supplication to the aggressor. But you have lost your government, liberties, material wealth, and many lives of your citizens. Given that such factors are partly constitutive of selves, you have been, in a real sense, spiritually transformed even if you have clung steadfastly to the principles of pacifism."[70] Thus, the view that "it would be fine if everyone renounced war in one grand gesture, the consequences could be grievous if only some do while others do not" apparently retains some vitality.

Third, the success of nonviolent resistance depends upon the good will of enemy soldiers, their capacity to sympathize with their captives and transform their own purposes.[71] Where the aggressor is deeply committed to its ends, perhaps reinforced by convictions that its purposes are divinely inspired or decreed by an order immanent in nature, it may resort to an all too common litany of draconian measures that would minimize the possibilities of success for nonviolent resistance.[72] Hence, a cruel turn: Unless we conceive of the power$_1$ of nonviolent resisters as defined fully by their continuing commitment to nonviolence as such, determined, evil aggressors still have major control over that power$_1$.

Fourth, if the success of nonviolent resistance is largely dependent on the moral convictions, sensibilities, and reactions of enemy soldiers, then the only practical way to cultivate the preconditions necessary for properly sensitive soldiers may be to produce and teach persuasive analyses of the normative conventions that set the boundaries of permissible behavior in wartime.[73] Holmes, of course, would counter quickly that a better way is to unsettle all preconceptions that war is acceptable under any circumstances, but questions remain about the practicality of such a strategy.

Fifth, the gradual all-encompassing societal transformations Holmes prescribes raise serious problems of transition. Given our starting point—a history that virtually sanctifies our military might; an economy based significantly on military production; media that have traditionally glamorized the force of cowboys in white hats, bend-the-rules policemen, righteous vigilantes, avenging superheros, and powerful athletes; our often justified mistrust of other nations; and an international community that is clearly not committed to principles of nonviolence—how do we attain a deep national commitment to nonviolence as a way of life? As Holmes well understands, this process is nothing short of a reimagination and reinvention of national character, and the entrenched institutional pressures legitimating the social and political status quo are numerous and mighty.

Moreover, even if massive numbers of citizens win others to their cause and the transition begins, what concomitant losses in national identity will we thereby suffer? It is easy to conjure a slobbering, war-mongering, violence-glorifying United States, a sort of serial killer writ large. But such a caricature conceals the positive aspects and other social contributions that may possibly accompany our commitment to forceful retaliation. These must at least be explored, psychologically and sociologically.

Accordingly, the problems of transition, which arise independently of the four earlier objections, can be summarized: How do we win enough societal assent to even establish a commitment to nonviolent transformation? Presupposing a commitment to do so, how do we make the transition? What, if anything, do we lose in the process?

Philosophy and Pedantry

Having raised these objections, however, I am struck by their crushing banality. Holmes would undoubtedly regard my objections as the reflex bleatings of conventional wisdom, lunacy leavened by cynicism. Rather than celebrating the tedious, degrading rhythms of history, he aspires to resuscitate the power$_1$ of nonviolence as a way of life. In short, he is acutely aware that he counsels nothing short of a societal (nonviolent) revolution and that he, like all other revolutionaries, is subject to charges of utopianism, impracticality, and vulgar idealism.

But surely he is correct in underscoring the poverty of the historically driven international military approach, especially in the age of nuclear armaments; in highlighting the massive, not merely few, numbers of innocent persons who perish during wartime; and in insisting that under such circumstances alternatives must be conceived and pondered. The Argument from Prevention, although embodying the apologetics of conventional wisdom, averts its gaze from even the possibility of nonmilitary alternatives. Indeed, its continued robustness depends on such a strategy. Accordingly, Holmes's paeans to nonviolent resistance, if nothing else, are challenging antidotes to unwarranted confidence in the conclusions of that argument.

It is unlikely, however, that massive social transformation will ensue from philosophical pedantry. Readers should by now be struck by the limitations of conceptual analysis in resolving the paramount issues at bar. Whether brandished by Holmes or by me, the favorite toys of analytic philosophy camouflage at least as much as they expose, obfuscate as much as they clarify. The dangers of reductionism, abstractness, absolutism, and infatuation with strictly binary alternatives imprison as much as empower analytic philosophers. Logic crunching, conceptual manipulation, and grand philosophical theory are unlikely to resolve adequately the dispute between advocates of the Argument from Prevention and Holmes. The crucial areas of disagreement turn more on empirical examinations and practical considerations, on understandings of social possibilities that are more likely to be chronicled than to be created by analytical scrutiny.

INDIVIDUALISM AND COMMUNITY

Garibaldi would have been baffled, perhaps even insulted, by serious appeals for passive resistance. Living in a world of emerging nation-states and incessant warfare, he would have interpreted pacifism as hopelessly unrealistic. Given the need for the unification of the disparate regions of Italy, their history of foreign invasion, and their legacy of cyclical rebellion and resignation, Garibaldi would have spurned pacifist appeals as defeatist, even cowardly.

Holmes, of course, would be quick to distinguish mere passivity from passive resistance. The latter involves concerted social effort that requires enormous determination, extraordinary mental toughness, and profound bravery. Moreover, there is a tremendous difference between the militarism Garibaldi experienced—one thousand redshirted guerillas forcing the capitulation of a regional government – and modern warfare with its potential for global nuclear destruction. Given the magnified horrors of modern conditions of war, Holmes would insist that passive resistance merits serious attention.

Successful passive resistance requires vital social organizations and unity unknown in Garibaldi's Italy, where the historical prerequisites of such organization and unity were lacking. Even though most modern thinkers would probably harbor deep skepticism of the possibility of successful passive resistance, the possibilities were even dimmer in Garibaldi's Italy. Where, as in the nineteenth-century *Mezzogiorno*, individuals are connected closely to their families and families are distanced from society, there are few, if any, robust social organizations capable of nourishing the concerted program demanded by passive resistance.

In fact, Garibaldi's military success and subsequent adulation by the masses tie in nicely with recurrent social themes of the nineteenth-century *Mezzogiorno:* the heroic, romantic actions of closely knit guerrillas righteously retaliating against larger, semiorganized military forces can be viewed as the vindication of the family writ large.

On a more general level, the interconnections of the chapters of this book become clearer: the ways individuals relate to their families, families relate to society, and society relates to the nation-state affect greatly the possible ways the nation-state can realistically confront the world. Under the extreme conditions of the nineteenth-century *Mezzogiorno* – where individuals identified closely with their families, families distanced themselves from society, and society was fragmented – the call for passive resistance to military invasion rings hollow.

In questions of the philosophy of war, the individual confronts several different, often conflicting communities. She faces the intimate aspirations of family; the stirring, history-laden, patriotic demands of country; and the more distant claims of the international order. Clearly, the individual – community continuum expands in several dimensions. In fact, only in the simplest cases is it ever merely one-dimensional. War multiplies the tensions, exhilarations, fears, and hopes invariably embodied by the continuum. Personal decisions that involve multiple dimensions of the continuum therefore require appreciation of particular context and the fine details of moral situation even more than usual.

Military conquest, especially when plausibly evaluated as the victory of the morally righteous over an irredeemably evil aggressor, vivifies a nation. It presents opportunities for expression of the deepest human emotions and, indeed, demands their revelation: unspeakable sadness and grief as loved ones perish; justified rage and vows of vengeance at the acts of the aggressor; undeniable experiences of making history as one participates courageously in a grand epic; intense spasms of self-esteem as precarious occasions to prove oneself to self and intimates are encountered and surpassed; and soul-searing intimacy as collective efforts at rebuilding national infrastructure transform the world, as in one's youth, into a forum of seemingly infinite possibilities.

Of course, military defeat produces our deepest feelings of shame: a lingering sense of historical impoverishment; convictions of inferiority, betrayal, and divine abandonment; a profound understanding of failure. The world becomes, as in death, a place without hope, pity, or compassion.

No wonder that so many people who have encountered large-scale war describe the event as their defining moment, the period when they felt most alive. Much was at risk. Apathy and collective narcolepsy were impossible. Prostrate, complacent faithlessness was not an available option.

My point is only to understand that as the postmodern cultural smog descends upon us—as we mimic Sysiphus in our routinized life of technical adjustments, as lived experiences are replaced by ersatz images and representations, as the pleasures of manual labor and of the body are increasingly enjoyed vicariously, as the commodification of the world intensifies—our sense of wonder and of possibility, our opportunities for intense human emotion, our very humanness are in jeopardy.

Under such circumstances, the pathology of war, as the struggle for feeling writ large, is a pathetic reminder of our historical condition. Accordingly, the ultimate success of nonviolent resistance and pacifism as a way of life depends on massive numbers of socially organized people understanding them as necessary remedies for postmodern somnambulance and the remorseless savagery of a world eclipsed.

In the terms of this book, in war the individual—community continuum is implicated most fully in all of its dimensions. The price of humanness rises astronomically. We understand viscerally, not merely rationally, the radical indeterminacy of life: the dread of cosmic exile and the longing for infinite redemption.

CHAPTER 5

THE SELF CONFRONTS ETHNICITY

Membership, Community, and Columbus

On October 15, 1992, I presented "Columbus and the Italian Americans" at a *Conversations across the Faculty* forum held at SUNY Fredonia to mark the five-hundreth anniversary of Columbus's landing in the Americas. At the end of my presentation, after the obligatory polite applause, the squeals of a thin, high-pitched voice resounded in the four-hundred-seat theater. My son, Angelo, who was then four years old, had jumped out of his seat and yelled, "That's my Daddy!" It was the proudest moment of my life.

I begin by recalling my presentation, which inspired my son in 1992, of Christopher Columbus as an Italian-American ethnic symbol. I then discuss ethnicity generally and provide the most current, reliable statistical analyses of Italian-American attitudes, behaviors, and ideology. Next I advance a normative ideal of ethnicity, an ideal in which group pride and solidarity do not degenerate into prejudice, in which a groups' past is honored but not sanctified as necessarily definitive of its future, in which a group celebrates its historical legacy without forsaking allegiance to its present homeland. Finally, I issue concluding remarks about the individual-community continuum.

COLUMBUS AND THE ITALIAN AMERICANS

When I was a child I sometimes sought counsel from my maternal grandfather. My grandfather was an immigrant without formal education who worked as a laborer. He never spoke or understood English. He could not read or write Italian or even his native Sicilian dialect. He was, one might say, illiterate in several cultures. Nevertheless, he appreciated my curiosity and pronounced naiveté, at least usually.

One day, in self-righteous outrage, I approached my grandfather and chronicled a series of complaints against Anglo-American historians. With my mother acting as translator, I said: "Grandpa, look at what happened to all the great Italian navigators. Cristoforo Columbo became 'Christopher Columbus.' Giovanni Caboto became 'John Cabot.' Sebastiano Caboto became 'Sebastian Cabot.' The Anglo-American historians turned all these guys into English butlers! For crying out loud, 'Sebastian Cabot'!"

My grandfather merely shrugged his shoulders and permitted a wry grin to grace his face. Instinctively, I knew that he regarded such indignities as beneath serious consideration and my outrage as wastefully misplaced. He, engaged in a daily, brutal struggle to survive, was immune to visionary appeals to "be all he could be." Only his Americani grandchildren, with their increased expectations of life's prospects, could think the surnames of historical figures worthy of such passion.

Then a cousin pointed out that I had ignored a few counterexamples. What about Amerigo Vespucci and Giovanni di Verranzano? The Anglo-American historians did not alter their names. What could account for this? At this point, my grandfather shook his head slowly. He was obviously saddened that his grandchildren were too dense to understand simple reality. Distressed, he nevertheless provided in stentorian tones the obvious answer: "Vespucci and Verranzano must have paid off the right people." For he knew only too well that in the New World, the rights and dignity of his people were always hostage to the demands of those entrenched groups holding social and political power. He knew it and he accepted it without rancor and without hope for change.

I write not to glorify Christopher Columbus, not to minimize the negative effects of his voyage on the indigenous population of the Americas, and not to impugn those who participate in anti-Columbus commemorations. But neither do I write in abject contrition for the numerous celebrations of the five-hundred-year harvest that followed Columbus's voyages. In fact, I will not address Columbus as a *historical* figure at all. Instead, I will approach only a small piece of the mosaic of Columbus's legacy: the symbolic function he serves for many Italian Americans. Unquestionably, Columbus symbolizes much for Italian Americans, and what he represents transcends by far his specific historical deeds.

The great wave of Italian immigration to the Americas occurred from the 1870s through the 1930s. The vast majority of these immigrants originated from southern Italy and Sicily. These typically uneducated and impoverished people did not arrive in the Americas with Columbus in their hearts and paeans of praise to him on their lips. Columbus was, after all, a native of Genoa, and to the disenfranchised sons and daughters of the *Mezzogiorno*, Genoa seemed as far away from their native villages as Singapore. Italy had only become a unified nation in the 1860s, and the new republic had lavished few benefits on the traditionally oppressed southern Italians and Sicilians. Accordingly, celebrations of various patron saints, especially those linked for generations with specific villages, held highest priority. Appeals from the new immigrants for the benedictions of Columbus were few and muted.

But this situation was soon to change. Upon arriving in the United States, the Italians and Sicilians were to suffer the familiar range of physical terrors and assaults on the soul that greet new immigrant groups. They learned quickly that the streets were not paved with gold and that their lives would not soon improve radically. Italian immigrants in the South and as far west as Colorado were lynched by the KKK and other white supremacy groups, along with African Americans and Jewish Americans, through the 1920s. The most notorious of these lynchings involved eleven Italian immigrants and occurred in New Orleans in 1891. The news of such brutality spread to all Italian-American communities in the United States. The New World had sent its message, and its meaning was clear.

Denied a sense of secure attachment to their newly chosen land, many Italian immigrants yearned for the day when they could accumulate enough money to return as aristocracy to their native villages. But this longing, too, would soon be recognized as an unrealistic dream. My maternal grandparents, for example, trying desperately to supplement my grandfather's wages as a laborer, engaged in small-scale production and sale of alcohol during Prohibition days. My grandmother forwarded all profits to a secret bank account in her native village in Sicily, where they hoped soon to return triumphantly. The master plan was foiled, however, when Mussolini rose to power and confiscated numerous accounts held by "foreigners." My grandparents' hopes of returning to Sicily and their days as outlaws ended in feckless disillusionment. Crime did not pay, at least this time.

No longer connected intimately with their birthplaces, nor yet accepted fully in the New World, the new immigrants lacked the credential of membership: a sense of belonging. Men and women without full and effective membership anywhere are stateless persons. Statelessness is a condition of infinite danger because it precludes a person from a guaranteed place in the collectivity and constantly subjects that person to fears of involuntary expulsion. Even where statelessness is not one's condition by law, even where one is permitted to apply for citizenship and naturalization, conditions of life can facilitate a de facto statelessness, an alienation of the spirit.

Under such conditions, the southern Italian and Sicilian immigrants begrudgingly put aside their longstanding provincial grievances and joined with one another and with northern Italian immigrants, and began to identify themselves as "Italian Americans." At some point they noticed the decidedly favorable press that the entrenched groups in the United States had bestowed upon Christopher Columbus: "discoverer of the New World," "courageous explorer," "founder of the land of tolerance and hope." Suddenly, at once and forever, Columbus was no longer merely a Genoese but an "Italian." Just like them. What greater claim to membership could they hope to lodge? One of them, an Italian, had "discovered" the very land which they themselves had recently chosen! Better still, there was no need to do all the difficult political work usually necessary to canonize a hero. After all, Columbus was already mythologized by the trusted historians of the Anglo-American world. He had even been honored by the Catholic Church, with its dominant Irish-American power structure, when in the 1880s the "Knights of Columbus" were formed. All that was needed was marginal adjustment, a little additional reinforcement: "In 1492, Columbus *the Italian* sailed that ocean blue."

The fine tuning of Columbus as symbol continued with political movements to declare a national holiday in his honor, complete with extravaganzas and parades. As early as the 1870s, Italian-American societies staged Columbus Day celebrations. In 1882 President Harrison declared October 12 a general holiday in commemoration of the four-hundredth anniversary of Columbus's voyage. By 1909 several states formally recognized Columbus Day as an annual holiday. In 1937 President Franklin Roosevelt issued a proclamation designating October 12 as Columbus Day. In 1968 that proclamation was extended to make October 12 a federal legal holiday.[1] Columbus Day became the Italian equivalent to the Irish St. Patrick's Day, without the green beer.

Columbus was now the most powerful symbol of security and badge of membership that an Italian American could wield. For example, when Mussolini, a dictator who was once praised highly by the media of the United States, declared war on France in 1940, anti-Italian sentiment in this country exploded. One way Italian Americans counteracted this venom was to change the names of many of their social clubs to "Columbus Clubs." The great navigator was the ultimate ethnic trump card.

I've sketched the past of Columbus as ethnic symbol, but what about the present? Italian Americans now find mixed blessings. Third- and fourth-generation Italian Americans rarely encounter the same social prohibitions that hindered their parents and grandparents: for decades no Italian American has been lynched simply because of his or her ethnicity; intermarriage is not only common but usual; there are no more signs that sneer, "Workers Wanted: White Men $1.50 per day, Niggers $1.40, Dagos $1.25." Yet insidious stereotypes of Italian Americans pervade the media, mirroring and legitimating much of the subtle prejudice Italian Americans still endure, especially first-, second-, and third-generation Italian Americans and those who have remained in their traditional urban ethnic sanctuaries. Today, those who identify themselves as Italian Americans occupy an eerie limbo: not oppressed explicitly enough to enjoy protected legal status, yet not so firmly entrenched as to constitute part of the power elite.

Worse, Italian Americans have been submerged in the cruel, overly broad category of "white Europeans," a category which eviscerates their particularity and renders their special grievances invisible. Italian Americans are given the shroud but not the substance of privilege. Apologists for this categorization peculiarly seek justification by referring to the existence of other grossly distorting categories. The effects are mighty and clear.

Columbus therefore remains our symbol of belonging, our badge of membership. Italian Americans do not know any more about Columbus, the *historical* figure, than other groups. But when references are made to Lief Erickson's voyage to the Americas, an alleged journey that occurred much earlier than 1492, some Italian Americans react defensively because they know instinctively that much more is at stake than who was the first "white European" to set foot here. When revisionists, often well-motivated by a concern for historical balance or for the untold stories of the indigenous population of the Americas, deride Columbus's legacy, Italian Americans sometimes respond defensively because they sense that their own status remains hostage to the social and political exigencies of the moment.

In any event, the Genoese navigator who had so little in common with the first wave of Italian immigrants to this country became, by dint of circumstances and desperation, a figure of paramount importance to them and their children. Accordingly, the present symbolic value of Columbus remains high for Italian Americans. We cannot relinquish that value easily. Don't expect it. And certainly don't demand it in service of a politically expedient agenda.

What about the future? Will new symbols emerge to diminish the need for Columbus? Will Italian Americans truly enter the privileged class, as other racial groups and newly arriving immigrants continue to suffer? Will the intermarriage rate of Italian Americans by itself obscure cultural identity? Will a balanced historical view of the legacy of 1492 eventually place Columbus in diminished favor? Is ethnic assimilation the price of full membership?

The answers to such questions require, among other things, an understanding and examination of the nature and functions of ethnicity.

ETHNICITY

There are numerous models of "ethnicity" in scholarly literature.[2] A *relational* model describes ethnicity not on the basis of the shared cultural properties of a group but as an aspect of intermural group relationships. Thus, ethnicity is the communication of difference by a group that perceives itself and is perceived by others as culturally distinct from members of other groups. The perception of difference is magnified by relatively limited personal contacts with non–group members. A *shared culture* model describes ethnicity on the basis of a group's common cultural properties: religion, customs, language, ideology of shared ancestry, biological self-perpetuation, values, kinship, cuisine, geographical locale, and so on. An *epistemic* model describes ethnicity on the basis of a group's subjective beliefs in its common descent because of similarities of physical type or of customs, or because of shared experiences and memories of colonization and migration. Members of the group recognize a boundary that, at least partially, delineates their identity: they participate in a consciousness of likeness.

Ethnicity, then, is not an univocal, brute fact of existence that unambiguously distinguishes different peoples. Ethnic groups are relationally located in social arenas and defined internally by specific understandings. They often emerge most vividly when perceived group interests are at stake. It is therefore probably best to view ethnicity not as a static characteristic but as a relational variable that overlaps with a host of other social phenomena and dimensions constitutive of personal identity: economics, nationality, class, gender, and social position. Accordingly, ethnicity is understood not as a fixed ontological category but as a social construction that often represents a search for identity and meaning in response to external socioeconomic circumstances. Individuals can amplify, downplay, or ignore their ethnicity in strategic response to various social situations.

It is a mistake to discount the public relations aspect of ethnicity: the extent to which people believe in, internalize, and extol ethnicity as a brute fact of biology or an undeniable mark of nature itself has significant effects on how groups experience ethnic identity. Such convictions translate into various behaviors that in turn modify social understandings.

Accordingly, ethnicity is neither merely a freely chosen social construction nor merely a fact of ancestry. Ethnic choice is constrained in at least two ways. First, external socioeconomic circumstances often circumscribe the range of ethnic possibility. Second, as heirs to the legacies of our forebearers, we arrive in the world endowed with cultural liabilities, vulnerabilities, entitlements, and expectations. Yet individuals, especially those who are descendants of immigrants, retain a significant degree of freedom to retain, ignore, or remake their ethnic contexts. Ethnicity emerges, as do most social constructions, as a unique combination of inherited constraints and cultural reinvention. Therefore, the ethnically based moral requirements generated by noncontractual partialism (see Chapter 1) can gradually fade away as the self is re-created.

I have no interest in arguing for a particular version of "ethnicity" nor will I attempt to define the term further. Whether ethnicity is based on the objective relations among groups, the subjective beliefs of various collectivities, or shared cultural traits,[3] it is clear that bounded differences, uniquely shared experiences, and distinctively common consciousness are germane to ethnic investigations. To imagine a world without such differences and particularities among humans is to conjure a nonethnic universe. Such a world might be better in some respects—it might better replicate the philosophers' fantasy of impartial, undifferentiated human concern—and perhaps worse in other respects—humans would approach a homogenized ideal that undermines specialness and serendipity—but it would not be our present world.

Who Are We?

→Although negative and positive myths, projections, images, and stereotypes of Italian Americans abound, there has been relatively little attention to empirical research of Italian-American group attitudes, attributes, and lifestyles.[4] Part of the problem is the self-perpetuating nature of myths and stereotypes: they are a comfortable shorthand to identify and imagine groups. Another part of the problem, however, is the dearth of current, comprehensive research on Italian Americans.

By 1991 Italian Americans constituted the sixth largest ethnic group in this country, behind Germans, British, African Americans, Irish, and Hispanics. If Hispanics are separated into their individual nationalities (e.g., Mexican, Cuban, Puerto Rican, and so on) then Italian Americans are the fifth largest ethnic group in this country.[5]

The National Opinion Research Center at the University of Chicago has conducted the most thorough and reliable empirical studies of Italian Americans over the past twenty years (see Appendix, p. 186).[6] The findings assess Italian Americans in relation to fourteen other ethnic, racial, and religious groups in the United States: Asian, British, African American, Eastern European, French, German, Hispanic, Irish, Jewish, Native American, Other whites, Others (nonwhite and non–African American), Polish, and Scandinavian.

Socioeconomic Indicators. Comparing Italian Americans to the other fourteen groups reveals that they slightly exceed the national average on education and occupational prestige and rank sixth in terms of average family income.

The Nature of the Family. Italian Americans are raised in more stable families, mainly because of relatively fewer deaths, involuntary separations, and divorces.[7] Italian Americans have the second lowest birth rate among all groups despite having a typical attitude toward ideal number of children. Clearly, one prevalent image of Italian American families as composed of clusters of children is not empirically confirmed.

Moreover, of all currently married Italian Americans only 33 percent have an Italian-American spouse, a percentage that is nevertheless above the national average of group intramarriage, 26 percent. However, of those Italian Americans born since 1940 only around 20 percent have an Italian-American spouse.[8]

Social Interactions. Italian Americans differ little from national averages: they do rank higher than average, fifth among all groups, in spending a social evening with friends or with parents. Most strikingly, they rank first in percentage of members who spend social evenings in a bar and second in percentage of drinkers. Traditionally, Italian Americans have manifested relatively high rates of alcohol use but low rates of drinking problems. Recent trends, however, suggest that problem drinking among Italian Americans has reached or slightly exceeded national averages.[9]

Politics. The National Opinion Research Center reports the following regarding Italian-American politics:

> In terms of political party identification, presidential vote, and political ideology, Americans in general and Italian Americans in particular, have moved to the right over the last two decades. In the early 1970s only 17 percent [of Italian Americans] were Republicans. This doubled to 35 percent presently. Most of this increase has been at the expense of the Democrats. In the early 1970s, 45 percent of Italian Americans were Democrats, while this has since fallen to 32 percent. Likewise, the identification as Independents also slipped slightly from 36 percent to 33 percent.[10]

In terms of political ideology, Italian Americans have come increasingly to identify themselves as conservatives: "These shifts to the right have brought Italian-Americans to near the very center of the political spectrum, midway between liberal, Democratic groups such as Jews and Blacks and conservative, Republican groups like [sic] British and German-Americans."[11]

Values and attitudes. The picture that emerges varies radically from the firmly established image of Italian Americans as patriarchal, authoritarian, and insular. In fact, for better or worse, Italian Americans are more permissive on sexual matters than other Americans, somewhat more approving of nontraditional roles for women, and less likely to approve corporal punishment for children. Accordingly, "Italian-Americans emerge as moderate liberals. In regards to sexual permissiveness, women's roles, abortion, and most other issues, they are somewhat more progressive than the national average. Typically, they are not far from the middle ground, but always lean to the liberal side."[12]

Paradoxically, over the past twenty or thirty years, as Italian-American social values and attitudes became more liberal and entrenched family restraints loosened, Italian Americans simultaneously became more politically conservative. Such changes, however, may be attributed to other correlates Italian-Americans experienced over this period: increases in education, occupational prestige, and family income.

Psychological well-being. Although the data from 1988 through 1991 report that Italian Americans have a perception of general happiness greater than the national norm, research findings from 1972 through 1987 consistently reported that Italian Americans expressed significantly less general happiness than the correlated national norms.[13] Since 1984 Italian Americans have expressed greater satisfaction with friends than other ethnic groups, currently ranking first among all groups, but they have been less likely than other Americans to report that their lives are exciting, currently ranking next to the bottom among all groups, above only African Americans. Since 1972 Italian Americans have not differed much from the national averages on expressions of satisfaction with their families.

The overall picture that emerges is that "while Italian-Americans do not differ greatly from non–Italian-Americans, their psychological well-being tends to be lower. The one key exception is their high satisfaction with friendships."[14]

Religious attitudes. Although the figures have dropped from 81 percent to 70 percent over the past twenty years, Italian Americans still report the second highest percentage of Roman Catholic affiliation among all groups. Their strength of religious identification and church attendance, however, are well below national norms. Italian Catholics are also somewhat more likely than other Americans to express so-called "progressive and compassionate" images of the supreme being.

The overall picture suggests that Italian Americans are "certainly not more traditionalist, authoritarian, and patriarchal than other Americans in their religious beliefs . . . [they] are neither especially strong nor traditionalist in their faith."[15]

How can we summarize this panoply of data? Tom Smith of the National Opinion Research Center concludes that

> Italian-Americans are distinctive in various ways. As one would have expected, they are much more likely than the average American to be Catholic, live in the Northeast, and reside in metropolitan areas. However, on these traits they have been becoming less different over time. But in other ways their distinctiveness is surprising. On many social, family, and religious attitudes Italian-Americans are moderate liberals, not patriarchs, traditionalists, or conservatives. This shows up in their support for equal treatment of women, sexual tolerance, and other progressive values. They also favor government spending for human services. In particular, Italian-Americans are strong backers of governmental health care programs.[16]

Smith highlights friendship as another distinctive feature of Italian Americans: "[Italian-Americans] are more satisfied with their friends than any other group is, the second most likely to see God as a friend rather than a king, and more likely to socialize with friends than other groups are. More than for other groups, friendships appear to play a vital role in the lives of Italian-Americans."[17]

A superficial reading of the data may lead one to suspect that robust Italian-American ethnicity has vanished. One might note a few interesting, marginal differences between Italian Americans and national norms but conclude that Italian Americans on the whole have assimilated mainstream American norms. Certainly when we examine two cardinal indicators of social position, education and occupation, we see that Italian Americans meet or slightly exceed national norms. Such indicators are important when we assess a group's qualifications for places in the labor market, the extent to which mainstream culture has successfully instilled dominant American values, and correlations with income and wider social prestige.

This obvious interpretation is persuasive, but it may hinder fuller understanding. First, it ignores how ethnic groups not merely internalize dominant norms but also influence them. Second, it obscures class differences. We are never fully identified merely by our ethnicity: socioeconomic class, gender, religion, occupation, generation, and primary leisure-time projects, among other things, also make us who we are. The data I describe here are not broken down by generation, socioeconomic class, and gender. Although they do paint a broad picture of contemporary Italian Americans as a whole, they fail to address numerous questions: What social differences, if any, exist between working-class Italian Americans and professional Italian Americans? Between Italian Americans who are urban dwellers and those who are residents of small towns? Is the only remaining robust Italian-American ethnicity the blue-collar vestiges we see caricatured drearily in the media?[18]

We would expect that Italian-American ethnicity would be more obvious among members of earlier generations, older cohorts, inhabitants of the remaining Little Italies in the northeast, and recent arrivals to the United States. But the foregoing data obscure our full understanding of possible intraethnic differences because they are categorized, understandably, at the highest level of generality.

For example, other research conducted in New York City has highlighted educational difficulties there among Italian-American youth, discrimination in faculty hiring within the City University of New York, and persistent interethnic conflict. An 1985 study conducted by Audrey Blumberg and David Lavin concluded, among other things, that

> Italian-American students in CUNY are younger than other CUNY students, more likely to be single, and more likely to be living with their parents. The educational achievements of Italian-American students' parents are below those of other students, especially in terms of college attendance. Italian-American students also hold lower educational hopes and ambitions for themselves than other CUNY students . . . also more than other CUNY students tend to regard college as vocational training rather than as broader education . . . also tend to work heavily outside of college, and tend to be in two-year colleges rather than four-year colleges in higher percentages than other white students . . . [such patterns] make it more difficult for Italian-American students to be involved in and integrated in the total campus experience enjoyed by many other students.[19]

A study conducted by Professor James Perrone in 1986 concluded that

Italian-American students place a very high value on being responsible, loyal, loving, honest, ambitious, and on true friendship, health, family security, and a comfortable life. They place very low emphasis on such values as an exciting life, a world at peace, a world of beauty, equality, national security, pleasure, religious salvation, social recognition, being forgiving, being imaginative, being logical, and being obedient. They place relatively little emphasis on the value of being intellectual, helpful, broadminded, and self-controlled.[20]

The Perrone study also revealed striking differences between Italian-American females and males. The research concluded that Italian-American females suffered greater stress than Italian-American males and than other males and females in general.

Female Italian-American students perceive themselves much more than other CUNY female students as feeling anxious or uptight, being overweight, feeling lonely, eating too much, wasting money, not being able to relax, having their parents interfering with their decisions, and "having the same thoughts over and over again" . . . the profile shows them to be extremely anxious and very depressed . . . very unhappy.[21]

Other studies conducted during this period on faculty at CUNY concluded, among other things, that "Italian-American faculty in CUNY are an 'endangered species'."[22] This statement came more than ten years after CUNY's chancellor had designated Italian Americans as an affirmative action category for faculty hiring.[23]

I cite this information not to support broad conclusions about the current plight of Italian Americans, nor to invalidate the data I described earlier. Rather, I advance this information to support my view that it is illegitimate to conclude that Italian-American ethnicity is a myth or that Italian Americans have been assimilated almost completely to mainstream culture. At the very least, interethnic conflict in the political scramble for scarce social resources, pockets of discriminatory hiring,[24] aspects of ethnically based anomie and alienation among Italian-American youth, educational difficulties, and media stereotyping persist. Such maladies may well be correlated to other class difficulties in urban settings and as such are perhaps not endured by the majority of Italian Americans in this country, but their tenacity admonishes us to eschew an overly sanguine picture of fully assimilated Italian Americans.

Whither We Goest? Images of Ethnicity

Do Italian Americans have a future as an ethnic group? At least four images of ethnicity recommend themselves as plausible answers: literal resemblance, cultural re-creation, symbolic ethnicity, and requiem for ethnicity. We might measure current Italian-American ethnicity by the *literal resemblance* of the behavior, attitudes, lifestyles, values, and so on of those who currently self-identify as Italian Americans to their first-generation ancestors, the great wave of immigrants who arrived between 1870 and 1930. Judged by this criterion, current Italian-American ethnicity is at best faint. Among other things, few Italian Americans now take seriously the powers of the *malocchio*,[25] the eerie presence of the *jettatore,* the efficacy of direct discourse with the statues of saints, the salutary effects of amulets, the appropriateness of highly ritualized and stratified social classes, and the necessity of tightly controlled dating and mating rituals. Huge gaps and distortions are manifested when we compare the collective consciousness of the first-generation immigrants with the group mindset of their descendants.

The literal resemblance image of ethnicity suffers from two obvious flaws. Specifically, it ignores the massive social and economic transformations that have occurred over the past 120 years in communication, technology, travel, availability of intergroup contact, and so on. It would be both a miracle and social disaster if the third, fourth, and fifth generations of an ethnic group that immigrated to an advanced and evolving culture resembled closely the first generation.[26] Such convergence would clearly make researchers curious about the complete failure of the descendants to transform or to secure any significant access to the dominant culture.

Moreover, the literal resemblance image exhibits a deeper, more general problem: it implicitly assumes that the characteristics of a specific ethnicity can be frozen in time. In the illustration here, for example, the image assumes that the first-generation immigrants embodied the defining essence of Italianism and thus necessarily serve as the measure for all future generations. This assumption, regardless which group or time period it privileges, is inherently arbitrary. Why should we confer upon the 1870 or 1890 or 1910 group of immigrants the honorific status of defining Italianism? We could just as easily choose earlier or later generations. Why not the inhabitants of Italy in 1700 or 1990 or 1650? Are the current citizens of Italy precise replicas of the Italian citizens of 1870? Not only does the literal resemblance image err by arbitrarily focusing on one generation as the timeless definer of ethnicity, it also aspires to artificially truncate a group's ability to evolve under the pressure of radically changing social circumstances yet remain ethnic. Given 120 years of change in the world and three or more generations of life in the United States, that those who currently self-identify as Italian Americans embody a group consciousness that varies strikingly from the collective consciousness of first generation immigrants is unremarkable and virtually inevitable.[27] More important, the distance between these two collective consciousnesses does not establish the absence of Italian-American ethnicity today.

A second image of ethnicity is *cultural re-creation*. This image accepts what the literal resemblance view denied: ethnicity is evolving and emergent. Thus, even though those who currently identify themselves as Italian-Americans are discernibly and articulably different from their first-generation ancestors, they may still constitute a distinct ethnic group.[28] But what is required for this possibility to be a reality? What must today's Italian Americans demonstrate in order to constitute a distinct ethnic group?

Here we must return to the definitions, the models, of ethnicity: bounded differences, uniquely shared experiences, and distinctively common consciousness are germane to ethnic investigations. For the claim of continued ethnicity to remain plausible, it must be the case that Italian Americans at least continue to manifest some differences from other groups,[29] some degree of felt solidarity with other Italian Americans, and some measurable degree of continuity with earlier generations. The continuity requirement may appear to renege on the force of my earlier critique of the literal resemblance image. The continuity requirement and the earlier critique, however, are consistent because here "continuity" does not imply "literal resemblance." The continuity requirement is fulfilled when we can discern and articulate a chain of transformation that links current Italian-American collective behavior, values, attitudes, and so on with the collective consciousness of the first generations. Accordingly, current Italian-American traits need not literally resemble the attributes of forebearers, they may instead be group cultural re-creations that respond to and affect changing social contexts.[30]

To accept the cultural re-creation image on the conceptual level, however, is not to determine whether a robust Italian-American ethnicity persists today. This determination requires empirical examination of a number of questions:

What, if anything, remains of common language, common culture, common psychology, common history, and common morality? Is there a distinctive Italian-American ethnic identity that sums up the group's history, its social structure, and the tone of its emotional relations? In short, are there group characteristics or familial patterns that solidify Italian Americans and distinguish them from other social groups? I confronted such questions earlier in this essay.

A third image is *symbolic ethnicity*. Here we find ethnicity not woven inextricably into everyday life, but experienced recreationally by conscious, intermittent choice. Whereas the cultural re-creation image embodied a transformed ethnicity still deeply constitutive of self, the symbolic ethnicity image emphasizes the general assimilation or indistinguishability of a group previously understood as robustly ethnic, but it also recognizes that many of the group's members may still dust off their ethnicity on special, voluntarily chosen occasions. The contrast between the two images is clear: the former describes ethnicity as a mostly unchosen part of personal identity that manifests itself daily and automatically, whereas the latter portrays a diluted ethnicity only marginally constitutive of self that reveals itself sporadically and volitionally.[31]

Symbolic ethnicity, if invoked infrequently and inconsistently, is thus more of a hobby that one can relinquish easily. The events that occasion symbolic ethnicity for Italian Americans are myriad: visits to an urban "Little Italy," participation in Columbus Day commemorations, genealogical research, special heirlooms or household objects that trigger reminiscences of family and the immigrant legacy, attendance at Italian feasts or traditional meals, sense of shared cultural inheritance with other Italian Americans, enrolling in a course in Italian-American history, wearing historically significant amulets, such as the *cornu*, but with transformed meaning.[32]

Because symbolic ethnicity can be turned on and off at will, it need not threaten nonmembers of the group and is thus almost always safe: a form of ethnicity that neither unsettles nor demands much of the self. The self's psychological and emotional investment in such ethnicity is always sheltered and dominated by wider everyday commitments, practices, and social roles. Accordingly, symbolic ethnicity can be understood as a compromise. The dominant culture and extant economic conditions socialize group members away from subcultural features that translated to felt differences, yet the group maintains a sense of its unique history and special origins.

A robust ethnicity includes several dimensions: *ethnic ancestry,* beliefs about the origins of one's ancestors; *subjective acceptance,* one's self-identification as an ethnic; *ethnic behavior,* experiential expressions of identity; and *salience,* the felt intensity and associated relevance of ethnic identity and behavior in a variety of social settings. Ethnic ancestry unaccompanied by subjective acceptance of ethnicity and salient ethnic behavior is empty. Ethnic ancestry and subjective acceptance of ethnicity without salient ethnic behavior is an effete form of symbolic ethnicity that lacks cultural content. Ethnic behavior unaccompanied by subjective acceptance of ethnicity is experienced as cultural limitation, even self-hate. It should be clear that ethnicity is not simply a brute fact of one's being; it also implicates individuals' choices made from the background of social influences and inherited constraints.[33]

The fourth image, however, spells a *requiem for ethnicity.* That is, it points out from an empirical vantage point that Italian Americans can no longer be plausibly described as a distinct ethnic group. This conclusion is drawn from one or more of the following observations: contemporary Italian Americans as a group manifest little, if any, literal resemblance to their immigrant forebears; Italian Americans exhibit few, if any, discernible cultural differences when compared to other groups; Italian Americans, at least those from the third generation and beyond, have little or no connection to the main transmitters of distinctive culture: Italian language, regional dialects, and first-generation immigrants; Italian Americans suffer no legal discrimination and have moved comfortably along the economic, educational, and occupational indices; the much heralded Italian-American family now resembles contemporary middle-class American families much more closely than it mirrors traditional families in the *Mezzogiorno;* the sheer facts of American birth, American education and socialization, increased geographical mobility, and a high intermarriage rate destroy prospects for continued Italian-American ethnicity.

The requiem-for-ethnicity position compels us to review and amplify certain social facts: of Italian Americans born since 1940 only 20 percent have Italian-American spouses; Italian Americans have the second lowest birth rate among the ethnic, racial, and religious groups studied in 1988 to 1991; from 1980 to 1990 Italian language speakers in the United States, although still ranking fourth among numbers of foreign language speakers in the country, decreased by 324,000, the greatest proportional decline of any foreign language in the United States;[34] Italian Americans now reflect national norms in years of schooling and in occupational prestige, while slightly exceeding the national norm in family income; as generations pass and Italian immigration to the United States dwindles, fewer and fewer Italian-American children grow up within living memory of the immigrant experience. A strong case can thus be made that Italian-American identity will soon disappear, if it has not already.

Nevertheless, numerous countervailing trends persist. First, as Italian-American education levels rise, so too do the number of faculty who might serve as public disseminators of Italian-American cultural legacy.[35] But will they so serve? Even if willing, can they find or create an eager audience among the young? Second, especially in large urban centers, group affiliations, some of them ethnic, generate political currency. In an atmosphere of scarce social resources, individuals without the moral and strategic support of group solidarity stand at a distinct disadvantage when pressing their claims. Third, ironically, the still prevalent negative stereotyping of Italian Americans[36] by the media can function to bring otherwise disparate Italian Americans together. Fourth, the general American yearning to get in touch with one's roots can be viewed as a reaction to the estrangement and isolation of American individualism. The re-creation of ethnicity or the vigorous practice of symbolic ethnicity serves as an antidote: individuals engage in larger collective projects in which identity is concrete and discernible despite geographical mobility, material progress, and other external changes in social conditions. Fifth, renewed ethnicity can help neutralize two common but self-defeating strategies of coping with our postmodern Western world: the cynical distancing that transcends the particularities of one's past but which is often accompanied by a devastating sense of loss of identity, and the narcissistic consumption that hopelessly strives to preserve a sense of self through material aggrandizement.[37]

In short, ethnicity can offer personal security and a sense of generational continuity as partial remedy for the fragmentation of daily life. Ethnic ideology, sometimes based on myths of familial intimacy and biological uniqueness and fueled by common history, can rekindle sentiments of wholeness and membership that soothe felt ruptures between the individual and mainstream society. Nurturing connections with smaller, more tractable groups mediate tensions between individuals, who feel powerless before the larger collectivity, and mainstream society, which is often perceived as inaccessible and abstract.

In support of such convictions, Susan Kellogg argues that

> Powerful forces at work in American society push people toward somewhat uniform behavior; at the same time, a retained sense of ethnic identity and separateness exists and is celebrated in literature, cinema and the theater, family and community rituals . . . Ethnicity is a symbol of group and family identity and history. Its power and persistence reside in its place in a conscious and unconscious discourse among ethnic group members about the distinctive history of a group, about what constitutes membership in an ethnic group, and about the role of families in sustaining that membership.[38]

Furthermore, there are other general trends, at least in terms of subjective acceptance of ethnicity, to counter the requiem for ethnicity. There have been, for example, increases in radio and television broadcasts in non-English languages, in ethnic studies courses in institutions of higher learning, in the interest of the young in their ethnic backgrounds, as well as a growing social sensitivity to ethnic concerns and a decrease in straightforward appeals for the assimilation of ethnic groups.[39] Moreover, data reveal that higher education levels, increased cosmopolitanism, and interethnic contact, instead of decreasing ethnic identification as conventional wisdom would have it, actually increase the probability of identifying oneself ethnically.[40]

Strikingly, intermarriage makes little difference for the subjective importance attached to ethnicity, and there is no correlation between persons who identify strongly as ethnics and endogamy.[41] Moreover, despite a high level of intermarriage among Italians Americans, one study concluded that "the Italians stand apart [from other major ancestry groups] for the strength of their desires to impart some ethnic identity to their children . . . this degree of concern . . . is largely attributable to the relative strength of ethnic identity in the Italian group and exists despite a high level of intermarriage."[42] In fact, data indicate that Italian Americans are more likely than most other ethnic groups in the United States to identify subjectively as ethnics, to be socially sensitive to ethnicity, and to report intense ethnic experiences.[43]

Still, it would be a mistake to discount the long-range effects of intermarriage on ethnic identity. The children of intermarriages embody an attenuated connection between ethnic identity and ethnic ancestry, are less likely to identify ethnically, and place less importance on ethnic background as such.[44] Moreover, the steady erosion of the geographical basis of ethnicity, in which members of an ethnic group lived, worked, and went to school in the same neighborhoods, decreases opportunities for the salient ethnic behavior that is necessary to transform mere ethnic self-identification into a robust ethnicity.[45]

My main point, however, is that once we liberate ourselves from a naive and suffocating literal resemblance conception of ethnicity, and once we understand the lingering value of ethnicity in a fragmented postmodern world, we must acknowledge possibilities, even needs, for ethnic cultural re-creation and symbolic ethnicity.

I am not in the business of prognostication and I lack clairvoyance, so I will make no attempt to foretell what Italian-American re-creation or level of symbolic ethnicity may develop. I seek only to mute the Muses who insist on chanting a requiem for Italian-American ethnicity. The end of Italian-American ethnicity remains only one among several possibilities for the future.

A NORMATIVE VISION OF ETHNICITY

As a normative vision, my ideal of ethnicity does not purport to describe what ethnicity has been or the conditions group consciousness must fulfill to be properly called an "ethnicity." My ideal is aspirational: to set forth a vision of ethnicity in which group pride and solidarity do not degenerate into prejudice, in which the group's past is honored but not regarded as necessarily definitive of its future, and in which a group celebrates its common legacy without forsaking allegiance to its adopted homeland.

This vision embodies both roots and wings.[46] It acknowledges roots as methodically essential for self-understanding, as necessary for knowing who we are and for savoring our shared genetic and historical legacy. It recognizes wings as prudentially required for ethnic emergence and adaptation to constantly changing social times: we cannot remain self-imprisoned by ancestral boundaries dialectically related to a social context much different from our own.

My normative vision begins with a simple proposition: humans are more similar than different. Burdened with universal basic physiological and psychological needs, confronting a common fate, and struggling against the same daily limitations, humans are strikingly similar regardless of geographical locale, race, religion, ethnicity, socioeconomic class, and political ideology. Accepting this proposition permits us to restrain our tendencies toward group exclusion and mindless assertions of master races or inherent ethnic superiority.

Closely related to this proposition is the slogan "pride not prejudice." The members of a group can walk tall and proudly without forcing members of other groups to stoop. Once we understand that we can celebrate a particular genetic and historical legacy without denigrating the legacy of others, we will perceive the persecution of other groups as demeaning eruptions of unrecognized self-hate and abject ignorance.

A robust ethnicity cannot lose itself in the universal and abstract, however. As I have already argued,[47] excessively universalistic moral theories that demand that we treat equally the desires and satisfactions of all humans degenerate into meaningless formalism. Such theories purchase their universality with unacceptable currency: they plunder individuals of their distinctive metaphysical constituents and thereby eviscerate personhood. Humans have a general moral requirement to preserve and maintain value; constituents of personal identity such as our inherited legacy, including our genetic make-up, family, nation, culture, and traditions, embody value; moral requirements are generated in part by the fact that as the repository of such value I am better placed than others to understand and preserve it simply by being who I am; and as the repository of that value I bear a special responsibility to a particular segment of the shared human heritage. Accordingly, my metaphysical constitution – who I am – has moral implications for what I must do.

I contend that certain moral imperatives do not arise from explicit, discrete volitional acts. Our inherited legacies do not merely partially define the particular people we are, they also represent aspects of the human spirit: limited to context but not confined to any particular one, internally transcendent as we struggle to loosen the boundaries of our finitude with full knowledge that we cannot secure full victory, and that if we could our triumph would destroy us;[48] adaptable to a variety of climatic, economic, and social environments but masters of none. Our group particularity, our ethnicity, is important not only for our own specific self-understanding but as a piece of a general human understanding: as another unique illustration of human possibility, struggle, adaptation, and limitation.

Ethnicity therefore should not be acknowledged sheepishly, reluctantly, or apologetically, but should be celebrated for its epistemic value for general human understanding. People who embody such ethnicity bear unique personal and human value. The past, our unique roots, constitute an irreplaceable link in the ongoing human story. We should honor the positive traditions of our ethnicities as a way of keeping the faith with the special value they represent.

But we must simultaneously beware of ethnic imperialism. I use the phrase to connote the belief that members of a specific ethnic group participate in an unitary essence or must embrace a single ideological perspective. Ethnic imperialism sprouts most frequently from within an ethnic group. It is a form of group-think and group-speak that insists that one is not really, for example, an Italian American unless he or she advocates position X or behaves in fashion Y. The essentialism—the firm conviction that group members share an inextricable nature—that underwrites such imperialism is both practically and theoretically flawed.

First, ethnic imperialism wrongly projects a biological unity that denies the hybridity of life. The southern Italian culture and genetic pool from which most Italian Americans descend embodied and transformed a host of influences: Arab, Greek, Norman, Saracen, Spanish. To presume a peculiar form of race purity is thus poor history and worse biology. Second, ethnic imperialism oddly adopts a version of the literal resemblance image, thereby tacitly and erroneously assuming that a particular ethnicity can be frozen in time once and forever. Third, ethnic imperialism demands a rigid orthodoxy of perspective that rests on the dubious foundation of a uniquely correct (Italian-American) answer to complex social and political questions. Such orthodoxy artificially truncates normative discourse and suffocates the transcendent aspects of human personality. Fourth, ethnic imperialism falsely insists that solidarity implies lack of conflict and presence of accepted dogma. In fact, we are better served by learning how to harness the energies of conflict for common purposes and to liberate ourselves from spuriously imposed dogma. Otherwise, instead of being nourished by roots, we will be shackled by self-imposed chains.

A normative vision of ethnicity presses emergent group possibilities as recognition of the transcendent aspirations of human personality: we cannot permit ourselves to accept one social context as definitive of our essence. Instead, we must simultaneously accept that we are by nature a context-bound species, but that no particular context can rightly define who we are.[49] We must acknowledge the people we are and strive to understand the social contexts we presently inhabit, but we must also reimagine ourselves and remake our contexts: roots and wings, situatedness and transcendence.

This project requires that we minimize self-deception. We should neither fall prey to negative ethnic stereotypes projected by the media nor react to such distortions by desperately creating fulsome group portrayals. Self-understanding, a necessary step toward salutary transformation, requires apprehension of a composite true picture of ourselves: flaws and perfections, embarrassments and glories.

Moreover, the project demands group outreach, particularly concerted efforts that will facilitate social equality. Part of the "walk tall without forcing others to stoop" aspiration is to eliminate interethnic and interracial competitions. We must work together to destroy the zero-sum game mentality: our triumphs necessarily require your defeats. Instead, a robust ethnicity envisions progressive social action that will raise our nation's collective consciousness of the special value and contributions of all ethnic and racial groups. Such action need not be accompanied by the melting-pot mentality that foresees the end of all older ethnicities and the formation of a unified American culture.

Admittedly, concerted action will be difficult in a social climate with increasingly scarce social resources and increasingly greater group demands. Moreover, the presence of paradox should be clear: one of the great sustaining forces for robust ethnicity is that, under present circumstances, group affiliations seem necessary to realize certain political and material benefits, whereas the vigorous group outreach I have sketched seems to aim at the elimination of the power of conflicting ethnic moral and political claims on the larger society. It would seem that group outreach strives to efface one of the very conditions that makes ethnicity necessary. How can a robust ethnicity consistently aspire to undercut a necessary condition for the survival of *any* ethnicity?

Although some tensions between the goal of continued ethnicity and group outreach will remain, we can unravel this paradox to a large extent. First, the persistence of a relative scarcity of social resources, with group demands exceeding national supplies, will ensure the continuation of some of the moral and political power generated by group affiliations. Second, the continuation of robust ethnicity, however, need not depend on the presence of such power: to call the continuation of interethnic rivalry for social goods a necessary condition of robust ethnicity is to overstate the case. Numerous other animating forces sustain ethnic affiliation. Third, a normative vision of ethnicity seeks to transform but not eliminate group affiliation: the call for group outreach aspires to moderate unnecessary intergroup hatreds while retaining elements of distinctiveness.

What, then, does a normative vision of ethnicity demand from its disciples? At a minimum, it compels us to promote vibrant symbolic ethnicity: initiating and participating in group and family events that remember, celebrate, and transmit our cultural legacy. Such events, which I sketched earlier, permit us to keep faith with the past and positively reinforce passions of solidarity. In short, a spirited symbolic ethnicity sustains traditions and cherishes familial continuity, thereby preserving an important aspect of collective human personality and heightening prospects for self-understanding. Ethnic group members specially placed to preserve and transmit these unique cultural legacies, such as those within living memory of the immigrant experience and those enjoying educational advantages, bear extra responsibility here.

Salient ethnic behavior can include such commonplace actions as eating ethnic foods, participating in specific holiday rituals, speaking the mother language or even spicing English speech with mother language words and phrases,[50] teaching children about their ethnic background, practicing relevant ethnic customs and traditions, attending ethnic festivals and celebrations, discussing ethnic background with another person, and feeling a special sense of relationship to someone else because that person shares an ethnic background. Less common but more ethnically intense actions include residing in an ethnic community; producing an ethnic magazine, newsletter, or play; teaching or enrolling in an ethnic studies course; engaging in concerted ethnically based political action; partaking in ethnic religious societies; and participating in ethnic social and cultural clubs.[51]

Ethnic social structures, such as families, neighborhoods, cultural clubs, and political organizations, are necessary to provide ready forums for salient ethnic behavior and thereby to sustain a vital ethnic identity that does not degenerate into weak symbolic ethnicity or mere subjective acceptance of ethnicity.[52]

Moreover, robust symbolic ethnicity requires group solidarity in resisting partial, perniciously negative media portrayals of the group. Such portrayals are partial to the extent that they disproportionately highlight one negative aspect of a group's contribution to the wider culture. When such portrayals become the predominant association the wider public makes with the group, serious distortion occurs that prevents accurate understanding of a group's cultural legacy and for which its perpetrators are morally culpable.

To make the point concretely: in this country, media have overwhelmingly embraced and projected the image of Italian American as gangster.[53] My objection is not that these practices are inherently wrong. I do not claim that media, either through self-policing efforts or through external censorship, should be prevented from projecting the image of Italian-Americans as gangsters. Clearly, some Italian Americans *are* members of organized crime. Given my earlier injunction that self-understanding, a necessary step toward salutary transformation, requires apprehension of who we are, it would be a mistake to outlaw negative images of any ethnic, religious, or racial group. Wrongdoing, however, emerges when such negative images become the predominant, virtually the only, media portrayal of a group, when the negative image becomes, by repetition and unimaginative association, and through the connivance of other socially reinforcing mechanisms, a defining feature of the group. In this fashion, a relatively minor group attribute is shamefully amplified into an essential group characteristic.

How many Italian Americans are members of organized crime? Estimates from federal law enforcement figures tell us that, at most, three or four Italian-Americans out of ten thousand are connected with organized crime.[54] Even factoring in our culture's fascination with violence and lawlessness, it is astounding that an activity engaged in by so few Italian Americans could evolve into such a prevalent media image.

Although Italian Americans should neither desire nor seek to compel the elimination of the Italian-as-gangster from media portrayals, we should insist that other, positive images emerge. Not images reluctantly concocted as appeasement, but images representative of what Italian-American ethnicity has been. It is not only the prevalence of the negative gangster image that inflates its associative effects, but also the absence of a proportionate number of positive images of who Italian Americans are. My objection, then, to the media is that not only do they relentlessly connect gangsterism, which is hardly the exclusive province of any particular group, with Italian Americans, but they rarely conceive Italian Americans on other, positive bases. Inexcusable, dangerous image distortion ensues. Robust symbolic ethnicity demands group solidarity in actively resisting this distortion.

Symbolic ethnicity, then, recognizes certain debts of gratitude and obligations of legacy to those who preceded us, who lived the immigrant experience, who fought to survive and flourish, thus paving the way for our fuller cultural membership. Again, the fulfillment of these requirements does not merely imply benefits for group members but also for collective humanity.

No bright line clearly distinguishes robust symbolic ethnicity from cultural re-creation. Symbolic ethnicity need not be an infrequent, inconsistent set of practices. As one becomes more and more involved in symbolically ethnic action, as such action constitutes and expresses more of one's central aspirations, one draws nearer and nearer to cultural re-creation. Of course, no single person or coterie can singlehandedly transform an entire group and thereby culturally re-create an ethnicity, but vibrant symbolically ethnic action engaged in by large numbers of people does offer precisely such possibilities for group transformation. If the arguments of this book are sound, efforts in these directions may be moral prescriptions and psychological necessities.

Some academic and popular writers, however, assail advocates of ethnicity for being anti-individualistic and for preaching a philosophy of balkanization and fragmentation.[55] Moreover, they contend that the apologists for ethnicity reverse the wisdom of existentialism, which insists that existence precedes essence, birth precedes identity. These writers claim that philosophers of ethnicity, instead, limit themselves by indulging fantasies of predestination. For example, Pete Hamill claims that "[philosophers of ethnicity believe that] American identities . . . are not shaped by will, choice, reason, intelligence, and desire but by membership in groups. They are not individuals but components of categories . . . And such categories . . . are destiny."[56] Finally, critics of ethnicity charge that philosophers of ethnicity ferment social divisiveness. Again, Hamill claims that "our side must be in conflict with their side. It's not enough to be an American; you must despise, attack, diminish, and empty the guts of those millions of other Americans who are not like you."[57]

These are at least three parts to this attack: ethnic philosophers are anti-individualist, they embrace a false notion of predestination, and they aggravate, or least tolerate, harsh social conflict among the various ethnic and racial groups. It would be gravely presumptuous of me to pretend to speak for all ethnic philosophers; I will confine my response to highlighting some of the previous arguments of this book. First, a sound normative ideal of ethnicity is not anti-individualistic. On the contrary, such an ideal aspires to mediate the tensions of the individualism – community continuum. Of course, ethnicity can be suffocating if viewed as the sole constituent of self; thus, ethnic philosophers must always recognize that distance from family and group affiliations is also a requirement of full human development. A robust ethnicity, however, offers a measure of security and stability in a fragmented world that is too large and remote to form a true community. Although it can never eliminate the existential conflicts of the human condition, ethnicity can alleviate feelings of uprootedness, re-create sentiments of wholeness, and nurture understandings of continuity with the past. Ethnicity, at its best, can mend the modern rupture between individual and society.

Second, I have explicitly rejected appeals to predestination, which are based either on embarrassing forms of literal resemblance ethnicity or on the assumption that groups cannot or should not transcend their historical context. The former view is both empirically inaccurate and grounded in an arbitrary starting point that wrongly freezes group convictions and behavior patterns forever. The latter assumption is trapped in false necessity and is untrue to the human need to remake historical contexts. Moreover, "will, choice, reason, intelligence, and desire" are not opposed to "membership in groups." On the contrary, will, choice, reason, intelligence, and desire are prerequisites, especially for the descendants of immigrants, for continued ethnicity. The traditions, convictions, social structures, and cultural celebrations necessary for a robust ethnicity cannot otherwise be sustained. The continued vitality of subjective identification as an ethnic, social sensitivity to ethnicity, and the salience of ethnicity are all largely dependent on will, choice, reason, intelligence, and desire. As an ethnic philosopher, I do not rest my conclusions on fatuous appeals to predestination.

Third, any form of ethnicity based on virulent group conflict or on perceptions of abject victimization reveals itself as malevolent or blind to historical nuance. As described earlier, a normative ideal of ethnicity cannot be grounded in hate of other groups or in the false convictions of a simplistic sociology. Moreover, contrary to Hamill's suggestion that ethnicity prevents us from being truly "American," it may well be true that self-identification as an ethnic has become a distinctive way of claiming to be an American. Thus, Richard Alba writes:

> In a society where racial cleavages remain profound and where ethnicity is revitalized by new, non-European immigrations, there are incentives to retain a specifically ethnic identity . . . ethnic identities have become ways of claiming to be American . . . [they] can be a means of locating oneself and one's family against the panorama of American history, against the backdrop of what it means to be American.[58]

Accordingly, Hamill's parody of ethnicity does not describe the theses of this book. In fact, his understanding of group affiliation is diametrically opposed to the robust ethnicity I advocate.

INDIVIDUALISM AND COMMUNITY

My questions were originally these: Will Columbus have a rosy future as an Italian-American ethnic symbol? Will new ethnic symbols emerge that will diminish the need for Columbus? Will Italian Americans truly enter the privileged class, as other racial groups and newly arriving immigrants continue to suffer? Will the intermarriage rate of Italian Americans by itself obscure cultural identity? Will a balanced historical view of the legacy of 1492 eventually place Columbus in diminished favor? Is ethnic assimilation the price of full membership in the United States?

I conclude that the answers depend on the way individuals, families, ethnic and religious groups, society, and the state negotiate the individualism – community continuum.

APPENDIX

The tables in this section are a compilation of research that was commissioned by the National Italian American Foundation and conducted by Dr. Tom W. Smith of the National Opinion Research Center at the University of Chicago. Italian Americans were surveyed in relation to fourteen other ethnic, racial, or religious populations in the United States over a 20-year span, including Asian Americans, British Americans, African Americans, Eastern European Americans, French Americans, German Americans, Hispanic Americans, Irish Americans, Jewish Americans, Native Americans, "other whites," "other non-white and non – African Americans," Polish Americans, and Scandinavian Americans.

SOCIOECONOMIC INDICATORS

	Italian Americans	*Non – Italian Americans*
Years of schooling	12.9	12.7
Occupational prestige	41.7	41.3
Family income	$32,615	$29,820

FAMILY COMPOSITION

	Italian Americans	*Non – Italian Americans*
Family Configuration		
Both parents present	83.0%	73.5%
Parents divorced	12.4	12.1
Marital Status		
Married	59.0	60.9
Ever divorced/separated	20.9	24.8
Children and Siblings		
Number of children ever had	1.3	2.0
Ideal number of children	2.5	2.5
Number of siblings	3.3	3.9

SOCIAL INTERACTIONS

	Italian Americans	*Non – Italian Americans*
Spending a social evening		
Almost daily with friends	44.6%	41.2%
Often with neighbor	23.3	23.8
Often with relatives	32.7	35.1
Often with parent	27.2	21.1
Often with sibling	17.9	18.9
Sometimes in a bar	54.2	46.6
Drinking Alcohol	80.1	68.3

SOCIAL VALUES AND ATTITUDES

	Italian Americans	Non–Italian Americans
Divorce should be easier to obtain	24.5%	26.6%
Premarital sexual relations are always wrong	15.3	27.4
Extramarital sexual relations are always wrong	74.1	78.4
Homosexual relations are always wrong	63.8	76.2
Legal abortion is acceptable if a woman does not want more children	50.3	43.2
Legal abortion is acceptable if a family cannot afford more children	54.2	46.2
Legal abortion is acceptable if a woman is unmarried and does not want to marry	55.0	43.3
I would vote for a woman for president	89.0	88.6
Women are less emotionally suited for politics than men	24.2	29.4
Women should run their homes, not the country	15.3	19.8
A woman working even if her husband is capable of supporting the family is acceptable	81.6	80.3
Spanking is necessary to discipline a child	66.9	78.1
Obeying parents should be a child's highest value	16.3	20.2
Elderly parents should live with their children	46.5	45.7
Marijuana should be legalized	20.7	17.5

Note: Percentages indicate level of agreement with the statements at left.

PSYCHOLOGICAL WELL-BEING

	Italian Americans	*Non – Italian Americans*
General happiness	34.5%	32.4%
Marital happiness	60.0	62.8
Job satisfaction	46.1	45.8
Financial satisfaction	29.0	29.7
Satisfaction with community	11.5	17.2
Satisfaction with family	41.4	42.0
Satisfaction with friends	33.7	31.1
Satisfaction with leisure-time activities	20.7	22.6
Satisfaction with health	28.0	24.4
Evaluation of health	25.2	31.9
General evaluation of life	39.9	44.9

Note: Percentages indicate level of satisfaction with the categories listed.

RELIGIOUS ATTITUDES

	Italian Americans	*Non – Italian Americans*
Currently Roman Catholic	70.2%	23.1%
Weekly church attendance	37.2	45.8
Having a strong religious identification	24.9	37.5
Feeling extremely close to God	30.4	31.5
Believing in life after death	71.5	79.0
God seen more as a mother	8.5	7.0
God seen more as a lover	15.9	12.6
God seen more as a spouse	12.5	9.3
God seen more as a friend	40.3	40.9

EPILOGUE

The findings of each chapter of this book are intimately related. *L'ordine della famiglia,* the image of *una buona femmina,* Italian and Italian-American anarchist experiences, Garibaldi as cultural hero, and Columbus as ethnic symbol are all dialectically intertwined. Moreover, they illustrate specific ways of struggling with the various dimensions of the individualism-community continuum.

In *l'ordine della famiglia* one finds tightly bound families trying to secure their destinies while acutely distrusting the wider society and the state. Because these families were relatively isolated from wider cooperative projects, the informal system of *compareggio* and the social practices of *una buona femmina* were necessary to increase prospects for familial self-sufficiency. Meanwhile, although occasional and atypical, anarchist insurgency stirred heroic-romantic impulses, sounded the human need to transcend context, and underscored vehement alienation from the state.

In this historical situation, Garibaldi emerged as a cultural hero not because of his professed radical ideology – the emancipation of women, the unification of Italy under the rule of a benevolent monarch, the call for a vigorous internationalism, and the transformation of the poorest class – but because his personal charisma, personification of righteous vengeance, instinctive displays of *rispetto,* and leadership of closely knit guerrillas retaliating against larger, semi-organized military forces represented the vindication of the family writ large.

When the great waves of southern European immigration to the Americas began, the transported sons and daughters of the *Mezzogiorno* reluctantly shelved their traditional provincial differences and became, along with northern Italian immigrants, Italian Americans. Confronting an alien and demanding social context in the New World, and a state that at once promised previously unimaginable material and social bounty and exacted a lofty spiritual price, the immigrants needed strategies to mitigate their cultural dissonance. Many seized upon the already established Christopher Columbus as ethnic symbol and credential of membership in the New World.

The various dimensions of the individualism-community continuum are thus dialectically related. The individual's connection to family, the family's perception of society, the society's link to the state, the state's relationship to the world, and the individual's self-identification as an ethnic reflect and sustain one another at the same time that each dimension seeks to mediate the tensions generated by the other dimensions. The self can discover no single, uniquely correct coping strategy for all sociopolitical contexts. The self, as it struggles with its simultaneous needs for a social context and for context-transcendence, cannot escape from the risks of the individualism-community continuum. In the words of existential philosophy, the self is condemned to its freedom and responsible for its choices.

Again, the fears and hopes embodied by the individual-community continuum partly define the human condition. Technological and ideological developments in the twentieth century, however, have radically exacerbated pressures emerging from the choices we must confront along this continuum. Many of us find ourselves alienated from the comforting, if often illusory, certitudes of the past. Marx, Freud, and Nietzsche had earlier disaggregated the redeeming unassailability of religious meaning by pressing their suspicions that latent economic, psychological, and cultural motives underwrite, indeed create, religious conviction. Later, the rise of fascism, Nazism, and early-stage socialism that aspired to communism amplified the risks inherent in state control of the individual and family. The explosive hegemony of instrumental reason and abstract systems of control facilitated a crisis of the spirit as anxiety became addiction. Refined technology mocked itself by producing weapons that threaten a humanly inspired apocalypse. Lived experiences, especially of the body, are too often eclipsed by ersatz media-inspired substitutes: virtual realities, blatant commodifications, and mere images understood vicariously. The enormous increase in information finds no parallel in expanded wisdom. Too many of us seem unable to reconnect with or to re-create wholesome realities. The human search for meaning is caricatured by capitalist hucksterism, pop psychology, the sham transcendence of a drug culture, and craven flight from individual responsibility. Cynicism and thorough skepticism are falsely enshrined as insight. The citadel of the self is under siege.

Amid the spiritual alienation and the cultural rubble lie possibilities for reemergence and transcendence: cultural deconstruction is rarely one-dimensional degeneration. Personal reconstruction and the search for meaning, necessary projects of human life, must begin with re-creations of the relationships most closely constitutive of self. It is to our nuclear and extended families, our intimate friends, and our ethnic connections that we must first turn. The human struggle for feeling and meaning must acknowledge the truths of blood: resistance surmounts resignation, passion conquers torpidity, concreteness trumps abstraction.

NOTES

1. Family Confronts Society

1. The *Mezzogiorno* refers to the regions of Italy south of Rome: Abruzzi and Molise, Campania, Apulia, Basilicata (Lucania), Calabria, and Sicily. I have seen Sardinia also included in the group. *"Mezzogiorno"* literally means "middle of the day" but also bears several rich connotations such as "the land that time forgot" and "where the sun always shines." This region has for centuries been the poorest but most intriguing part of Italy. It is estimated that over 80 percent of the Italian immigrants to the United States came from the *Mezzogiorno*.

2. Most of my general account of the family structure in Italy comes from four excellent books: Richard D. Alba, *Italian Americans: Into the Twilight of Ethnicity* (Englewood Cliffs: Prentice-Hall, 1985); Luigi Barzini, *The Italians* (New York: Atheneum, 1964); Richard Gambino, *Blood of My Blood* (New York: Anchor Books, 1974); Jerre Mangione and Ben Morreale, *La Storia* (New York: Harper Collins, 1992).

3. Gal. 5:14

4. Matt. 19:19, echoing Lev. 19:18. The parable of the good Samaritan, told in answer to the question, "And who is my neighbor?" (Luke 10:29), implies that the commandment applies to any fellow human: thus "neighbor" must be construed globally.

5. "Teachings of Mo Tzu" in Yu-lan Fung, *A Short History of Chinese Philosophy* (New York: Macmillan, 1960).

6. Ibid., 92.

7. William Godwin, "Enquiry Concerning Political Justice" (1798), quoted in Don Locke, *A Fantasy of Reason* (London: Routledge, 1980), 168.

8. Peter Singer, "Is Racial Discrimination Arbitrary?" *Philosophia* 8 (1978):197 (emphasis added).

9. For a valiant attempt to show that Kantianism is compatible with a robust notion of personal relations see Barbara Herman, "Agency, Attachment, and Difference," *Ethics* 101 (1991):775–797.

10. John Hardwig, "In Search of an Ethics of Personal Relationships," in George Graham and Hugh LaFollette, eds., *Person to Person* (Philadelphia: Temple University Press, 1989), 72.

11. Jan Narveson, "On Honouring Our Parents," *Southern Journal of Philosophy* 25 (1987):77.

12. Thus, Peter Singer, one of the strictest impartialist-utilitarians concedes: "Subordinate principles giving members of families responsibility for the welfare of others in the family . . . will be derivable from the principle of equal consideration, *if* everyone's interests are best promoted by such arrangements; and this is likely to be the case if, first, people are more knowledgeable about the interests of those close to them and more inclined to work to see that these interests are catered for, and, second, if the distribution of resources between families and between nations is not so unequally distributed that some families or nations are simply unable to provide for themselves the means to satisfying interests that could be satisfied with ease by other families or nations." "Racial Discrimination," 198–199 (emphasis added).

13. Thus, Barbara Herman argues: "In acting from a motive of connection I must also recognize that I am in circumstances in which action is morally required, be willing and able to act even if connection wavers, and act only on the condition that the particular action I am moved to take is permissible." "Agency, Attachment, and Difference," 777.

14. Thus, in John Rawls's "original position," an ideal and impartial vantage point, where everyone is shrouded by a "veil of ignorance" from particular knowledge about, among other things, their own age, gender, ethnic, racial, religious circumstances, it is possible that some principle of partiality would be selected. *A Theory of Justice* (Cambridge, Mass.: Harvard University Press, 1971).

15. Singer, "Racial Discrimination," 199.

16. James Rachels, "Morality, Parents, and Children," in George Graham and Hugh LaFollette, eds., *Person to Person* (Philadelphia: Temple University Press, 1989), 49.

17. Ibid., 46.

18. Ibid., 48.

19. Thomas Donaldson, "Morally Privileged Relationships," *Journal of Value Inquiry* 24 (1990):4.

20. Ibid., 5.

21. Marcia Baron, "Impartiality and Friendship," *Ethics* 101 (1991):838.

22. Thus, James Rachels, who embraces a version of moderate contingent impartialism, writes: "Bonds of affection are more than just instrumental goods.

To be loved is to have one's own value affirmed; thus it is a source of self-esteem. This is important for all of us, but especially for children, who are helpless and more vulnerable than adults . . . Loving relationships provide individuals with things to value, and so give their lives . . . meaning." "Morality, Parents, and Children," 54–55.

23. Ibid., 56.

24. Ibid., 59 (emphasis added).

25. "You may provide the necessities for your own children first, but you are not justified in providing them luxuries while other children lack necessities. Even in a fairly weak form [one in which necessities are broadly defined], this view would still require much greater concern for others than the [partialist] view that is most common in our society." Ibid., 60.

26. As Thomas Donaldson argues: "There is something about the particularity of [my present friends, family members, and other intimates] which helps ground the value and the commitment of the friendship; and which would be lost by substitution. Your friendship is with a particular person. This goes beyond the mere fact that the value must be grounded in a particular relationship." "Morally Privileged Relationships," 6.

27. Hugh LaFollette, "Personal Relationships," in Peter Singer, ed., *A Companion to Ethics* (Oxford: Basil Blackwell, 1991), 328. Moreover, it is through special personal relations that we learn much about morality that would otherwise be obscured from us. See, for example, Martha C. Nussbaum, *Love's Knowledge* (New York: Oxford University Press, 1990), 44 ("Bonds of close friendship or love (such as those that connect members of a family, or close personal friends) are extremely important in the whole business of becoming a good [moral] perceiver . . . one learns to see aspects of the world that one had previously missed. One's desire to share a form of life with the friend motivates this process.")

28. As John Hardwig puts it: "Characteristically and normatively, the appropriate motive for action in personal relationships is simply that we want to do these things. Persons pursue whatever *ends* they have simply because they want to . . . in a personal relationship, I and my well-being are ends of yours." "An Ethics of Personal Relationships," 75.

29. Thus, Hardwig insists that in personal relations "neither party magnanimously or ignominiously sacrifices personal interests, but the two interests are not independent, not really even two. For your ends are my ends too. The distinction between giving and receiving thus collapses . . . conflicts of interest are conflicts within myself, a very different thing from a conflict of interest with

someone separate from me . . . I see myself, in part, as part of a larger whole that is *us* . . . if our relationship does end, I will have to alter my conception of myself and my well-being." Ibid., 76–77.

30. Bernard Williams writes that to require a person to calculate impartiality would be to "alienate him in a real sense from his actions and the source of his action in his own convictions . . . to neglect the extent to which *his* actions and *his* decisions have to be seen as the actions and decisions which flow from the projects and the attitudes with which he is most closely identified. It is thus in the most literal sense an attack on his integrity." J. J. C. Smart and Bernard Williams, *Utilitarianism, For and Against* (Cambridge: Cambridge University Press, 1973), 116.

31. John Cottingham, "Ethics and Impartiality," *Philosophical Studies* 43 (1983):90.

32. Thus John Kekes remarks on the value of personal transformation: "Personal morality is like artistic creation: what is being created is oneself. The moral life is the attempt to realize an ideal conception that one has imaginatively understood, to make oneself into the kind of person that one's ideals call for . . . what matters is how the agent goes about transforming himself, and thus how he differs from others. Impartiality, in this context, would render the moral endeavor absurd." "Morality and Impartiality," *American Philosophical Quarterly* 18 (1981):298–299. Kekes also addresses the need for social non-fungibility in morality: "The moral force of impartiality is inversely proportionate to the intimacy of the moral nexus to which it is supposed to apply. Intimate personal relationships involve the participants' recognition of each other as *special, noninterchangeable* individuals, because they, and only they, have certain particular idiosyncratic qualities, or combinations of them." "Morality and Impartiality," 300 (emphasis added).

33. John Cottingham, "The Ethics of Self-Concern," *Ethics* 101 (1991):800.

34. In fact, Cottingham describes impartialism as dangerously, not exhilaratingly, utopian: "If adherence to [impartialism] is either impossible or else so far beyond the bounds of the feasible as to belong in the 'ethics of fantasy', then its coherence as an ethical ideal collapses . . . it is to make the subject matter of ethics relate to some wholly hypothetical ideal world, a world of nonhumans, rather than to see its task as the constructing of a rational blueprint for how, in this world, human beings can best live." Ibid., 801.

35. See, for example, Nussbaum, *Love's Knowledge*, 37 ("One point of the emphasis on [moral] perception is to show the ethical crudeness of moralities based exclusively on general rules, and to demand for ethics a much finer

responsiveness to the concrete."); Barry Hoffmaster, "Can Ethnography Save the Life of Medical Ethics?" in Earl R. Winkler and Jerrold R. Coombs, eds., *Applied Ethics* (Oxford: Basil Blackwell, 1993), 376 ("Moral decision-making is a search for a feasible, appropriate response to a particular situation, not the application of a method that in virtue of its extreme generality is insensitive to the particularities that structure the situation. There is no homogeneous unifying conception of rationality in morality – or anywhere else for that matter."); Michael Philips, "How to Think Systematically about Business Ethics," in Winkler and Coombs, eds., *Applied Ethics*, 187 ("Many philosophers . . . deny that 'morality' is a proper name for a supercode. There is no supercode. The term 'morality' stands to moralities as the term 'language' stands to languages . . . The proper terms of evaluation for moral standards are not 'true' and 'false' but rather 'reasonable' or 'unreasonable.' ")

36. Many philosophers argue for the priority of the concrete and particular over the highly abstract and general. See, for example, Earl R. Winkler, "From Kantianism to Contextualism: The Rise and Fall of the Paradigm Theory in Bioethics," in Winkler and Coombs, eds., *Applied Ethics*, 352, 355, 344 ("The real problem [in moral decision making] lies in an inadequate and oversimplified conception of moral reasoning as the application of principles to concrete issues . . . it is dominantly the interpretation of cases that informs our understanding of principles rather than principles guiding the resolution of difficult cases . . . Applicable moral principles will derive mainly from [appeal to relevant historical and cultural traditions, with reference to critical institutional and professional norms and virtues], rather than from ethical theory on the grand scale."); Nussbaum, *Love's Knowledge*, 69, 311 ("Principles are authoritative only insofar as they do not err with regard to the particulars. And it is not possible for a formulation intended to cover many different particulars to achieve a high degree of correctness . . . frequently we will reject an abstract theoretical account for being at odds with the concrete perceptions of life and feeling.").

37. Donaldson, "Morally Privileged Relationships," 9.

38. Christina Hoff Sommers argues that strict contractualism is radically counterintuitive when describing the extent and nature of human obligations: "[Contractualism] means that there is no such thing as filial duty per se, no such thing as the special duty of mother to child, and generally no such thing as a morality of special family or kinship relations . . . most people think we do owe special debts to our parents even though we have not voluntarily assumed our obligations to them . . . many people believe we owe special consideration to

our siblings even at times when we may not *feel* very friendly to them. But if there are no special duties [beyond those voluntarily assumed], then most of these prima facie requirements . . . should be looked upon as archaic survivals to be ignored in assessing our moral obligations." "Philosophers Against the Family," in George Graham and Hugh LaFollette, eds., *Person to Person* (Philadelphia: Temple University Press, 1989), 95.

39. Raymond A. Belliotti, "Honor Thy Father and Thy Mother and to Thine Own Self Be True," *Southern Journal of Philosophy* 24 (1986):149–162; "Parents and Children: A Reply to Narveson," *Southern Journal of Philosophy* 26 (1988):285–292; "Blood is Thicker Than Water: Don't Forsake the Family Jewels," *Philosophical Papers* 18 (1989):265–280.

40. Ibid.

41. Christina Hoff Sommers captures the unreliability of affection as a ground for moral duties: "[Some] philosophers set aside special [familial] duties, replacing them with an emphasis on friendship, compatibility, and interpersonal love among family members. This has a disintegrative effect. For if what one owes to members of one's family is largely to be understood in terms of feelings of personal commitment, definite limits are placed on what one owes. For as feelings change, so may one's commitments, and the structure of responsibility within the family is permanently unstable." "Philosophers Against the Family," 101.

A somewhat different route would be to ground the moral requirements in question in duties of gratitude. One could argue that a beneficiary owes such duties to her benefactors and that these duties require actually feeling grateful as well as acting on that feeling. Instead of perceiving gratitude as merely a feeling that is beyond the beneficiaries' control, this view insists that we can influence our beliefs, attitudes, and desires. Thus, we have control over whether we feel and act grateful, and we are morally responsible for cultivating the proper sentiments and performing the appropriate actions. See, for example, Fred R. Berger, "Gratitude," *Ethics* 85 (1975):298–309. This view is persuasive but it fails to account for situations in which benefactors render benefits without praiseworthy motives. Why should I feel grateful to someone who benefited me without praiseworthy motivation? I am not simply addressing cases in which benefactors contribute from mixed motives, but still with substantial benevolence, for it can still be argued in such cases that duties of gratitude are appropriate. I am concerned, instead, with cases in which benefactors contribute with little, if any, benevolence. I want to argue, and the Conservation of Self Principle and Principle of Preservation permit me to argue, that in such cases beneficiaries still owe duties to their benefactors. I do not, however, believe that grounding the moral requirements in question in duties of gratitude would permit me to cover such cases. Accordingly, I have not employed that strategy.

42. Eddy M. Zemach, "Love My Neighbor as Thyself or Egoism and Altruism," *Midwest Studies in Philosophy* 3 (1978):151–154.

43. Narveson, "On Honouring Our Parents," 68.

44. Ibid., 66.

45. Anthony Cortese, *Ethnic Ethics* (Albany: SUNY Press, 1990), 157.

46. Narveson, "On Honouring Our Parents," 65–66.

47. Edward C. Banfield, *The Moral Basis of a Backward Society* (Glencoe, Ill.: Free Press, 1958). This book is the culmination of Banfield's research in Montegrano in the province of Lucania.

48. Ibid., 85.

49. Ibid.

50. The seventeen implications are as follows: "(1) No one will further the interest of the group or community except as it is to his private advantage to do so. (2) Only officials [not private citizens] will concern themselves with public affairs, for only they are paid to do so. (3) There will be few checks on officials, for checking on officials will be the business of other officials only. (4) Organization (deliberately concerted action) will be very difficult to achieve and maintain. (5) Office-holders, feeling no identification with the purposes of the organization, will not work harder than is necessary to keep their places; professional people and educated people generally will lack a sense of mission or calling. (6) Law will be disregarded when there is no reason to fear punishment. (7) Office-holders will take bribes when they can get away with it; whether they take bribes or not, it will be assumed by society that they do. (8) The weak will favor a regime which will maintain order with a strong hand. (9) The claim of any person or institution to be inspired by zeal for public rather than private advantage will be regarded as fraud. (10) There will be no connection between abstract political principle and concrete behavior in the ordinary relations of everyday life. (11) There will be no leaders and no followers. (12) [Citizens] will use their ballots to secure the greatest material gain in the short run. (13) [A citizen] will value gains accruing to the community only insofar as he and his are likely to share them. He will vote against measures which will help the community without helping him. (14) The voter will place little confidence in the promises of the parties. (15) It will be assumed that whatever group is in power is self-serving and corrupt. (16) There will be no

strong or stable political machines in society. (17) Party workers will sell their services to the highest bidders." Ibid., 85–104. This parcel of behavior, according to Banfield, both describes current social interaction in Montegrano and precludes the people from making the reforms necessary for socioeconomic progress.

51. See, for example, William A. Douglass, "The South Italian Family: A Critique," *Journal of Family History* 5 (1980):338. ("Central to the amoral familism debate is the question of the typicality of Montegrano within the Italian South. Banfield himself was equivocal on this point.") Several social scientists, however, find Banfield's descriptions of behavior in Montegrano essentially accurate for the Italian South. See, for example, J. Davis, "Morals and Backwardness," *Comparative Studies in Society and History* 12 (1970): 340, 343; Frank Cancian, "The South Italian Peasant," *Anthropological Quarterly* 34 (1961):1, 2 ("Montegrano can be taken as representative of the mountain peasant community."); Leonard Moss and Walter Thompson, "The South Italian Family," *Human Organization* 18 (1959):35, 38 ("In most areas of the South, it is the neolocal nuclear family which serves as the primary focus of the individual."); Constance Cronin, *The Sting of Change: Sicilians in Sicily and Australia* (Chicago: University of Chicago Press, 1970), 85 ("Banfield's statement is as true in Sicily as it is in Apulia. It is clear by now that the nuclear family is the cornerstone of Sicilian social organization and the most fundamental of Italian organizations.")

52. See, for example, Roy A. Miller, "Are Familists Amoral? A Test of Banfield's Amoral Familism Hypothesis in a South Italian Village," *American Ethnologist* 1 (1974):515, 533 ("The ethos of the community does not reduce to the rule of amoral familism . . . this rule alone does not accurately represent the villager's orientation toward extrafamilial social behavior . . . Since the concept of amoral familism appears to characterize neither the total ethos of a typical Southern village nor the more specific orientation to action of its men, it is difficult to see how it can be maintained that this concept can explain South Italian poverty and backwardness."); Lydio Tomasi, *The Italian American Family* (Staten Island: Center for Migration Studies, 1972), 11 ("Banfield is not justified in qualifying this familism as 'amoral,' because in the psychocultural and economic context in which Southern Italians are now considered, that is the only possible morality."); Joseph LaPalombara, *Democracy Italian Style* (New Haven: Yale University Press, 1987), 99, 100 ("[Banfield's] reading of southern Italy, as Italians themselves were later to complain, was somewhat gratuitous and reeked of stereotypes . . . [his] real puzzlement was that these southern

Italians had not behaved as would Kansas farmers, with whom he actually compared them . . . he somehow assumed that where there occurs government indifference or incapacity, and particularly where citizens are inclined to place most of their ills at the feet of a 'thief of a government,' something like a pioneer spirit will intervene to take up the slack. That is not how the process and the drama of politics are played out in Italy.")

53. See, for example, Alessandro Pizzorno, "Amoral Familism and Historical Marginality," *International Review of Community Development* 15/16 (1966): 55, 59, 61, 63 ("Even if the Montegranians did everything suggested [by Banfield], even if everything humanly possible was done, the conditions in Montegrano would not improve . . . the Montegranians are right in not doing anything, because no one is silly enough to do things that serve no purpose . . . [the people] renounce collective, or community, action, not because they are afflicted with amoral familism, but simply because this collective action would bear no fruit in those conditions . . . the cause [of alleged backwardness] should be sought in objective conditions [such as class relations and poverty] which are independent of the present action of the Montegranians.")

54. See, for example, William Muraskin, "The Moral Basis of a Backward Sociologist," *American Journal of Sociology* 79 (1974): 1484, 1489, 1491, 1492, 1494 ("Banfield's analysis ignores 'objective reality,' the external social and economic forces that impinge upon people. The concept of amoral familism presupposes that the inhabitants of southern Italy behave as they do because of processes going on within the confines of their own minds . . . [But] people sometimes do what they despise. They live as best they can despite their ideals, values, and psychological needs . . . All of [Banfield's] examples are more persuasive as proof that the peasants . . . are 'realistically' adapting to the sociopolitical-economic environment of their world than that they have a value system or psychological framework that determines their behavior . . . [His book] is packed with evidence that the people of Montegrano have little or no choice at all . . . Banfield has falsely assumed that values, ideals, and needs can be discovered from how people act without reference to the external constraints that confine them."); Juliet du Boulay and Rory Williams, "Amoral Familism and the Image of Limited Good," *Anthropological Quarterly* 60 (1987):12, 13 ("Banfield's contrast [between the morality of the Montegranesi and his projected ideal] is, however, extremely partial; for the morality to which he appeals in making it is a universalistic morality, whereas the moral imperatives of peasant societies are commonly of a different order, for example, not to universal categories but to particular relationships . . . there are often other

goods envisaged in peasant life, equally removed from the world of commodities, which are not necessarily moral goods at all, but rather fall into the category of symbolic values, or relate to possessions which are common and indivisible. Thus the concepts of amoral familism and limited good are selective views of peasant value systems.")

55. Some side with Banfield and claim the basic form of the southern Italian family is nuclear. See, for example, J. Davis, *Land and Family in Pisticci* (London: Athlone Press, 1973); I. Cinel, *From Italy to San Francisco* (Stanford: Stanford University Press, 1982); Moss and Thompson, "South Italian Family"; Cronin, *Sting of Change;* C. Johnson, *Growing Up and Growing Old in Italian-American Families* (New Brunswick: Rutgers University Press, 1985); Virginia Yans-McLaughlin, *Family and Community: Italian Immigrants in Buffalo, 1880–1930* (Ithaca: Cornell University Press, 1977).

The more persuasive view, in my judgment, is that the basic form of the southern Italian family was extended. See, for example, R. Bell, *Fate and Honor, Family and Village* (Chicago: University of Chicago Press, 1979); Paul Campisi, "Ethnic Family Patterns: The Italian Family in the United States," *American Journal of Sociology* 53 (1948):444; Leonard Covello, *The Social Background of the Italo-American School Child* (Leiden: E.J. Brill, 1967); F. Gross, *Il Paese: Values and Social Change in an Italian Village* (New York: New York University Press, 1973); Lydio Tomasi, *The Italian American Family* (Staten Island: Center for Migration Studies, 1972); Rudolph Vecoli, "Contadini in Chicago," *Journal of American History* 51 (1964):404; Richard Gambino, "Italian Americans: Today's Immigrants, Multiculturalism, and the Mark of Cain," *Italian Journal* 7 no. 6 (1993): 42, 43 ("The family system of old south Italy was far from amoral, and so is its evolved form in the USA today. It was one of extended families linked beyond blood both by arranged marriages and by a system of *comparatico* to form a complicated network . . . a 'community' system which Banfield incorrectly saw as lacking.");

Nicholas J. Esposito does an excellent job of trying to reconcile these conflicting views by demonstrating the soundness "of defining family structure . . . not in terms of a single variable such as household structure, but in terms of a number of variables and operational definitions which provide a more thorough and valid description of family structure." "Family Structure in Rural Southern Italy," Richard N. Juliani and Philip V. Cannistraro, eds., *Italian Americans: The Search for a Useable Past* (Staten Island: American Italian Historical Association, 1989), 147. Esposito considers a variety of variables and concludes that "Southern Italy exhibits a number of characteristics which are associated with extended familism; viz., a rural setting, a family-based economy, property as land, close proximity of relatives' residences, etc. Values and attitudes regarding marriage, children, divorce, and illegitimacy likewise are best interpreted to indicate traditional familism . . . all of [the relevant information] says that Southern Italian families are extended; none of it says they are nuclear." 146–147.

Paul Ginsborg describes the contemporary nouthern Italian family in this way: "The average size of families in the southern cities has remained much greater than elsewhere in Italy. The concept of maximizing the number of persons available for the labor market is still stronger than any idea of limiting family size in order to conserve resources . . . The family remains a necessary refuge from a hostile environment; the lack of *fede pubblica* (civic trust) continues to bedevil southern society . . . Kinship networks . . . have remained as strong as ever." *A History of Contemporary Italy: Society and Politics, 1943–1988* (London: Penguin, 1990), 416–417, 418.

56. See, for example, Louis J. Gesualdi, "A Documentation of Criticisms Concerning Amoral Familism," in Richard N. Juliani, ed., *The Family and Community Life of Italian Americans* (Staten Island: American Italian Historical Association, 1983), 129, 131. ("Southern Italy's culture is not the cause of its under-development, but is on the contrary a consequence and a means of adapting to it . . . Values are more a dependent than independent variable. The ethos 'amoral familism' is the result of an impoverished society and not a cause of its impoverishment."); Thomas McCorkel, "Review of *The Moral Basis of a Backward Society*," *American Anthropologist* 61 (1959):133–134; Sydel F. Silverman, "Agricultural Organization, Social Structure, and Values in Italy: Amoral Familism Reconsidered," *American Anthropologist* 70 (1968):1, 3, 17 ("The ethos is a consequence rather than the basis of these social characteristics; they, in turn, have their foundation in the agricultural system . . . although the ethos validates a social system, changing the ideas alone will not alter the social system. Similarly, the social structure (and also the ethos) will respond to changes in the agricultural system, but the latter will not be fundamentally altered merely by manipulating the social structure . . . the Southern Italians are 'prisoners' not of their ethos but of their agricultural system."); du Boulay and Williams, "Amoral Familism," 12 ("The ideas of amoral familism or limited good do not, in the view of some, generate patterns of behavior, but are themselves generated, together with the appropriate behavior, by processes of social control . . . by agricultural organization . . . or by objective limitations on economic opportunity . . . [still] cooperation in political associations is not

always impeded . . . and there may be important forms of collaboration between spiritual kinsmen).

57. See, for example, Donna R. Gabaccia, *From Sicily to Elizabeth Street* (Albany: SUNY Press, 1984), 3, 10 ("Sicilians also strongly desired social ties to people outside [the nuclear family] and they had clear rules defining moral social behavior outside the nuclear family. They wanted close and harmonious social ties to their *casa* of close relatives. Under special conditions, they also sought ties to their more distant kin, called the *parenti* . . . nineteenth-century Sicilians were not amoral familists; Banfield was wrong in his historical reasoning."); Joseph Lopreato, *Peasants No More* (Scranton, Penn.: Chandler, 1967), 225–246 (arguing, among other things, that Banfield's analysis is misleadingly "ahistorical."); Douglass, "South Italian Family," 339–340.

58. My conclusions are based on analyzing the literature listed in notes 47 through 57 above. By "mutually constitutive" and "dialectical" relationships I mean interdependent and mutually sustaining ones. By "linearly causal" I mean a simple "A causes B" relationship. By "causal priority" I mean, in this case, that economic forms have greater causal impact on the family ethos than vice versa, although causality is still not simply linear or in one direction only.

59. Booker T. Washington quoted in Mangione and Morreale, *La Storia*, xv.

60. Karl Marx quoted in Mangione and Morreale, *La Storia*, 58.

61. Rudolph Bell, *Fate and Honor, Family and Village: Demographic and Cultural Change in Rural Italy since 1800* (Chicago: University of Chicago Press, 1979), 113.

62. Barzini, *The Italians*, 198.

63. Richard Alba describes the situation in this way: "The name *campanilismo* refers to the town bell, *il campanile*, implying that the margin of this world was where the bell ceased to be heard. Except for the military service of the men, which gave them a taste of the wider world, it was not unusual for a peasant to spend his or her entire life within this boundary, with infrequent visits to neighboring towns and villages and few or none at all to larger urban places." *Italian Americans*, 30.

64. Thus, Barzini writes: "In the outside world, amidst the chaos and disorder, [Italians] often feel compelled to employ the wiles of underground fighters in enemy-occupied territory. All official and legal authority is considered hostile by them until proved friendly or harmless: if it cannot be ignored, it should be neutralized or deceived if need be." *The Italians*, 202.

65. Ibid., 199.

66. See, for example, Roberto Unger, *Passion: An Essay on Personality* (New York: Free Press, 1984), 95, 100 ("The desire for the tangible expression of mutual acceptance—from sexual union to the elaborate development of a life in common—repeatedly conflicts with acquiescence in the distinctive selfhood of the other person . . . The problem of our mutual fear and our mutual need is worked out in the life of the passions, which ring the changes on the relations between our reciprocal and infinite longing for one another and our reciprocal and infinite terror."); Duncan Kennedy, "The Structure of Blackstone's *Commentaries*," *Buffalo Law Review* 28 (1979):205, 212 ("The goal of individual freedom is at the same time dependent on and incompatible with the communal coercive action that is necessary to achieve it. Others . . . are necessary if we are to become persons at all—they provide us with the stuff of ourselves and protect us in crucial ways against destruction . . . But at the same time . . . the universe of others . . . threatens us with annihilation.")

2. The Gendered Self Struggles with the Family

1. Lydio F. Tomasi, *The Italian American Family* (New York: Center for Migration Studies, 1972), 9.

2. Ibid., 14.

3. "The Italian peasants themselves attributed greater prestige and importance to male contributions to the family economy. A wife's clearly defined family and household responsibilities included obedience to her husband, family loyalty, thrift, and, most important, childbearing . . . Peasants looked disdainfully at wives who left the home to work, and few did so unless poverty required it . . . Even [a wife's] household powers—always subject to [her husband's] will—accrued to her by default. A Sicilian study reports, for example, that the father's 'authority in his house is final, and there is no official redress to his commands.' " Virginia Yans-McLaughlin, "A Flexible Tradition: South Italian Immigrants Confront a New Work Experience," *Journal of Social History* 7 (1974):431.

F. G. Friedmann pulls no punches in explaining the male peasant's attitude toward women: "Though we may find deep in the heart of the peasant a feeling of respect toward women, it is a feeling which seems to refer to the maternal function in general than to one's own wife in particular. As a rule, the wife is treated as a useful possession since she represents working power as well as the capacity to satisfy man's most elementary desire of possession . . . The woman . . . takes on a symbolic meaning. This becomes most strikingly evident in attitudes toward virginity – symbol of symbols – in which the elements of precariousness, of possession, and of dignity are clearly present. "The World of 'La Miseria'," *Partisan Review* (March-April 1953):221, 222.

Colleen Johnson presses home several themes: "The mother is viewed as the center or heart of the family; without her, the family would cease to exist . . . her image has been so extolled that in Italy it is linked to the Madonna . . . Characteristics of the mother include seriousness of purpose, purity, chastity, and self sacrifice . . . the immigrant father stood above other family members as the ultimate source of social control . . . his superior position was maintained by the enforcement of respect for his role as provider and protector of the family. "The Maternal Role in the Contemporary Italian-American Family," in Betty Boyd Caroli, Robert F. Harney, and Lydio F. Tomasi, eds., *The Italian Immigrant Woman in North America* (Toronto: Multicultural History Society of Ontario, 1978), 237.

See also Corrado Gini and Elio Caranti, "The Family in Italy," *Marriage and Family Living* 16 (1954):360 ("The woman's participation in extrafamilial economic life is rather infrequent. The Italian woman, before and after marriage, is essentially a housewife. The man sees in her the mother of his children, then the housewife; the functions of sweetheart, advisor, and comforter seem minor, probably because in the lower classes they are not separate from the first two.").

4. Tomasi, *Italian American Family*, 14; Paul J. Campisi, "Ethnic Family Patterns: The Italian Family in the United States," *American Journal of Sociology* 53 (1948):444 – 446.

5. Richard Gambino, *Blood of My Blood* (New York: Anchor Books, 1974), especially 160 – 182.

6. Ibid., 164, 166, 168.

7. See, for example, Virginia Yans-McLaughlin, "Patterns of Work and Family Organization: Buffalo's Italians," *Journal of Interdisciplinary History* 2 (1971):307 ("There are a number of ways in which homework did not challenge Old World family organization. The mother's roles as arbiter of household organization and tasks and as disciplinarian and child-rearer were reinforced by her economic position as manager of the domestic undertaking, be it artificial flower-making, basting, or sewing. Because she still had not become, in the strict sense of the term, a wage earner, she presented no clear threat to her husband's authority and power. The basic unit of homework industries continued to be just as it has been in the Old World – the family, not the individual."); Cynthia R. Daniels, "No Place Like Home," in Joseph L. Tropea, James E.

Miller, and Cheryl Beattie-Repetti (eds.), *Support and Struggle: Italian and Italian Americans in Historical Perspective* (Washington, D.C.: Proceedings of the 17th Annual Conference of the American Historical Association, 1984), 94, 110 ("Through the homework system these women could care for children at the same time they earned an income; they could bring needed income into the family without challenging their husband's identity as the 'head' of the household . . . by retaining the stability of the family, women were at least promised (if not assured of) a kind of long range security that the labor market could never provide.")

8. Yans-McLaughlin, "Patterns of Work," 303 ("Because tradition bestowed upon the mother great prestige, authority, and power (frequently including control of the household budget), south Italian peasant family organization was not purely patriarchal. Male superiority and paternal control, however, were the norm.")

9. "[At funerals] women mourn dramatically, even histrionically. They mourn for the whole family. It falls upon them to express the bereavement of the entire clan. They do not merely weep. They rage against death for the harm it has done to the family. The more mature the women, the more extreme their behavior. Under other conditions of adversity these same women respond by steeling themselves. When necessary to the preservation of *l'ordine della famiglia,* they can press back tears and emotions and present a stony determination to the world that can even outdo the stoic aspect of their men." Gambino, *Blood of My Blood,* 161.

10. Yans-McLaughlin, "Patterns of Work," 312 ("Why was family disorganization minimal and why were female-headed families rare among Italian-Americans? First, Italians had strong cultural and historical traditions regarding their women's role which survived long after emigration. The male continued to dominate in spite of his own unemployment and despite the existence of certain matriarchal privileges within the south Italian family. The conservatism of female employment patterns is clear evidence for continuing male domination.")

11. "Immigrant women . . . regarded such behavior as living outside the parents' home, going out on dates, informality in public settings, and open quarreling with family elders as the ways of *puttane* ('whores'). They warned their young daughters . . . to come right home after school. And they fought the Americanization of the girls to a draw. The girls succeeded in becoming American in form but remained Italian in substance. Theirs is a conflicted personality, and one which in turn now causes tension between them and *their* daughters." Gambino, *Blood of My Blood,* 175.

See also Helen Barolini (ed.), *The Dream Book* (New York: Schocken Books, 1985), 11 ("Daughters [of immigrant women] assert a need for self-identity and want to free themselves from the past patterns; in their self-actualization they *must* react against their mothers; and in denying the value of the mother's role by their rebellion against it, they lay upon themselves a heavy and terrible conflict."); Elizabeth Ewen, "City Lights: Immigrant Women and the Rise of the Movies," *Signs* 5 (no. 3 supplement) (1980):S50 ("Unlike their mothers, the immigrant daughters' sense of self, although halting and incomplete, was directed outward. American society was based on a different conception of family life which demanded that adolescents identify with a social world outside the domain of family. Access to that world was dependent on having time and money for the use of the self. The price of admission to new culture was the negation of old-world notions of womanhood."); Arlene Mancuso, "Women of Old Town," in Caroli, et al., eds., *The Italian Immigrant Woman*, 320 ("The feminist outcry for self-fulfillment, power, and autonomy does not deeply touch [the Italian American woman in 'Old Town'], for she already has these things. She is well aware of her critical importance to the family unit. Contrary to her middle-class contemporaries, she does not lean on her husband or on 'the experts' to fulfill status needs or to solve problems. For this she has her extensive kinship and friendship networks.")

12. Gambino, *Blood of My Blood*, 162.

13. Ibid., 163.

14. Ibid., 170 ("As a female moved through the stages, she was first as a child an apprentice in womanhood. Upon her marriage she was a responsible woman who fulfilled economic, cultural, and more strictly family roles. In her motherhood and her old age she became progressively more a teacher of womanhood to her daughters, daughters-in-law, nieces, goddaughters, and grandchildren.")

15. Barolini, *Dream Book*, 10.

16. Ibid., 10–11.

17. Ibid., 16 ("There is a dark underside to the bright picture of the compact Italian American family life so extolled by sociologists and onlookers: there are men caught in low-paying, demeaning jobs who vent their frustration and rage on wives and children; there are fathers who have deserted families to go west to seek that illusory fortune they left their land for; there is divorce, cruelty, long bitter marriages, and the brutalization of their children and women by unhappy men.")

18. Ibid., 15. Barolini, however, is not above taking cheap shots. For example, she claims that "Gambino has woven an illusion. His model woman

does not exist; and, if she did, she is no longer desirable to those educated and socially evolving Italian American males (like himself) who have committed exogamy, fleeing her company and the *miseria* mentality for Jewish or Wasp wives. For one of the most verifiable phenomena of Italian American men is that, in their zest for upward mobility, they marry outside their group." This diatribe is embarrassing. First, of those Italian Americans born after 1940, about 80 percent commit exogamy. Thus this "transgression" is not confined to males. Second, Barolini conjures venal motivations supporting the phenomenon, but the reasons for exogamy (in all ethnic groups) are much more complex. Third, she hurls an unnecessary and unfair *ad hominen* at Gambino himself.

19. Ibid., 16. One wonders, however, if Barolini would confer the same understanding toward Italian immigrant men ("*men* who are harsh, cruel, crushing, unfeeling. They are embittered and malevolent; and given the strictures of their own lives, there is plenty of reason why.")

20. Ibid., 17–18.

21. Gambino, *Blood of My Blood*, 169.

22. This description, of course, also applies to Italian immigrant men.

23. Elisabetta Vezzosi, "The Dilemma of the Ethnic Community," in Tropea, et al., eds., *Support and Struggle*, 86.

24. Vezzosi puts it this way: "America represented the discovery of mechanisms of socialization and solidarity between women produced by working in the factory, as well as the discovery of their own identity outside of the family. Abandoning in part the ancestral conditioning of the mother-country, these women realized concepts such as 'individuality' and 'personal happiness' formerly unknown. Pride in their work and the instinct of workmanship began to appear for the first time." Ibid., 87. Moreover, American "social workers tried, by organizing numerous clubs, to stimulate the capacity of women immigrants to develop their own individuality and to improve their personal and family lives." Ibid., 89. Maddalena Tirabassi adds that "often women became the active agents of change within the family, in trying to assume American values and cooperating with American social workers when conflicts overcame them." "Emancipation Through Americanization?" in Joseph V. Scelsa, Salvatore J. LaGumina, and Lydio Tomasi, eds., *Italian Americans in Transition* (New York: Proceedings of the 21st Annual Conference of the American Italian Historical Association, 1988), 81.

25. There was, however, a steep price for such change: "As women moved from the constricted family-dominated culture to the more individualized values of modern urban society, the form and content of domination changed, but new

authorities replaced the old. In the name of freedom from tradition, they trapped women in harsh forms of sexual objectification and bound them to the consumerized and sexualized household." Ewen, "City Lights," S65.

26. Tirabassi, "Emancipation," 82.

27. "The choice . . . was that of escaping the meshes of the ethnic community emancipating herself from ancestral limitations and restrictions of the mother country and to 'Americanize' herself, or remain caught in these meshes, the immobile custodian of values that in the new country no longer existed. The community was asked to redefine these values through new responsibility and acceptance of the altered power structure within the family and the community itself . . . The choice and change were lengthy processes. Vezzosi, "Dilemma of Ethnic Community," 90.

28. See, for example, Emiliana P. Noether, "The Silent Half," in Caroli, et al., *The Italian Immigrant Woman*, 99. ("[After their men departed for the New World] many [southern Italian] women, for the first time in their lives, found themselves with enough money to feed themselves and their children. Decision-making in the family and relations with the outer world now depended upon them . . . when they were reunited with their menfolk the relationship between the dominant male and the previously submissive and silent female must have subtly changed." 8); Micaela di Leonardo, *The Varieties of Ethnic Experience* (Ithaca: Cornell University Press 1984) ("I could not connect . . . the image of the Italian Family—stolid, inward-looking, preventing the mobility of its children—with my clear evidence of an array of economic strategies, including risk-taking and planning for the future, and a variety of gender and household structure patterns.")

But compare this to Humbert S. Nelli, *From Immigrants to Ethnics: The Italian Americans* (New York: Oxford Press 1983), 132 ("The father, the interpreter of family needs and interests, held the highest status. He was highly authoritarian and a strict disciplinarian who ruled the home with a firm hand. No one in the family was allowed to undertake an enterprise without obtaining the father's permission.")

29. di Leonardo, *Ethnic Experience*, 116 ("My field materials lead me to believe that [the claim that white ethnic families are stable and patriarchal] is as baseless for Italian-Americans as are the other claims about ethnic families we have found wanting. It is in part a result of the confusion of the present with the ethnographic present—the use of old family studies as if they represented contemporary life. It is in larger part the result of the confusion of ethnic symbols with ethnic behavior.")

Regarding the "old family studies" see Leonard Covello and Francesco Cordasco, *The Social Background of the Italo-American School Child* (Totowa, N.J.: Rowman and Littlefield, 1972), 154, 209, 214 ("The leadership of the family was based on several principles . . . As long as he was the main provider, as long as he was healthy in body and mind, his rule and authority were unquestioned. But old age or feeble mentality definitely terminated his role as the representative of the family tradition. But no less important was his status as a married male . . . Outwardly, the family organization was under the domination of the father, but this domination was based upon the principle of submission by the rest of the family, rather than rational acceptance and recognition of his rights. The domination of the father was based on fear inculcated in all members of the household . . . the authority of the southern Italian father was valid not so much *per se,* as because of the superior status of the male.")

30. Ann Cornelisen, *Women of the Shadows* (Boston: Little, Brown, 1976), 219, 222.

31. Susan G. Berkowitz, "Familism, Kinship and Sex Roles in Southern Italy," *Anthropological Quarterly* 57 (1984):87.

32. Ibid.

33. "[Women's influence] is always essentially a derivative or indirect power and influence, exercised, if not always through, then in the name of appropriate males . . . [A woman's] social identity is an extension of her connections with relevant males . . . Alone, without a husband, the same woman would only be a *povera disgraziata,* a poor soul pitied by all." Ibid., 88–89.

34. Ibid., 88.

35. Robert Anthony Orsi, *The Madonna of 115th Street* (New Haven: Yale University Press, 1989), 145, 147. ("Older married women with children were the centers of power and authority in the private matriarchy of Italian Harlem. dominating the lives of the members of their domus, defining tradition, called upon to heal and condemn, to express anger and approval, making important decisions for their sons and daughters and grandchildren." 143.)

36. Ibid., 120. ("The powerful women of the community were expected to show an absolute respect for their husbands and sons in public, even though everyone in the community knew that such subservience was theater." 133.)

My maternal grandparents' home was located in a village containing numerous first- and second-generation Italian immigrants and, for what it is worth, I never observed the extreme forms of deference (e.g., kissing father's hand, bowing in public) noted in Orsi's book.

37. See also Mancuso, "Women of Old Town," 314. ("While some authors have described [the immigrant family] as father-dominated and mother-centered, it may also be viewed in terms of public images and private workings. The father is the public representative of the family. He is the breadwinner, the defender of family honor, the voice of the family in external affairs. The mother is the central figure in the running of the family unit. She cares for the family in all areas, makes decisions 'for the family.' Her domain is pervasive, and not challenged by the husband.")

38. "Who had the real power here—the women who had to uphold the standards of the domus or the men who put them to the test? Again, women seem trapped by the power assigned them in the domus, their authority linked to an inescapable dialectic of aggression and resentment. Their power, although it is real, is also their powerlessness." Orsi, *The Madonna*, 139.

39. "One source [of struggle] was the subtle but real alienation that existed between the Italian-born generations and their Italian American children, a conflict that was always exacerbated by the extreme demands for conformity and submission within the domus. Other conflicts arose out of the nature of the structure of the domus itself. Individuals felt suffocated by the unrelenting demands for intimacy and self-sacrifice made by its members." Ibid., 108.

40. "The internal conflicts generated by the structure and demands of the domus extended into other areas besides the sexual and involved other struggles than those between generations. Fierce rivalries rage among particular members of the domus for power and authority." Ibid., 117.

41. "The life of the domus was lived very closely and with an intense inward preoccupation: its members insisted on living close together, visiting each other frequently, and socializing with other members of the domus. Individuals had no privacy, which reflected in part the economic realities of Italian Harlem, but also the priority of the domus, which interpreted privacy as hostility and rejection." Ibid., 113.

42. "The fortunes of an individual person, as such, were of no concern to anybody because, in distress or in good fortune, the individual was always appraised as representative of some family." Covello and Cordasco, *Social Background*, 178.

43. "The individual thus located in the world by blood ties was not, and could not be, an isolated self: the self in Italian Harlem was a self-in-connection . . . the individual could not exist apart from the domus and remain a human being." Orsi, *The Madonna*, 82.

44. For example, "adult women in the second generation, while adopting the language, dress, and manners of the broader culture, retain the social structure of the immigrant group on primary levels of family formation and kinship. Whatever the outward changes are, they cannot deeply penetrate the family structure." Mancuso, "Women of Old Town," 316.

45. Accordingly, "almost all the gestures of rebellion . . . actually strengthened [the domus's] power, which was like an oriental finger trap—the more one struggled to get out, the more entangled one became . . . The young woman who secretly withheld part of her paycheck was acknowledging the power of the domus over her. The same is true of the young man who dreaded his parents' matrimonial plans for him but would not tell them he was dating a non-Italian woman. In both cases, the public power of the domus remained unchallenged. It was impossible to escape into the streets and parks of Italian Harlem because these too had been incorporated into the extended domus . . . Rebellion would mean the end of [daughters'] hopes to marry and have a domus of their own; it could bring scandal to the family, ruin to themselves. As a result of all this pressure, young women internalized the values and expectations of the domus even more completely than their brothers did." Orsi, *The Madonna*, 124–125, 143.

46. "The persistence of the domus as southern Italians understood it generated terrible burdens of guilt, anxiety, anger, and frustration in the lives of the men and women of Italian Harlem. They simply could not escape or change the domus—they were trapped. The survival of the domus also meant survival of a kind of historical, culturally institutionalized neurosis, a domus obsession, which the Italians of Harlem had to suffer along with other Italian Americans. All was not well in the domus of Italian Harlem." Ibid., 129.

47. "Even if one is always a man or a woman, one is never *just* a man or a woman. One is young or old, sick or healthy, married or unmarried, a parent or not a parent, employed or unemployed, middle class or working class, rich or poor, black or white, and so forth . . . Experience does not come neatly in segments, such that it is always possible to abstract what in one's experience is due to 'being a woman' from that which is due to 'being married', 'being middle class' and so forth." Jean Grimshaw, *Philosophy and Feminist Thinking* (Minneapolis, Minn.: University of Minnesota Press, 1986), 84–85.

48. Ibid., 17.

49. Finally, Grimshaw argues that "the assumption of multiple female 'realities', all of which are 'valid' and none of which have any claim to be regarded as more adequate than any other, cannot provide a way of conceptualizing things such as oppression, exploitation, the domination of one social

group by another." Ibid., 102. Thus, insofar as feminism aspires to conceptualize precisely such notions, this strategy fails.

50. Kimberle Crenshaw, "Demarginalizing the Intersection of Race and Sex," in Alison M. Jaggar, ed., *Living With Contradictions* (Boulder: Westview, 1994), 44–45.

Deborah King echoes such themes: "For black women, the personal is bound up in the problems peculiar to multiple jeopardies of race and class, not the singular one of sexual inequality . . . Feminism has excluded and devalued black women, our experiences, and our interpretations of our realities at the conceptual and ideological level . . . The assumption that the family is by definition patriarchal, the privileging of an individualistic worldview, and the advocacy of female separatism are often antithetical positions to many of the values and goals of black women." "Multiple Jeopardy: The Context of a Black Feminist Ideology," in Alison M. Jaggar and Paula S. Rothenberg, eds., *Feminist Frameworks* (New York: McGraw-Hill, 1993), 228–229.

51. Esther Ngan-Ling Chow makes this point in the context of Asian-American women: "Broadening feminism implies that sisterhood is inclusive regardless of one's race, class, background, national origin, sexual preference, physical condition, and life-style." "The Feminist Movement," in Jaggar and Rothenberg, eds., *Feminist Frameworks*, 217.

52. For a contrary view see Elizabeth Rapaport, "Generalizing Gender," in Louise M. Antony and Charlotte Witt, eds., *A Mind of One's Own* (Boulder: Westview, 1993), 138 ("MacKinnon's feminism is not reductionist. She is not committed to the view that gender identity or gender oppression has political primacy. MacKinnon can maintain with perfect consistency that all women share as women certain common traits or experiences; that the proper tactical or strategic response to multiple oppression cannot be determined a priori and should not be presumed to be the same in every context; and that it is not for white women to tell black or Native American women where their duty or interest lies in circumstances of conflict.")

Maybe so, but MacKinnon spends precious little time addressing such issues. This lack of attention suggests that she has effectively marginalized the relevant issues. Regardless of whether we can rehabilitate her theory to accommodate such issues, MacKinnon has pushed them, whether consciously or not, from the center of her feminist agenda. And that is significant.

53. See, for example, Naomi Scheman, "Though This Be Method, Yet There Is Madness in it," in Antony and Witt, (eds.), *Mind of One's Own*, 166 ("That epistemology presents itself as universal, a universal defined by pre-

cisely that which is not different in the ways that some are defined as different: women . . . people of color . . . the disabled . . . gays and lesbians . . . none of these categories is natural or ahistorical, and they all came into existence as strategies of regimentation and containment.")

54. Louise M. Antony, "Quine as Feminist," in Antony and Witt, (eds.), *Mind of One's Own*, 213–214 ("As with all unrealistically high standards, they tend to support the status quo—in this case, received opinion—by virtue of the fact that they will only be invoked in 'controversial' cases, i.e., in case of challenge to familiar or received or 'expert' opinion. Since the standards are unreasonably high, the views tested against them will invariably be found wanting; since the only views so tested will be unpopular ones, their failure to pass muster serves to add additional warrant to prevailing prejudices, as well as a patina of moral vindication to the holders of those prejudices, who can self-righteously claim to have given 'due consideration' to the 'other side.' ")

55. Sally Haslanger, "On Being Objective and Being Objectified," in Antony and Witt, (eds.), *Mind of One's Own*, 106 ("The norm of aperspectivity . . . functions to mask the power of the objectifier, thereby reinforcing the claim that the observed differences between men and women are a reflection of their natures. By this move the objectifier casts gender differences as asocial and amoral: We aren't responsible for things' natures, so morality has no foothold. And because we cannot change something's nature, there is nothing to be done about it anyway.")

56. Black feminists state this forcefully. See, for example, Patricia Hill Collins, "Toward an Afrocentric Feminist Epistemology," in Jaggar and Rothenberg, eds., *Feminist Frameworks*, 94–95 ("For any body of knowledge, new knowledge claims must be consistent with an existing body of knowledge that the group controlling the interpretive context accepts as true . . . scientists aim to distance themselves from the values, vested interests, and emotions generated by their class, race, sex, or unique situation . . . Such criteria ask African-American women to objectify themselves, devalue our emotional life, displace our motivations for furthering knowledge about Black women, and confront in an adversarial relationship those with more social, economic and professional power.")

57. Haslanger, "Being Objective and Being Objectified," 101.

58. Haslanger answers in the negative, ibid., 115 ("We should reject the ideal of assumed objectivity . . . for the suggestion that we might endorse it while working to undermine the existing social hierarchy leaves us in an unmanageable position . . . If we accept the norms of assumed objectivity as

binding on us, then our efforts at social change would be, by its lights, not only unmotivated but unjustified.")

59. Scheman, "Though This Be Method," 162.

60. "In order to apply a rule neutrally in future cases, one must discern a priori what the differences and similarities among groups are . . . one must first abstract the essential and universal similarities among humans; one must have strict assumptions about human nature as such. Without such an abstraction, there is no way to talk about what differences in treatment are arbitrary and which are justified. Underlying this approach is the correspondence theory of truth: The sovereign's judgments are valid only when they reflect objective facts . . . there must be a list of sex differences that matter and those that do not. Notice, however, that abstract universality by its own terms cannot arrive at such a list. It has no 'bridge to the concrete' by which to ascertain the emerging and cultural qualities which constitute difference." Ann C. Scales, "The Emergence of Feminist Jurisprudence: An Essay," *Yale Law Journal* 95 (1986):1377.

61. Catharine A. MacKinnon, "Feminism, Marxism, Method and the State: An Agenda for Theory," *Signs* 7 (1982):537. (Emphasis in original.)

62. MacKinnon, "Feminism, Marxism, Method and the State: Toward Feminist Jurisprudence," *Signs* 8 (1983): 645.

63. Ibid., 658 ("If objectivity is the epistemological stance of which women's sexual objectification is the social process, its imposition the paradigm of power in the male form, then the state will appear most relentless in imposing the male point of view when it comes closest to achieving its highest formal criterion of distanced aperspectivity. When it is most ruthlessly neutral, it will be most male.")

64. Scales, "Emergence of Feminist Jurisprudence," 1400–1401.

65. Ibid., 1401.

66. Ibid.

67. Ibid., 1402–1403. Most of Scales's remarks are directed to legal contexts. It is not clear, however, whether Scales is attacking any real, influential philosopher of law. Those philosophers, such as Ronald Dworkin and H. L. A. Hart, who do accept objectivity in law have more subtle accounts of right answers and judicial discretion than the clumsy versions of mechanical jurisprudence that seem to be the focus of attacks by proponents of feminism unmodified. See, for example, Raymond A. Belliotti, *Justifying Law* (Philadelphia: Temple University Press, 1992), 44–107.

But the point may be that preoccupation with traditional Rule of Law virtues blinds us to the fluidity, contextuality, and pluralistic interpretations of social reality. Thus, an advocate of feminism unmodified might argue that even in a radically egalitarian or female dominated state, adherence to Rule of Law adjudication would be misconceived from the outset.

68. MacKinnon says that "Feminism must grasp that male power produces the world before it distorts it. Women's acceptance of their condition does not contradict its fundamental unacceptability if women have little choice but to *become* persons who freely choose women's roles. For this reason, the reality of women's oppression is, finally, neither demonstrable nor refutable empirically. "Agenda for Theory," 542.

MacKinnon is aware of the potential vacuity in claiming that women who oppose her views are victims of false consciousness: "Not all women agree with the feminist account of women's situation, nor do all feminists agree with any single rendition of feminism . . . what is the point of view of the experience of all women? Most responses in the name of feminism . . . either (1) simply regard some women's views as 'false consciousness,' or (2) embrace any version of women's experience that a biological female claims as her own. The first approach treats women's views as unconscious conditioned reflections of their oppression, complicitous in it . . . But if both feminism and antifeminism are responses to the condition of women, how is feminism exempt from devalidation by the same account? . . . The false consciousness approach begs this question by taking women's self-reflections as evidence of their stake in their own oppression, when the women whose self-reflections are at issue question whether their condition is oppressed at all. The second response proceeds as if women are free . . . So our problem is this: the false consciousness approach cannot explain experience as it is experienced by those who experience it. The alternative can only reiterate the terms of that experience." MacKinnon, "Toward Feminist Jurisprudence," 637 n. 5.

There is much in this quotation that is perspicacious and that would be applauded by a mainstream analytic philosopher. The question is this: Does MacKinnon heed her own counsel? Or does she end up descending into the quagmire of "the first approach" when she rebukes her critics as "collaborators"? See, for example, MacKinnon, *Feminism Unmodified* (Cambridge, Mass.: Harvard University Press, 1987), 198–205, 216–228.

69. MacKinnon, "Toward Feminist Jurisprudence," 637.

70. Ibid.

71. Ibid., 638.

72. Katharine T. Bartlett, "MacKinnon's Feminism: Power on Whose Terms?" *California Law Review* 75 (1987): 1562.

73. Ibid., 1563.

74. MacKinnon, *Feminism Unmodified*, 198–205, 216–228.

75. Bartlett, "MacKinnon's Feminism," 1563.

76. MacKinnon, "Toward Feminist Jurisprudence," 640.

77. Ibid., 638.

78. "MacKinnon's failure to acknowledge that not every fact related to women's experience neatly and unreservedly supports her thesis of male dominance not only reduces the persuasiveness of her work, but demonstrates an effort to control and objectify her subject that is characteristic of the male world she otherwise so firmly rejects . . . She claims to speak for all women, yet dismisses in disgust as 'collaborators' those who don't think and act in accordance with her own views." Bartlett, "MacKinnon's Feminism," 1564.

79. "They are also a notorious philosophical quagmire, involving such problematic notions as self-deception, unconscious motivation, foreseen but unintended consequences, coercive offers, and even 'false consciousness.' Unfortunately, feminists can sometimes find no way around this quagmire." Alison M. Jaggar, "Introduction" in *Living With Contradictions*, 8.

80. "MacKinnon talked about how male domination is an *almost* metaphysically perfect system. It seems to me what she presents *is* a metaphysically perfect system and therefore one that is unreal . . . it defines women as having no power, and if by definition women are those without power, then go home and lock the door because there is no possibility for change." Ellen C. DuBois, "Feminist Discourse, Moral Values, and the Law," *Buffalo Law Review* 34 (1985):70.

81. MacKinnon, *Feminism Unmodified*, 195. Although the criticism that MacKinnon tacitly relies on a notion of "authenticity" is recurrent, it is not clear that the charge is well-founded. See, for example, Ruth Colker, "Feminism, Sexuality, and Self: A Preliminary Inquiry into the Politics of Authenticity," *Boston Unversity Law Review* 68 (1988):217, 220 n. 8 ("MacKinnon never takes a position on the concept of authenticity explicitly in her scholarship. However, when I asked her about the concept when she presented a paper . . . she responded that she found the concept unhelpful.")

82. See, e.g., Katherine O'Donovan, "Engendering Justice: Women's Perspectives and the Rule of Law," *University of Toronto Law Journal* 39 (1989):139.

83. "I do not myself find MacKinnon's thesis that sexual exploitation is the life force or linchpin of gender inequality persuasive. Although sexual relations may commonly exhibit the dominance and submission patterning she de-

scribes, MacKinnon has not shown why sexual exploitation should be regarded as the primary cause rather than an effect of gender hierarchy." Rapaport, "Generalizing Gender," 134.

84. MacKinnon, "Agenda for Theory," 529–534, especially 532.

85. Although not clearly an exponent of feminism unmodified, Robin West captures part of the contrast between feminist jurisprudence and "male" versions of legal theory: "Feminist legal scholars insist it is the heart and not the head, the ability to particularize, not generalize, one's *sensitivity* to context, and not one's ability to transcend it, the ability to connect . . . not the ability to 'see past' differences to some universal essence, which is the basis of . . .'The Rule of Law.' " "Love, Rage and Legal Theory," *Yale Journal of Law and Feminism* 1 (1989):101, 102.

86. Moreover, MacKinnon wrongly extrapolates from observations about the socially created world to the world as a whole. "The basic strategy of MacKinnon's argument—a strategy all too common among feminist theorists—is deeply flawed. The strategy is to take a powerful analysis of how the social world has been shaped by male power and desire, and to extend this analysis to the world as a whole . . . If we claim, however, that the power that has determined gender categories is the *same power* that has determined all categories, then we deflate the social analysis of this power with the simple thought that much of what the world is like is not within the control of people, societies, cultures, languages, etc." Haslanger, "Being Objective and Being Objectified," 112.

87. Epistemological foundationalism is the view that our knowledge claims can ultimately be tested by certain foundational truths which themselves are immune from revision. Such foundational truths may be indubitable (incapable of consistently being doubted), self-evident (beyond and not in need of rational demonstration), incorrigible, or presuppositions of rationality itself. Metaphysical realism is the view that reality is mind-independent and admits of one true description, and that humans arrive at truth insofar as their propositions about the world copy or correspond to reality. Metaphysical realism often appeals to a notion of inherent essences—"things-in-themselves"—and sometimes appeals to a special human cognitive faculty (for example, intuition) by which we grasp these essences.

88. Antony, "Quine as Feminist," 200. ("The first lesson is that all theorizing *takes some knowledge for granted.* Theorizing about theorizing is no exception . . . we cannot expect to learn *from our philosophy* what counts as knowledge and how much of it we have; rather we must begin with the

assumption that we know certain things and figure out how that happened . . . a second lesson . . . requires us to give up the idea that our own epistemic practice is transparent to us . . . It requires us to be open to the possibility that the processes that we actually rely on to obtain and process information about the world are significantly different from the ones our philosophy told us had to be the right ones." 202.)

The rationalists (e.g., Descartes, Leibniz, Spinoza) emphasized the power of a priori reason to grasp substantive truths about the world. The empiricists (e.g., Locke, Berkeley, Hume), on the other hand, stressed experience as the main source of knowledge.

89. See, for example, Thomas Kuhn, *The Structure of Scientific Revolutions*, 2d ed. (Chicago: University of Chicago Press, 1970); Paul Feyerabend, *Against Method: Outline of an Anarchistic Theory of Knowledge* (London: New Left Books, 1975).

90. "A completely 'open mind,' confronting the sensory evidence we confront, could never manage to construct the rich systems of knowledge we construct." Antony, "Quine as Feminist," 211.

91. "[This is] a watershed insight common to several overlapping philosophical traditions whose progenitors include John Dewey, Ludwig Wittgenstein, and Rudolf Carnap: The world can be described in alternative ways bespeaking distinctive theoretic purposes. We confuse the social ontology of our theories with the way the world really is only to the detriment of our understanding of both theory and the world." Rapaport, "Generalizing Gender," 139.

92. Antony, "Quine as Feminist," 214.

93. Ibid.

94. Richard Bernstein, "Pragmatism, Pluralism, and the Healing of Wounds," *American Philosophical Society Proceedings* 63 no. 3 (1989):10.

95. Ibid., 16.

96. Ibid., 16–17.

97. Ibid., 15 ("For there is a danger of *fragmenting* pluralism where . . . we are only able to communicate with the small group that already shares our own biases, and no longer even experience the need to talk with others outside of this circle. There is a *flabby* pluralism where our borrowings from different orientations are little more than glib superficial poaching. There is a *polemical* pluralism where the appeal to pluralism . . . but becomes rather an ideological weapon to advance one's own orientation. There is a *defensive* pluralism, a form of tokenism, where we pay lip service to others 'doing their own thing' but are already convinced that there is nothing important to be learned from them.")

98. See, for example, Belliotti, *Justifying Law,* 9–14.

99. "[My book] is a personal interpretation. The book represents *my* view of *my* people." Gambino, *Blood of My Blood,* vii.

3. The Individual Resists the State

1. By far the best article written on this topic is Nunzio Pernicone, "Anarchism in Italy, 1872–1900," in Rudolph J. Vecoli, ed., *Italian American Radicalism: Old World Origins and New World Developments* (Staten Island: American Italian Historical Association, 1972):1–29.

2. When the provisional French government withdrew from Paris in March 1871, after some of its troops had fraternized with the populace, the Paris National Guard unexpectedly found itself holding state power. The Central Committee of the guard held a special election. A third of the elected members to this Paris Commune were manual workers and most of these were activists in the French branch of the First International. The Paris Commune was a two-month, unplanned experiment in popular governance that numerous leftists valorize as the precursor of extended democracy.

3. In the words of Nunzio Pernicone: "Like most of their contemporaries, they accepted the mistaken belief that the Commune had been a socialist experiment undertaken by the International Workingmen's Association. Because of this presumed link with the Commune, the prestige of the International soared among young Italian republicans." "Anarchism in Italy," 5.

4. Ibid., 6.

5. Ibid., 6.

6. Ibid., 9.

7. Ibid., 9–10.

8. Ibid., 10.

9. Ibid., 10–11.

10. Ibid., 10.

11. Ibid., 12 ("As the anarchists grew increasingly isolated from the masses and from each other, the scope of their activities tended to shrink accordingly. The insurrectionary undertakings of the 1870s could not be repeated in the 1880s . . . instead of collective action, anarchists now placed great emphasis on individual acvton, i.e., terrorism. Yet for all the rhetoric about dynamite and daggers, the Italian anarchists never produced a terrorist movement worthy of the name.")

12. Ibid., 13.

13. This position is in contrast to spontaneity theory, which held that the spontaneous, self-emancipatory efforts of workers, undertaken when the proper objective historical conditions were in place, were the best fuel for social change. According to spontaneity theory, organizations tended to reinstate leadership by elites and thus reinforce social hierarchy.

14. Pernicone, "Anarchism in Italy," 14–15.

15. The *Fasci dei Lavoratori* was a popular workers' cooperative movement that began with local strikes of farm and sulfur workers and slowly spread throughout Sicily achieving the effect of a general strike. Some individual members, against the advice of their leaders, engaged in significant destructive of public property. In 1894 Prime Minister Crispi dispatched forty thousand soldiers and imposed martial law in Sicily. See Jerre Mangione and Ben Morreale, *La Storia* (New York: Harper Collins, 1992), 81–85.

16. Pernicone, "Anarchism in Italy," 15.

17. Ibid.

18. Ibid., 16.

19. Ibid., 17.

20. Ibid.

21. Ibid.

22. Ibid., 18.

23. Ibid.

24. Ibid.

25. Peter G. Ciano, "The Moral Imprint of Early Twentieth Century Italian-American Radical Labor," *Proteus* 7 (1990):25–31, 25.

26. Melvyn Dubofsky, "Italian Anarchism and The American Dream: A Comment," in Vecoli, ed., *Italian American Radicalism*, 52 ("Why examine anarchism among Italian immigrants in the U.S., the vast majority of whom were drawn from the Mezzogiorno and Sicily, the regions of the 'old Kingdom' least penetrated by anarchist men and ideas?")

27. Paul Avrich, *Sacco and Vanzetti* (Princeton: Princeton University Press, 1991), 46.

28. Pernicone, "Anarchism in Italy," 1. Avrich, *Sacco and Vanzetti*, 45–46 ("The first anarchist groups in the United States sprang up during the 1880s, rooted in the large-scale immigration of the period. Most of the immigrants were of peasant and artisan stock, the anarchists not excepted. The initial group, formed in 1885 in New York City, which became the leading center of Italian anarchism in America, was called the *Gruppo Socialista Anarchico Rivoluzionario Carlo Cafiero* . . . From New York the movement spread rapidly

as the immigrants increased in number. At first, it was concentrated in the large port cities on the eastern seaboard, where the newcomers tended to settle. By the early 1890s, accordingly, we find Italian anarchist groups in such places as Boston, Philadelphia, and Baltimore . . . the movement gradually filtered westward, with circles appearing in Pittsburgh, Cleveland, and Detroit, as well as in Chicago . . . by the mid 1890s, groups were established on the Pacific Coast, the first, in San Francisco.") See also Mangione and Morreale, *La Storia*, 248 ("Of the ten thousand Italians [in Paterson at the turn of the century], two thousand called themselves anarchists.")

29. Pernicone, *Anarchism in Italy*, 1 ("Every important [Italian] leader made a point of visiting [the United States]: Franceso Saverio Merlino in 1892; Pietro Gori in 1895; Errico Malatesta in 1899 and Luigi Galleani in 1901. Galleani, who remained active in the United States until his deportation in 1919, figured so prominently in the development of the movement that the mainstream of Italian anarchism in America might well be described as 'Galleanista.' "). Avrich, *Sacco and Vanzetti*, 48–49 ("Galleani during the first two decades of the twentieth century, was the leading Italian anarchist in America . . . His powerful rhetoric and vision of total freedom raised his listeners to a high pitch of enthusiasm . . . a visitor from France [said] 'I have never heard an orator more powerful than Luigi Galleani . . . His voice is full of warmth, his glance alive and penetrating, his gestures of exceptional vigor and flawless distinction.' ")

30. Avrich, *Sacco and Vanzetti*, 49–50. Mangione and Morreale, *La Storia*, 248, 281–282.

31. Pernicone, "Anarchism in Italy," 2.

32. Avrich, *Sacco and Vanzetti*, 51.

33. Nunzio Pernicone, "Carlo Tresca: Life and Death of a Revolutionary," Richard N. Juliani and Philip V. Cannistraro, eds., *Italian Americans: The Search for a Usable Past* (Staten Island: American Italian Historical Association, 1989), 216–235, 217.

34. Compare with Avrich, *Sacco and Vanzetti*, 53 ("Almost all Italian anarchists, and especially the Galleanists, disdained conciliatory measures and piecemeal economic and social change. Achieving limited improvements, they argued, would only blunt the revolutionary ardor of the workers, weaken their will to resist, and delay the final overthrow of capitalism. Impatient with the reformist methods of socialists and liberals, they espoused more militant tactics . . . Because of this, the Italian anarchists did not play a conspicuous role in the organized labor movement.")

35. Ciano, "Moral Imprint," 25–26.

36. Ibid., 26.

37. Ibid.

38. Pernicone, "Anarchism in Italy," 2.

39. Ibid.

40. For example, labor unrest or strikes in Paterson in 1902, Barre in 1908, Hopedale in 1913, Plymouth in 1916, Lawrence in 1912 and 1919, New York City in 1922, Passaic in 1926.

41. Mangione and Morreale, *La Storia*, 296.

42. Ibid., 299 – 301. "The Sacco and Vanzetti case was a crossroads for the Italian immigrants and their children. Significantly, it was during this period that some of the young and ambitious turned their energies to crime rather than politics or honest work as a way out of the ghetto." 299. The authors have a point, but it would be a mistake to draw firm causal connections between the outcome of the Sacco-Vanzetti affair and subsequent Italian-American crime. If Sacco and Vanzetti had been vindicated would the relevant segment of Italian Americans have refrained from their criminal activities during Prohibition Days? Quite unlikely.

What about Sacco and Vanzetti? Avrich reminds us that "Both men . . . were social militants, advocates of relentless warfare against government and capital. Far from being the innocent dreamers so often depicted by their supporters, they belonged to a branch of the anarchist movement which preached insurrectionary violence and armed retaliation, including the use of dynamite and assassination. Such activities, they believed, were replies to the monstrous violence of the state." *Sacco and Vanzetti*, 56 – 57.

But were they guilty of the crimes for which they were accused? Most writers have argued that they were not guilty. See, for example, Herbert Ehrmann, *The Case That Will Not Die* (Boston: Little, Brown, 1969); Roberta Feuerlicht, *Justice Crucified* (New York: McGraw-Hill, 1977); Osmond Fraenkel, *The Sacco-Vanzetti Case* (New York: Knopf, 1931); Felix Frankfurter, *The Case of Sacco and Vanzetti* (Boston: Little, Brown, 1927); Eugene Lyons, *The Life and Death of Sacco and Vanzetti* (New York: International Publishers, 1927); Louis Joughin and Edmund Morgan, *The Legacy of Sacco and Vanzetti* (New York: Harcourt Brace, 1948). Some have argued that Sacco was guilty but Vanzetti was innocent. See, for example, Francis Russell, *Tragedy in Dedham* (New York: McGraw-Hill, 1962) and *Sacco & Vanzetti* (New York: Harper and Row, 1986); James Grossman, "The Sacco and Vanzetti Case Reconsidered," *Commentary* (Jan. 1962). A few insist that they were both guilty. See, for example, Robert Montgomery, *Sacco-Vanzetti* (New York: Devin-Adair, 1960). At least one book feigns neutrality but is implicitly condemnatory: David Felix, *Protest* (Bloomington: Indiana University Press, 1965).

For what it is worth, I am firmly convinced that the two men were at least *legally* (if not factually) innocent and that their trial constitutes a textbook illustration of procedural injustice.

43. Mangione and Morreale, *La Storia*, 301. I must note that Sacco and Vanzetti have finally achieved a limited vindication: in August 1977, Governor Dukakis of Massachusetts declared the fiftieth anniversary of their execution as Sacco and Vanzetti Memorial Day.

44. Pernicone, "Anarchism in Italy," 3. Mangione and Morreale, *La Storia*, 301–303.

45. Avrich, *Sacco and Vanzetti*, 51. ("What [Galleani] expressed was not a social philosophy as much as a cry of indignation, a call for militants to resist, by force if necessary, the regimentation and bureaucratization, the brutality and corruption, of the prevailing system.")

46. For an excellent introduction to such issues see J. Roland Pennock and John W. Chapman, eds., *Anarchism: Nomos* 19 (New York: New York University Press, 1978).

47. Petr Kropotkin, "Anarchism," *Encyclopaedia Brittanica*, 11th edition, vol. 1, 914.

48. Rather than viewing the rejection of government as logically entailing the other widely shared anarchist propositions, or vice versa, view them as intertwined and mutually sustaining. The rejection of government, however, may have a degree of causal priority.

49. See, for example, Robert Nozick, *Anarchy, State, and Utopia* (New York: Basic Books, 1974).

50. Mikhail Bakunin, *Statism and Anarchy* (1873) in Paul Berman, ed., *Quotations from the Anarchists* (New York: Praeger, 1972), 27.

51. Thus, the Russian-born American anarchist Emma Goldman (1869–1941) wrote: "Anarchism . . . leaves posterity free to develop its own particular systems, in harmony with its needs. Our most vivid imagination cannot foresee the potentialities of a race set free from external restraints. How, then, can anyone assume to map out a line of conduct for those to come? We . . . must guard against the tendency to fetter the future. *Anarchism* (1910) in Berman, *Quotations*, 35.

52. Bakunin, *Letters to a Frenchman* (1870) in Berman, *Quotations*, 173.

53. Max Stirner, *The Ego and His Own* (1845) in Daniel Guerin, *Anarchism: From Theory to Practice* (New York: Monthly Review Press, 1970), 27–28.

54. Ibid., 28–29.

55. George Woodcock, "Max Stirner," *Encyclopedia of Philosophy* (New York: Macmillan, 1967), vol. 8, 18.

56. Woodcock, "Anarchism," *Encyclopedia of Philosophy* (New York: Macmillan, 1967), vol. 1, 113.

57. Guerin, *Anarchism*, 17. Proudhon, although viewing the electoral process as counter-revolutionary, sometimes strayed from his principles in practice: "In June 1848 he let himself be elected to parliament . . . during the partial elections of September 1848 and the presidential elections of December 10 of the same year, he supported the candidacy of Raspail . . . in 1863 and 1864, he did advocate returning blank ballot papers, but as a demonstration against the imperial dictatorship, not in opposition to universal suffrage." 18.

58. Ibid., 45–46.

59. Ibid., 64.

60. Proudhon, *Philosophie du progres* (1853); George Woodcock, "Pierre-Joseph Proudhon," *The Encyclopedia of Philosophy* (New York: Macmillan, 1967), vol. 6, 508.

61. "[A revolutionary] must share our conviction that woman, different from man but not inferior to him, intelligent, working, and free like him, must be declared his equal in all political and social rights; and that in free society, religious and civil marriage must be replaced by free marriage." Bakunin, *Program of the Fraternity* (1865), in Berman, *Quotations*, 200.

62. "I am not a communist because communism concentrates all the powers of society and absorbs them into the State, because it leads inevitably to the centralization of property in the hands of the State, while I want to see the State abolished . . . I want society, and collective or social property, to be organized from the bottom up through free association and not from the top down by authority of any kind." Bakunin, quoted in Guerin, *Anarchism*, 22.

63. Ibid., 36.

64. Woodcock, "Anarchism," 114.

65. Carlo Cafiero, *Anarchy and Communism* (1880), in Berman, *Quotations*, 31.

66. Woodcock, "Anarchism," 114.

67. Ibid.

68. Bakunin, *The Paris Commune and the Notion of the State* (1871), in Berman, *Quotations*, 160–161.

69. Errico Malatesta, *L'Agitazione* (1897), in Berman, *Quotations*, 162.

70. Emma Goldman, *The Place of the Individual in Society* (1934), in Berman, *Quotations*, 162.

71. In this vein, Donald McIntosh describes anarchism: "[No anarchist] has been so utopian as to seek to eliminate all forms of coercion from human relations. What is anathema to all is not compulsion itself, but any form of compulsion which proceeds from a position of supremacy—from a superior to a subordinate. In fact, the relation of superior to subordinate is opposed just as vehemently if no compulsion whatsoever is involved. Among the various kinds of government only anarchism does not involve the imposition of the will of the higher on the will of the lower. It is the passion for equality, not freedom, that lies behind the anarchist temper of mind." "The Dimensions of Anarchy," in Pennock and Chapman, eds., *Anarchism*, 247–248.

72. Ibid., 261–262 ("To eliminate all political authority must lead in the following directions: The principle of unanimity . . . The community must be very small in size . . . Technology must be simple . . . The division of labor must be minimized . . . Social cohesion must be high . . . Individualism must be low.")

73. Roberto Unger, *Passion: An Essay on Personality* (New York: Free Press, 1984), 7–10.

74. Ibid., 3–5, 20–22, 95–100.

75. Ibid., 86.

76. Ibid., 22–39, 53–55, 57–62, 65–67, 69–76. The heroic ethic attracts those who combine devotion to collective tasks with skepticism about the possibility of moral insight. Assuming a task at the margins of society and often in violation of some of its norms, the hero engages in limit-breaking activity. As he assigns unconditional value to a conditional task, he exalts pride at the expense of faith and disengages himself from ordinary concerns. Fusion with an impersonal absolute accepts a contrast between our illusory phenomenal world, where the principle of individuation holds sway, and the plane of absolute reality, where distinctions between individuals and things vanishes. Seen most clearly in Hinduism and Buddhism, adherents take either the path of the recluse or accept their social role while remaining aloof from it. Confucianism adheres to a particular list of social relations and ordering of the emotions. Viewing people as completely defined by fixed social roles and a particular political order, this ethic mistakes a specific system of social order as the solution to conflicting conduct and assertion. The Christian-romantic ethic puts personal attachments up for grabs, acknowledging that the qualities realized in

faith, hope, and love override the claims of given social categories and that advances in self-understanding occur as we open ourselves to personal encounter. It is beset by a deep ambivalence between a moralistic obsession with fixed rules and a fantasy of the super-individual who defies all obstacles while asserting his will.

77. Ibid., 53–64.

78. Ibid., 62.

79. Ibid., 24–25.

80. Ibid., 24.

81. Ibid., 32–39.

82. James Boyle, "Modernist Social Theory," *Harvard Law Review* 98 (1985):1066, 1073–1074; Drucilla Cornell, "Toward a Modern/Postmodern Reconstruction of Ethics," *University of Pennsylvania Law Review* 133 (1985):291, 296, 328, 356–358.

83. Cornell, "Toward a Reconstruction," 356.

84. For Unger, the standard of proof applicable to his account must emerge from experience itself. Some critics, however, are unconvinced by his method. See, for example, Ernest Weinrib, "Enduring Passion," *Yale Law Journal* 94 (1985):1825, 1828, 1833 ("Modern science, Unger argues, merely disqualifies the classical mode of normative argument as a procedure of science, but leaves it intact as a method of normative inference . . . Unger requires a means of prying the method of arguing from fact to value loose from its underlying justification. Thus, his second move is to assert that the slide from fact to value responds to an inescapable human need. The practice is so intimate a part of our history, he argues, that no mode of inquiry will establish its validity. Only a radical and terminal skepticism unwilling to accede to the possibility of knowledge would lead us to challenge so ingrained a practice . . . By infusing the transcendence of context with value, he immediately transforms the basis of right, which is conceptually anterior to the notion of good, into a good to be pursued. Not only is this movement from is to ought unsupported by any argument commensurate with its significance, but its use here undermines the radicalism of contextuality by incorporating it into the conceptually posterior moment of goodness.")

85. Roberto Unger, *Social Theory: Its Situation and Its Task* (Cambridge: Cambridge University Press, 1987), 9, 165–169. Unger identifies Foucault, Gramsci, and Dewey as ultra-theorists.

86. Ibid., 168–169.

87. See, for example, Bernard Yack, "Book Review: Toward a Free Marketplace of Social Institutions: Roberto Unger's 'Super-Liberal' Theory of

Emancipation," *Harvard Law Review* 101 (1988):1961, 1967–1970 (1988). For the view that the entire Critical Legal Studies movement generally merely restates the problem of our existential dilemma see Christopher H. Schroeder, "Liberalism and the Objective Point of View," in J. Roland Pennock and John W. Chapman, eds., *Justification: Nomos* 28 (New York: New York University Press, 1986), 1108–1109.

88. See, for example, Thomas Kuhn, *The Structure of Scientific Revolutions*, 2d ed. (Chicago: University of Chicago Press, 1970); and Paul Feyerabend, *Against Method: Outline of an Anarchistic Theory of Knowledge* (London: New Left Books, 1975).

89. See, for example, Unger, *False Necessity: Anti-Necessitarian Social Theory in the Service of Radical Democracy* (Cambridge: Cambridge University Press, 1987), 572.

90. Unger, *Passion*, 5, 11–15.

91. Roberto Unger, *Plasticity into Power* (Cambridge: Cambridge University Press, 1987), chapter 3.

92. Unger, *Passion*, 259.

93. Weinrib, "Enduring Passion," 1840.

94. Unger, *False Necessity*, 587.

95. Roberto Unger, "The Critical Legal Studies Movement," *Harvard Law Review* 96 (1983):561, 584, 672–673.

96. Friedrich Engels explicitly used the term "false consciousness" in his letter to Franz Mehring, July 14, 1893, in Marx and Engels, *Selected Works* (Moscow: Progress Publishers, 1968), 690 ("Ideology is a process accomplished by the so-called thinker consciously, it is true, but with a false consciousness. The real motive forces impelling him remain unknown to him; otherwise it simply would not be an ideological process. Hence he imagines false or seeming motive forces.")

97. Unger, "Critical Legal Studies," 580.

98. For example, the ideal of "democracy" is normally thought to be paramount in the sphere of "country," the ideal of "private community" in the sphere of "family," and the ideal of "contract and technological hierarchy" in the sphere of "work." Moreover, each of these ideals has certain institutional embodiments (three-branch representative government, nuclear family, management/workers, respectively). By developing new institutional embodiments for our abstract ideals we may efface their distinctive spheres of domain. For example, "democracy" may extend to "work," or "contract" may extend to family. In the process, personal relations are emancipated from vested social hierarchy and division. Ibid., 578–581.

99. Law would reflect four kinds of rights: (1) immunity rights would establish the nearly absolute claim of individuals to personal invasions. Such rights would include civic rights of political organization, expression, and participation; welfare entitlements; and options to withdraw functionally or physically from the established order. (2) Destabilization rights are collective entitlements which enable the disruption of established institutions and social practices in order to avoid the vesting of entrenched power. Their aim is the disruption of social hierarchy and division. (3) Market rights represent "conditional and provisional claims to divisible portions of social capital." In contrast to capitalist regimes, market rights will not be viewed as the paradigm of "rights," but will instead be a subcategory of rights. (4) Solidarity rights protect expectations that arise from the mutual reliance and vulnerability that characterize personal relations. The effect of such rights would be to ensure that good faith loyalty and reciprocity characterized the formation of contracts. Unger, "Critical Legal Studies," 598–600, 612, 640.

100. The organization of government would be formed in light of three aspirations: The branches of government should be multiplied to ensure that every feature of the social order is subject to destabilization and broadly based conflict; conflicts among these increased branches of government should be resolved by principles of priority among the branches and by appeal to the electorate. The principles of priority would aim at resolving impasses clearly and quickly, and the political party in office must have a real opportunity to implement its programs. Ibid., 592–593, 596.

As for law, Unger advocates use of "deviationist legal doctrine." This method is similar to the "loose form of criticism, justification, and discovery that is possible with ideological controversy itself." For Unger, abstract concepts such as "right," "economic market," and "freedom," have many possible specific institutional embodiments. Although philosophers using the analytic tools of conceptual analysis may purport to discover the dictates of Reason and, miraculously, demonstrate how the present institutional structures of democratic-centrist regimes are more or less morally sound, in fact, this is an exercise in false necessity. For things can well be otherwise.

The proponent of deviationist legal doctrine looks at pockets of doctrine outside the acknowledged core of law and tries to extend the use of that peripheral doctrine. For example, in the law of contracts the principle "every contract must be entered into with good faith" is peripheral to the acknowledged core principle "every contract must involve arms' length bargaining." By extending the use of the peripheral principle and marginalizing the hitherto core principle, the law of contracts changes considerably and certain balances of social power are altered as a result. Ibid., 577–580.

101. Ibid., 595.

102. See, for example, William A. Galston, "False Universality," *Northwestern University Law Review* 81 (1987): 751, 758–759, 761–762; Cass R. Sunstein, "Routine and Revolution," *Northwestern University Law Review* 81 (1987):869, 890.

The jurisprudential version of this criticism would highlight Unger's apparent failure to understand the virtues of the stability of the Rule of Law: constraints on rampant discretion; security in forming expectations and predictions over time; protection of civil liberties through general applications of law; and its contribution to economic efficiency.

103. See, for example, Cornel West, "Between Dewey and Gramsci: Unger's Emancipatory Experimentalism," *Northwestern University Law Review* 81 (1987):941, 942–943, 950–951; David E. Van Zandt, "Commonsense Reasoning, Social Change, and the Law," *Northwestern University Law Review* 81 (1987):894, 938–940.

4. The Nation Encounters the World

1. Christopher Hibbert, *Garibaldi and His Enemies* (London: Penguin, 1987), 6–7. See also, Frank J. Coppa, "Giuseppe Garibaldi: Italian Patriot with an International Vision," in Rocco Caporale, ed., *The Italian Americans through the Generations* (Staten Island: American Italian Historical Association, 1986), 49–55. ("It was Mazzini who taught Garibaldi about the unity of the human race and convinced him that the Italians were a Messianic people destined to initiate a new epoch of the human race. A prophet of a new order and religion, Mazzini truly believed that the destiny of Italy was intertwined with that of the entire world." 50.)

2. Hibbert, *Garibaldi and Enemies,* 18 ("For twelve years, first at sea and then on land, he fought his way along this new path that the republic of Rio Grande do Sul and afterwards the republics of Santa Caterina and Uruguay, had opened for him. Shipwrecked, ambushed, shot through the neck, captured, imprisoned, strung up by the wrists for attempting to escape and refusing to say who had helped him, marching exhausted for days on end through the jungle with nothing to eat but the roots of plants, and riding at night over the cold sierras, through suffering, violence and the unquestioned belief that he was 'helping the cause of nations,' he grew to love the wild and trackless immensities of the continent where he was serving so invaluable an apprenticeship.

Throughout his later life he looked back with pride and a kind of sad longing to those days.")

3. Ibid., 22. See also Denis Mack Smith, ed., *Garibaldi* (Englewood Cliffs: Prentice-Hall, 1969).

4. Hibbert, *Garibaldi and Enemies*. ("Cavour's perseverance and skill in manipulating men and situations to his own ends, his instinctive flair for recognizing the crucial and decisive moment after long periods of patient waiting, his cunning, not to say, unscrupulous opportunism, so carefully concealed behind the comfortable, frank, beard-fringed face and the small spectacles of a far less astute master of expediency, were all, at least in part, recognized by the King [Victor Emmanuel] and valued by him." 136; "Cavour's habit of saying one thing to one man and something else to the next, his willingness to contradict himself twice on the same day, his skill in persuading so many different men that he had as many different motive . . . his subsequent desire to rationalize his actions and idealize his motives make it impossible, of course, to reveal in a clear light any sort of consistent attitude." 194.)

5. Ibid., 199.

6. Smith, *Garibaldi*, 63 ("Garibaldi was outlawed like a brigand or a rebel, just for trying to do once again what he had been so applauded for doing in 1860. He was then seriously wounded in an engagement with the Italian army at Aspromonte in Calabria during which some on both sides were killed. The soldiers did not even call upon him to surrender before opening fire . . . it was the most terrible moment in Garibaldi's life. Some of his men who surrendered were at once executed without trial . . . Garibaldi reacted with extreme bitterness . . . As it was thought too dangerous to punish him or even bring him to trial, he was then 'pardoned' and set free.")

7. Hibbert, *Garibaldi and Enemies*. (" 'The making of Italy was to prove a victory for the intellectuals, the liberals, the middle classes; not for the uneducated, who hardly knew what the word *Italy* meant; not for the poor, who felt its presence only in higher taxes and conscription; not for those who lost a paternal, protective ordering of society to gain a more grasping competitiveness in which the weaker went to the wall . . . There can be little doubt that Garibaldi's prestige among ordinary people helped to obscure what was really happening until they were too late to resist it.' " 149; "There was bitter feeling—later to grow so bitter that the whole conception of the Risorgimento was condemned— that the North has stripped the South of its riches, ignored its claims and abandoned it to poverty." 334.)

8. Ibid., 183 ("Those who inhabited this sun-scorched island [Sicily] felt themselves a world apart from the rest of Italy, as indeed they were. Geographically, racially, traditionally, they were different and they felt proud to be different.")

9. Ibid., 363 ("His idealistic, romantic socialism, his belief that people must be loved before they could be ruled, his supposition that the fulfillment of nationalist ambitions in Europe would be followed by a federal union, his persistent advocacy of benevolent dictatorship to replace for a time the corruption of self-seeking politicians and ineffectual parliaments, were all seen as typical Garibaldian fantasies.")

10. Ibid., 7. Smith, *Garibaldi*, 88 ("Garibaldi was then a man of 38, of medium height, well-proportioned, with fair hair, blue eyes, a Greek nose and a Greek chin and forehead . . . His beard is long . . . His movements are graceful. His voice has a splendid and melodious softness . . . he seems absent-minded and a person of more imagination than calculation; but, once mention the word independence, or that of Italy, and he becomes a volcano in eruption.")

11. Smith, *Garibaldi*, 175 ("Garibaldi lacked a capacity for self-criticism. He was too innocent. No doubt he took himself too seriously; and no doubt there was too little thinking and too much declamation in his pronouncements. But he was incorruptible, even by power.")

12. Hibbert, *Garibaldi and Enemies*, 322.

13. Smith, *Garibaldi*. ("One thing which did a great deal of harm to Giuseppe Garibaldi was his habit of thinking all men honest, and his assumption that everyone was as selfless and devoted to their country as he was," 135; "He was the most loving, the least hating of men . . . one may freely defy the world to trace an act of meanness or a deed of cruelty, or even a deliberately unkind word, to the man himself . . . Unfortunately, his trust in men—and women—transcended all discretion." 151.)

14. Hibbert, *Garibaldi and Enemies*, 32–33.

15. Smith, *Garibaldi*, 93 ("He not only never was known to avail himself of his many opportunities of even allowable personal profit, and has always strictly prevented his men from pillaging or otherwise misconducting themselves.")

16. Hibbert, *Garibaldi and Enemies*, 214–215.

17. Ibid., 363. Smith, *Garibaldi*. ("Some of Garibaldi's first decrees as Dictator of Sicily were measures of social reform dealing with land redistribution and popular education." 43; "He campaigned for universal suffrage, for female emancipation, for reduced taxes on the poor, and for reduced expenditure on the army." 80.)

18. Smith, *Garibaldi*, 163.

19. Ibid., 169 ("The skill with which he made himself the idol of the common people, with his instinctive knowledge of their wishes and their changeableness, and the fact of his attending religious ceremonies [despite his intense anti-clericalism] to the great scandal of his volunteers, all this shows his political shrewdness . . . he could impose his will on nobles and common people alike.")

20. Hibbert, *Garibaldi and Enemies*, 61. The rules also seem to reflect Garibaldi's strong anticlericalism.

21. Ibid., 234 ("He denounced in unmeasured terms the want of good faith, indeed, the infamy, of the Royal authorities in allowing the foreign mercenaries, whilst a flag of truce was flying, to attack the Italian troops, who had orders to discontinue fire . . . in defiance of every principle of military honour.")

22. Robert L. Holmes, *On War and Morality* (Princeton: Princeton University Press, 1989). The view that it is impossible for both sides to act justly in war may not be in fact so banal. Given the ambiguity of the antecedent justness of a cause or claim in many cases, and the fuzziness of when preemptive strikes are permissible, there are at least imaginable instances when two conflicting sides could both act in good faith and, given the available evidence, stake reasonably but conflicting claims to the moral high ground.

23. See, for example, Michael Walzer, *Just and Unjust Wars* (New York: Basic Books, 2d ed., 1992), 32–33.

24. Holmes, *War and Morality*, 181.

25. Ibid., 181, 190.

26. Walzer, *Just and Unjust Wars*, 43, 135–137.

27. Holmes, *War and Morality*, 187.

28. Ibid.

29. Ibid., 186.

30. Ibid.

31. Ibid.

32. Ibid., 184.

33. Ibid., 189–210. The doctrine of double effect states, roughly, that an act that brings about foreseen evil effects is morally permissible if and only if the act also produces good effects that outweigh the bad effects, the act is not inherently immoral, the evil effects are not the means to the good effects, and only the good effects are intended. Critics of this doctrine charge that we cannot distinguish our intentions so clearly, nor can we distinguish means from ends so easily. Moreover, the more closely the two effects of the act are connected the

less plausible is the moral agent's claim to intend one but not the other. Holmes argues that "in fact no action whatsoever is prohibited by the principle of double effect so long as one acts from a good intention." 196. This statement is too strong, but I agree with critics who argue, in effect, that the doctrine slices the bologna too thinly.

34. Ibid., 211–212.

35. Ibid., 186.

36. Ibid.

37. Richard Wasserstrom, "On the Morality of War," John Arthur, ed., *Morality and Moral Controversies* (Englewood Cliffs: Prentice-Hall, 3rd ed., 1993), 112. Wasserstrom concedes later that "in war, no less than elsewhere, the knowing killing of the innocent is an evil that throws up the heaviest of justificatory burdens. My own view is that in any major war that can or will be fought today, none of those considerations than can sometimes justify engaging in war will in fact come close to meeting this burden." 112–113.

38. Ibid., 111.

39. Ibid., 110–112; Walzer, *Just and Unjust Wars*, 155; James P. Sterba, "Reconciling Pacifists and Just War Theorists," in Sterba, ed., *Morality in Practice*, 4th ed. (Belmont: Wadsworth Publishing, 1994), 541.

40. Holmes, *War and Morality*, 195.

41. Ibid., 200.

42. Ibid., 211.

43. Ibid., 213.

44. Ibid., 200.

45. Ibid., 201.

46. Ibid.

47. Ibid., 208–209.

48. Ibid., 209.

49. Ibid., 210.

50. Ibid.

51. Ibid.

52. Ibid., 210–211.

53. See, for example, Raymond A. Belliotti, "Negative Duties, Positive Duties, and Rights," *Southern Journal of Philosophy* 16 (1978):581–588; "Contributing to Famine Relief and Sending Poisoned Food," *The Philosophical Forum* 12 (1980):20–32; "Negative and Positive Duties," *Theoria* 47 (1981):82–92; "Killing, Letting Die, and Thomson," *Critica* 14 (1982):61–74.

54. Belliotti, "Negative and Positive Duties," 84.

55. Otherwise, "[if morality did require the same level of sacrifices to help those in need as it does to refrain from killing] it would result in virtually the complete elimination of the distinction between supererogatory and obligatory acts; its adoption could result in a severe blow to personal autonomy as the hopes, desires, goods, and life projects of each individual would *always* be subject to the adverse circumstances and social situations of others; it entails the practical impossibility of anyone becoming a saint or martyr, since we could only hope, at best, to be fulfillers of duties and no more; and the standard of morality would be set so high that virtually no one would be considered a moral person, since few could fulfill all their duties." Ibid., 84 n.2.

56. Belliotti, "Killing, Letting Die, Thomson," 68.

57. But one of Holmes's points has not been addressed. Isn't he correct when he avers that we do not have a right to the aid of others, whereas we do have a right that others refrain from killing us? And would not that difference be enough to morally distinguish killing from letting die? I answer the first question affirmatively, but the second question negatively. See "Negative Duties, Positive Duties, and Rights," *Southern Journal of Philosophy* 16 (1978):581–588. See also the other articles cited in note 53 above.

58. Holmes, *War and Morality*, 211.

59. Ibid.

60. My position does not embrace the doctrine of double effect. It assumes only that there is *some* distinction to be made between direct and incidental aspects of an agent's ends. Even Holmes accepts the presence of such as distinction. See ibid., 211.

61. Ibid., 287.

62. Ibid., 263–264.

63. Ibid., 269.

64. Ibid., 270.

65. Ibid., 273.

66. Ibid.

67. Ibid., 274.

68. Ibid., 278.

69. Ibid., 290.

70. I am reminded of the portion of *Raging Bull* when then middleweight boxing champion Jake LaMotta, badly beaten and disfigured by the punches of Sugar Ray Robinson, sneers after the fight is stopped: "You didn't knock me down, Ray, you didn't knock me down." Although Jake was "unconquered" in

some sense, the fact remained that he lost his title and endured a frightening battering.

71. Walzer, *Just and Unjust Wars*, 331.

72. "Nor would civilian resistance work well against invaders who sent out squads of soldiers to kill civilian leaders, who arrested and tortured suspects, established concentration camps, and exiled large numbers of people from areas where the resistance was strong to distant and desolate parts of the country." Ibid., 332. Walzer makes the point quite nicely that under such circumstances nonviolent resistance to resolute enemies becomes indistinguishable from violence against oneself. Ibid.

73. Ibid., 335.

5. The Self Confronts Ethnicity

1. Anthony James DelPopolo, Sr., "The Making of a Holiday," *Ambassador* 13 (Spring 1992):14–17. ("Public Law 90–263, passed by both houses of Congress and signed by President Lyndon Johnson in 1968, set the observance of Columbus Day on the second Monday in October. The law became applicable to all federal employees and to the District of Columbia, and the holiday is observed in most states on this day." 17.)

2. See, e.g., Thomas Hylland Eriksen, *Ethnicity and Nationalism* (London: Pluto, 1993), 1–17, 33–35; Francis X. Femminella, "The Ethnic Ideological Themes of Italian Americans," in Richard N. Juliani, ed., *The Family and Community Life of Italian Americans* (Staten Island: Italian American Historical Association, 1983), 109–120 ("The underlying basis of ethnicity is a commonality built upon a shared 'ideology' which may be real or fictitious . . . consisting of a real or putative ancestry, memories of a shared historical past, etc. . . . may include a common language or dialect, a common place of origin, a common territory, a unique way of life, a set of religious doctrines or dogmas, kinship patterns, phenotypical features, a consciousness of kind, or any combination of these." 110); Michael Novak, *The Rise of the Unmeltable Ethnics* (New York: MacMillan, 1972), 32 ("Besides a person's own private history, choices, and conscious desires, there operate in him the metaphors, memories, instincts, tastes, and values of a historical people. These traces are not simple, direct, clear, univocal. Each ethnic tradition is multiform, persons within it vary, and one generation commonly reacts against the tastes and methods of its predecessor.")

3. "A list of characteristics, attitudes, traits, values and norms wherein no single trait or theme need be either unique or distinguishing, but where rather,

the complex as a whole, that is the total configuration (including internal contradictions and discontinuities) and their stylistic expression, is what sets the group apart." Francis X. Femminella, "The Ethnic Ideological Themes of Italian Americans," in Richard N. Juliani, ed., *The Family and Community Life of Italian Americans* (Staten Island: American Italian Historical Association, 1983), 115; "We are not trapped by our past, or victims of it. We are in many ways free from it, even 'enlightened' from it. But we are also the fruit of it. We did not spring full-blown like some Venus from the sea." Novak, *Unmeltable Ethnics*, 34.

4. One of the more interesting studies is Phylis Martinelli and Leonard Gordon, "Italian Americans: Images Across Half a Century," *Ethnic and Racial Studies* 11 (1988):319–331. ("Generic Americans, often translated into 'WASPS,' exhibited the most consistent trait clustering selections of any group. For each of the four studies [spanning 1932–1982] cited the three, positive leading traits for 'Americans' of 'industrious', 'intelligent', and 'materialistic' stayed the same . . . Clearly, the overall image of Italian Americans, while faded in terms of the 1932 stereotypes [impulsive, passionate, quick-tempered], does not match that of the core Americans after a half century." 327.)

5. Tom W. Smith, *A Profile of Italian Americans: 1972–1991* (Washington, D.C.: National Italian American Foundation, 1992), 2.

6. "The National Data Program for the Social Sciences has been monitoring trends in American society since 1972. It is the largest and longest-running research effort supported by the Sociology Program of the National Science Foundation. Each year since 1972 (with the exceptions of 1979 and 1981) the National Opinion Research Center at the University of Chicago has conducted the General Social Survey (GSS) to examine how American society works and what social changes are occurring. The GSSs are full-probability samples of adults (18 +) living in households in the United States. Interviews are conducted in person. The annual response rates have ranged from 73.5% to 79.4% and have averaged 76.6%. Each GSS interviews about 1500 respondents and across the 18 surveys from 1972–1991 27,782 people have been interviewed. For more details on sampling and survey design see James A. Davis and Tom W. Smith, General Social Surveys: 1972–1991: Cumulative Codebook. Chicago: NORC, 1991." Ibid., 99.

7. "Despite the traditional picture of the Italian-American family [as patriarchal, parent centered, large and extended, stable, and close], that image is both out of date and out of focus . . . The current Italian-American family shows increasing disruption. Fewer Italian Americans are currently married now

(59%) than in the early 1970s (69%) . . . The decline in the proportion married in part comes from an increase in divorces. In the early 1970s 13% of Italian Americans had been divorced. This rose to 22% in the mid-1980s, but has since leveled-off at 21% presently." Ibid., 10–11.

8. "Intermarriage is a two-edged sword for ethnic groups. On the one hand high intermarriage indicates that a group is being accepted by other groups in society. Low intermarriage levels usually result from prejudice and overt segregation. On the other hand, high intermarriage means that ethnic heritages are being blended together and ethnic identification becomes more complicated." Ibid., 3.

9. "Traditionally this high level of alcohol use was not a problem for Italian Americans because their alcohol consumption was social and culinary and not symptomatic of serious drink [*sic*] problems. In fact, [a study conducted in 1980] found Italian Americans to have the lowest level of problem drinking among eight ethnic groups. But a problem may now be arising. In the late 1970s 19% reported that they sometimes drink more than they think they should. This has moved up to 27% presently. Over the same period non–Italian Americans reporting drinking 'too much' declined from 27% to 23%." Ibid., 13.

See also Hugh Klein, "Contemporary Italian-American College Student Drinking Patterns," in Joseph V. Scelsa, Salvatore J. LaGumina, and Lydio Tomasi, eds., *Italian Americans in Transition* (Staten Island: American Italian Historical Association, 1990), 177–187. ("The Italian-American students surveyed not only drank frequently and fairly heavily, but they also experienced a fairly large number of problems resulting from their alcohol use . . . not only are Italian-American students more likely [than non–Italian-American student drinkers] to suffer from alcohol problems as a result of their drinking, but they are also more likely to suffer from more of these problems as well . . . Perhaps only by holding on to (or indeed, regaining) their ethnic heritage will Italian-Americans be able to escape from the pitfalls of alcohol abuse that are otherwise likely to plague them in future years." 185–186.)

10. Smith, *Profile of Italian Americans*, 17.

11. Ibid.

12. Ibid., 16.

13. Ibid., 23.

14. Ibid.

15. Ibid., 9.

16. Ibid., 24.

17. Ibid., 25.

18. [Some social scientists insist that] ethnicity is for the working class . . . It is also primarily understood in terms of a traditional, Old World culture." Donald Tricarico, "The 'New' Italian-American Ethnicity," *Journal of Ethnic Studies* 12 (1984):75.

"Some influential social scientists and historians maintain that the ethnicity of Italian Americans . . . is being continually reduced as they move into the middle class . . . the more they attain, the less they are Italian American . . . ethnicity is a function of class position and being an Italian American depends on being a member of the working class . . . The association of ethnicity and class has been far too simply drawn, and scholars may have created their own stereotype of the Italian American subculture as an exclusively working class experience. It is not clear that membership in the middle class precludes serious and meaningful expressions of ethnic group membership, that is, personal values, patterns of behavior, and interpersonal relationships that go beyond merely 'symbolic ethnicity.' " Richard N. Juliani, "The Position of Italian Americans in Contemporary Society," in Jerome Krase and William Egelman, eds., *The Melting Pot and Beyond: Italian Americans in the Year 2000* (Staten Island: American Italian Historical Association, 1987), 68–69.

19. Reported in Richard Gambino, *Italian-American Studies and Italian-Americans at the City University of New York* (New York: Faculty Fellow Report to John A. Calandra Institute, 1987), 88. Reflecting on studies conducted about ten years earlier, the Gambino report concludes that "the profiles . . . present a picture of Italian-American students at CUNY who feel alienated from the faculty, staff, and other students at their respective colleges, are generally unenlightened and unmindful of issues in the larger community, are overstressed regarding their employment commitments outside the college (particularly males), have too irrational an anxiety about their appearance and other issues of self-worth (particularly females), and who experience severe feelings of loneliness which are aggravated by the contrast of their academic careers with their parents lack of academic achievement, and by the general difficulty Italian-American young people have in establishing personal independence from their close, and in many case, 'enmeshed' families." 96.

20. Ibid., 89.

21. Ibid., 92.

22. "Unless CUNY lures many more junior Italian-American faculty, the presence of Italian-Americans in the faculty in the future will drop far

below its low 1985 figure of 5%." Ibid., 73. Moreover, "Italian-American females are an underrepresented minority within an underrepresented minority." 74.

23. In 1976 Chancellor Kibbee's directive stated: "I am designating Italian-
Americans as an affirmative action category for this University in addition to
those so categorized under existing federal statutes and regulations." Ibid., 70.

24. "The degree of Italian American political attainment at the highest
levels of the federal government remains low . . . Italian Americans have
achieved greater political success in elected and appointed positions in local
and state government . . . [Moreover,] Italian Americans remain far underrepresented in positions of corporate power in comparison to their proportion of
the general population." Juliani, "Position of Italian Americans," 66–67. See
also Martin N. Marger, *Race and Ethnic Relations* (Belmont, Calif.: Wadsworth,
1985), 108–109.

25. One who has the powers of *malocchio* ("evil eye") can cast a malevolent
spell, which often acts as a disease, onto another person or object simply by
gazing upon it. The *jettatore* is the personification of mysterious malevolence.
His mere presence negatively disorders the world. His female counterpart is the
strega ("witch"). See, e.g., Lawrence DiStasi, *Malocchio* (San Francisco: North
Point Press, 1981); and Giuseppe Pitre, "The Jettatura and the Evil Eye," in
Alan Dundes, ed., *The Evil Eye* (New York: Garland, 1981), 130–142.

26. What traits and themes characterized southern Italian peasants?
Francis X. Femminella summarizes them as follows: "Family centered . . .
attached to their geoecological environment . . . *campanilismo*, a village mentality . . . [mutual] suspicion . . . quarrelsome . . . self-critical . . . very distrustful . . . infinitely generous . . . [belief in] destiny . . . independent . . .
[belief that] to act for oneself in a highly individualistic way is simultaneously to act for one's family . . . active, hard working . . . enterprising . . .
courageous . . . fidelity to a goal . . . passion . . . sense of drama . . . *fare be-
lla figura* [to create a good impression, to understand that personal matters
necessarily involve family] . . . [demand for] *respetto* [respect]." "Ethnic Ideological Themes," 115–116.

I note these traits not necessarily to endorse Femminella's observations, but
to give an example of what, to some people, constitutes the *contadino* ideal.

27. Some writers, however, argue that some Italian-American cultural traits
persist through the generations. See, for example, Valentine J. Belfiglio, "Cultural Traits of Italian Americans Which Transcend Generational Differences,"
in Rocco Caporale, ed., *The Italian Americans Through the Generations* (Staten

Island: American Italian Historical Association, 1986), 126–135. ("Experiments imply that there are significant cultural traits, transcending generational differences, which distinguish Italian Americans from non-Italian Americans. The most important of these traits include: The possession of an Italian surname or maiden name; Membership in the Roman Catholic Church; Pride in the achievements of Italy in the fields of music and art; Knowledge of customs pertaining to the preparation, cooking, and eating of Italian cuisine; A preference for Italian folk music over all other kinds of folk music . . . [However,] an 'Italian consciousness' does not depend upon any of these factors. Rather, they merely facilitate the formation or maintenance of an ethnic identity. What is essential, is a group perception of having accomplished important things in the past, and the desire to accomplish them in the future. Ethnic identity depends upon common values and sympathies. Many Italian Americans appear to share an unconscious constellation of feelings, thoughts, perceptions, and memories, based upon similar experiences in childhood, which give rise to common ideas and images." 133.)

28. "Ethnic groups are continually recreated by new experiences. Assimilation operated on immigrant groups in different ways to make them distinct . . . [but] the ethnic subsociety can exist [in terms of social dimensions] even after it has lost most of its distinctive cultural attributes." Concetta A. Maglione Chiacchio, "Current Patters of Socialization and Adaptation in an Italian American Community," in Jerome Krase and William Egelman, eds., *The Melting Pot and Beyond: Italian Americans in the Year 2000* (Staten Island: American Italian Historical Association, 1987), 274.

29. For a better idea of some such interethnic differences see Femminella, "Ethnic Ideological Themes," 117–119. Novak argues that such differences are salutary, even necessary: "the threat today is from homogenization, a coercive sameness, a dreary standardization . . . the emergence of 'rational' universal values is dysfunctional since it detaches persons from the integration of personality that can be achieved only in historical symbolic communities . . . People uncertain of their own identity are not wholly free . . . The world is mediated to human persons through language and culture, that is, through ethnic belonging." *Unmeltable Ethnics*, 229.

30. "An ethnic group . . . is a collectivity within a larger society. A new ethnicity, then, is not simply appropriated by the group (i.e., a process of self-redefinition), it also reflects the perceptions and judgments of significant others. To this extent, ethnicity is 'achieved' in a dialogue between the ethnic group and the wider society." Tricarico, " 'New' Italian-American Ethnicity," 85. ("Three

options [for cultural re-creation] are 'particularly discernible.' One constructs an identity in terms of the life of the Italian 'contadino,' or peasant. A second is grounded in the immigrant experience and emphasizes the values of 'la famiglia' and hard work. A third is the so-called 'Renaissance motif' whereby a 'direct kinship is established between second and third generation Italian-Americans and such renowned figures as Dante, DaVinci, and Michalangelo.' " 81.)

31. Regarding symbolic ethnicity generally, Susan Kellogg argues that "the particular history, or histories, of an ethnic group plays a strong role in the way the group fashions its identity now . . . each ethnic group has its own history and folk model of that history . . . 'summarizing' symbols . . . are symbols which express succinctly, yet powerfully, fundamental themes or ideas in a cultural system . . . ethnic identity sums up a group's history, especially critical events, its social structure, and the tone of emotional relations, especially within the family, that are thought to be characteristic of the group. The identity functions here in a public context because it contrasts 'the group' with other ethnic groups." "Exploring Diversity in Middle-Class Families: The Symbolism of American Ethnic Identity," *Social Science History* 14 (1990):27–41, 36–37.

32. The *mano cornuto* is the sign of the cuckold made with the hand. The *cornu*, or Italian horn, had many functions. For example, it was often worn on a chain around the neck to ward off evil forces, particularly the power of the *malocchio*. In the 1970s it enjoyed a resurgence as a symbol of Italian-American ethnicity.

33. Richard D. Alba, *Ethnic Identity: The Transformation of White America* (New Haven: Yale University Press, 1990), 37, 38, 75, 303.

34. Source: Census Bureau. This decline in language use has spurred several proposals aimed at the revival of the Italian language in the United States. See, for example, Gianclaudio Macchiarella, "Italian in the United States," *Italian Journal* 7, no. 1 (1993):57–62; Gianclaudio Macchiarella, "A Resource Center for the Diffusion of Italian Language and Heritage: A Proposal," *Italian Journal* 7, no. 4 and 5 (1993):47–50; Louis Caesar Brunelli, "The *Lingua Nostra* Project," *Italian Journal* 7, no. 6 (1993): 45–47. ("The Italian language is the very symbol and vehicle of Italian culture and ancestry." 45.)

35. "A refurbished group identity has largely come about through the efforts of Italian-American intellectuals who have contributed images and articulated ideas relating to selected aspects of the cultural heritage. This has become the basis for 'new generalizations about the group' . . . with respect to both past and present. It is largely corroborated by significant others as patrons

of the ethnic heritage, which has come to include the Italian-American experience (i.e., 'the neighborhood') now that the group no longer comprises a large and viable lower class. Earlier forms of group identity have not been displaced, rather, new layers have been superimposed on the old." Tricarico, " 'New' Italian-American Ethnicity," 88.

36. "A stereotype, shared by the mass media and our own personal acquaintances, that emphasizes organized crime, spicy foods, flashy clothes, strong emotions, great sexuality, physical appearance and violence remains all too familiar." Juliani, "Position of Italian Americans," 65.

"Of the major ancestry groups [addressed in this study], Italians seem to possess the greatest number of stereotypes. These run the gamut from preconceptions of physical appearance and mannerisms ('big noses' and 'talk with their hands'), to family life ('family oriented' and 'good with children'), to the Mafia ('they all have something to do with organized crime')." Alba, *Ethnic Identity*, 141–142.

37. See, for example, Eriksen, *Ethnicity and Nationalism*, 151 ("A great number of critical analyses of modern society accuse capitalism and large-scale society of encouraging this fragmented, unpolitical and nihilistic kind of social identity.")

Donald Tricarico puts it this way: "An identification with ethnic origins has been widely perceived as an antidote for the alienation and anomie of contemporary society. With the eclipse of other symbolic universes, an ethnic experience – with its myths, icons, and rituals – can perhaps succeed to 'break up the ordinariness' of modern life." " 'New' Italian-American Ethnicity," 91.

38. Kellogg, "Exploring Diversity," 29. ("There are three other [in addition to commercialization, industrialization, rise of consumerism, aging of population, declining birthrate, rising divorce rate, and changing roles for women] powerful trends in contemporary American life which move the middle class toward uniformity: a tendency to recall the 1950s as the Golden Era, the suburbanization of the middle class, and its long-term but increasing emphasis on individualism." 32.)

39. Alba, *Ethnic Identity*, 16, 307.

40. Ibid., 58, 73, 114, 308. ("Ethnicity may be part of the 'cultural capital' imparted by advanced education – the repertoire of cultural codes that highly educated persons acquire in order to be able to establish prompt and effective communication in diversified social worlds not strongly bounded by kinship and locality." 58.)

41. Ibid., 181–182, 204.

42. Ibid., 193.

43. Ibid., 59–61, 70–71, 137–138, 193.

44. Ibid., 206.

45. Ibid., 302.

46. I use this expression as a tribute to Joseph Giordano, whom I first heard use it.

47. See Chapter 1.

48. To completely transcend our finitude and liberate ourselves from contextuality itself would destroy our humanity. ("She [an athlete] shouldn't wish to be without the human body and its limits altogether, since then there is no athletic achievement and no goal; but it seems perfectly reasonable, in any particular case, to want, always, to be better, stronger, faster, to push against those limits more successfully. It is the paradox of a struggle for victory in which *complete* 'victory' would be disaster and emptiness – or, at any rate, a life so different from our own that we could no longer find ourselves and our valued activities in it." Martha C. Nussbaum, *Love's Knowledge* (New York: Oxford University Press, 1990), 381.)

49. See my discussion of Roberto Unger's work in Chapter 3.

50. "For purposes of [ethnic] boundary demarcation, fluency in an ethnic language may not even be necessary. The use of words and phrases from a mother tongue in an English conversation can remind others of a shared ethnic background, a form of 'ethnic signalling.' " Alba, *Ethnic Identity*, 84–85.

51. Ibid., 75, 79, 303.

52. Ibid., 208.

53. "Organized crime can be usefully thought of as an American institution, a sector of the economy providing illicit goods and services and serving as a channel for ethnic mobility. It is, to be sure, a stigmatized institution, whose participants are branded with the mark of unrespectability and whose proffered opportunities for power and money entail great risk, including the possible loss of one's life. For these reasons, it attracts chiefly the members of low-standing ethnic groups. Their ethnic backgrounds are a disadvantage added to the usual difficulty of achieving more than modest mobility through legitimate routes . . . they may perceive that the opportunities of illicit enterprise outweigh its risks." Richard D. Alba, *Italian Americans: Into the Twilight of Ethnicity* (Englewood Cliffs: Prentice-Hall, 1985), 95.

54. Richard Gambino argues: "If we use the only figure ever given by a federal agency – the *Report on Organized Crime* by the President's Commission on Law Enforcement, 1967 – admittedly an old and controversial figure, there

were 5,000 people involved in organized crime. Assuming all of them were Italian-Americans, *this is 0.0004 percent of the Italian-American population according to the 1980 Census* (the first census that included all generations of ethnic groups instead of only the foreign born and their children) or *0.0003 percent of the Italian American population according to the 1990 Census.*" "Italian Americans, Today's Immigrants, Multiculturalism, and the Mark of Cain," *Italian Journal* 7, No. 6 (1993):42–44, 42.

Gambino should not have included the term "percent" after 0.0004 and 0.0003. His figures are based on dividing 5,000 by 12 million and 15 million respectively. He once gave an even lower figure: 0.00025. See *Blood of My Blood* (New York: Anchor Books, 1974), 300–301. This figure, however, assumed that there are 20 million Italian Americans in the United States of America.

How many Italian Americans reside in the United States? Figures given range from 10.1 million (Smith, *Profile of Italian Americans,* 2) to 12 million (Juliani, "Position of Italian Americans, 62) to 15 million (National Italian American Foundation Inc. [NIAF], *Washington Newsletter* 9 (February/March 1993): 2). The Juliani figure purportedly represents the 1980 U.S. Census, whereas the NIAF figure reports the results of the 1990 U.S. Census. Gambino's new estimates correlate with the census figures and conclude that three or four Italian-Americans in 10,000 are members of organized crime. This estimate is probably sound. Andrew Rolle also cites 5,000 as the number of gangsters involved in organized crime. See *The Italian Americans: Troubled Roots* (New York: Free Press, 1980), 109. But suppose we take the lowest figure cited for the Italian-American population, 10 million, and suppose we *double* the 1967 federal figures on organized crime members: the inflated number would be 10,000. Let us suppose further, contrary to fact, that all members of organized crime are Italian American. Still, even with these unsupported assumptions unfavorable to Italian Americans, only 0.001 of the Italian American population would be members of organized crime! Of course, one can be involved in criminal activity without being a member of organized crime: if I am convicted of murder tomorrow that makes me a criminal but not necessarily a member of organized crime. So it might be argued that Italian-American criminality unrelated to membership in organized crime syndicates also contributes to the negative image of Italian Americans as lawless. This strategy, however, is unsuccessful because there is no evidence suggesting that Italian Americans are involved in such criminality in greater proportions than other ethnic and racial groups.

55. See, for example, Pete Hamill, "End Game," *Esquire* (December 1994): 85–92. ("Almost a hundred years after the last great immigration wave changed the face of American society, vast numbers of Americans—including, sadly, the best-educated—are again being taught to identity themselves with the qualifying adjectives of race, religion, ethnicity, and gender. The idea of the melting pot is dismissed as cultural genocide, replaced by a social worker's version of predestination." 88–89.)

Hamill cites favorably the work of the following academic and popular writers as generally supporting his thesis: Arthur M. Schlesinger Jr., Gertrude Himmelfarb, Michael Walzer, Allan Bloom, William A. Henry III, and Robert Hughes.

56. Ibid., 89.

57. Ibid. Unfortunately, despite the broadness of his attack on ethnic philosophers, Hamill specifically identifies only two of the alleged culprits: Catharine MacKinnon (see Chapter 2) and CUNY professor Leonard Jeffries Jr.

58. Alba, *Ethnic Identity*, 318–319.

INDEX